Storytellers, Saints, and Scoundrels

CONTEMPORARY ETHNOGRAPHY

Series Editors
Dan Rose
Paul Stoller

A complete list of books in the series is available from the publisher.

Storytellers, Saints, and Scoundrels

Folk Narrative in Hindu Religious Teaching

Kirin Narayan

PENN

University of Pennsylvania Press
Philadelphia

Publications of the American Folklore Society
New Series

General Editor, Patrick Mullen

10 9 8 7

Published by
University of Pennsylvania Press
Philadelphia, Pennsylvania 19104-4011
Fifth paperback printing 1997

Library of Congress Cataloging-in-Publication Data

Narayan, Kirin.
  Storytellers, saints, and scoundrels: folk narrative in Hindu
religious teaching / Kirin Narayan.
      p.   cm.—(University of Pennsylvania Press contemporary
ethnography series)
  Bibliography: p.
  Includes index.
  ISBN 0-8122-8119-5—ISBN 0-8122-1269-X (pbk.)
    1. Storytelling—Religious aspects—Hinduism.   2. Asceticism—
Hinduism.   3. Hindus—Folklore—History and criticism.   4. Tales—
India—History and criticism.   5. Hinduism—Customs and practices.
I. Title. II. Series.
BL1215.585N37   1989
598.08'82945—dc20   89-31363
                                                           CIP

Map design by Anne Marie Palagano

For Swamiji, Ba, and Rahoul,
whose words and works live on.

Contents

Acknowledgments

Thanks first to Swamiji, who allowed me to undertake this project, and to all those around him who contributed their insights. From here, gratitude spirals out into many arenas of my life. My parents, Didi and Narayan Contractor, each read, reread, and listened to me reading parts of this work; their considered comments are on a continuum with the encouragement that has brought me to where I now stand. Alan Dundes, my adviser, also painstakingly read the entire dissertation on which this book is based not just once but twice. This is an example of his expansive generosity that will be recognized by all who have worked with him. My editors Dan Rose and Paul Stoller pored through whatever I sent them, strengthening both my literary aesthetics and my good spirits with their frequent calls and notes. I am grateful, too, for the perspicacious readers they chose: A. K. Ramanujan and Susan Wadley, whose comments were extremely helpful. Ann Gold's spirited evaluation of the manuscript was also central to my revisions. And finally, Patricia Smith lent her sensitive eye to cut what was cumbrous from the final version.

Without the affection and encouragement of Reinhard and Jane Bendix, this project may never have come to pass. Other friends who read the manuscript in part or in its entirety, and who bolstered my spirits when they sagged, are: Manuela Albuquerque, Gerald Berreman, Maya Narayan, Kevin Dwyer, Claudia Henrion, Niloufer Ichaporia, Eugene Irschick, Smadar Lavie, Victor Perera, Renato Rosaldo, Nobuko Yamada, and Carolyn Young. I am also grateful to Robert Schine for sharing his computer expertise, and Jonathan Price for discussing the nearly finished manuscript.

I received excellent comments during oral presentations of this material at the Department of Anthropology at the University of Chicago, the Department of Folklore and Folklife at the University of Pennsylvania, the School of Social Science at Hampshire College, the Conference on Religion in South Asia at Amherst College, and an informal gathering of the faculty at Middlebury College. There are too many people involved here to name individually, but my thanks to all of them. They may recognize the repercussions of their words in these pages.

None of this would have been possible without financial support. I lived in Nasik between June and September 1983 and July and October 1985. I am extremely grateful for a National Science Foundation Graduate Fellowship, a U. C. Berkeley Graduate Humanities Research Grant, and a Robert H. Lowie Fellowship, which sponsored my trips. A Charlotte W. Newcombe Dissertation Writing Fellowship allowed for a precious year of undistracted writing, and the Social Science Research Council supported my travel to their sponsored conference on Religion in South Asia. Middlebury College smoothed the process of revisions with student help and the use of campus facilities. My thanks to all these institutions and the individuals who compose them.

A Note on Transliteration

Transliteration for the Hindu tradition brings up divergences between Sanskrit and Hindi conventions, and between scholarly and everyday Indian usage. I have settled on a compromise for the interested nonspecialist reader, sacrificing technical precision for readability. So I use *ch* and *chh* instead of the common *c* and *ch; sh* for both *ś* and *ṣ*. In most cases I drop the ending "a" of Sanskrit transcription, unless this is a word which has become well known in its Sanskrit form: *dharma,* for example, instead of the *dharam* which was actually pronounced. For deities, names, and titles I have followed a standard nontechnical form that omits diacritical marks: hence Krishna rather than Kṛṣṇā, Ram rather than Rāma, Swamiji rather than Svāmījī. I have not italicized words like Guru, ashram, and karma which are now also in English currency. Characters in stories are named without italics or diacritics: a *sādhu* becomes the Sadhu and so on.

A few guidelines for conventions I actually use: *a* should be pronounced as in "but"; *ā* as in "car"; *i* as in "lick" and *ī* as in "leek"; *u* as in "put" and *ū* as in "soon." A *t* is soft, as in "path," while *ṭ* is hard, like "pat." In all cases, an *h* following a consonant means that it is aspirated. An *ṛ* and *ṇ* involve a retroflex flap.

A hazard of settling on a system of transliteration that seeks to accommodate different conventions is that occasionally the sources I cite use spellings different from mine. I hope that my readers will bear with any inconsistencies in the text.

Introduction

Swamiji lay in his deck chair. His legs, bare below the knee, were out-stretched, but his eyes were alert. He was chatting with the assembled company about other Gurus. He had told us anecdotes about an eccentric saint, then about a child who was proclaimed to be the reincarnation of a popular Guru by some people but dismissed by others as a fraud. Like any day when Swamiji's doors were open, a motley array of visitors was present: Indians from various regions and castes, and a handful of Westerners. I sat among these visitors, cross-legged against the wall on the women's side of the room. A breeze lifted the curtains behind the deck chair and, suspended in the moment, I set my notebook and tape recorder aside to relax into the flow of Swamiji's colloquial Hindi. Yet I was soon shaken out of my lulled state, for Swamiji, leaping to another topic with his usual dexterity, now announced that there was a difference between the educated and uneducated. At this point his eyes, blurred and magnified by heavy glasses, became fixed on me.

"Suppose you and I are walking on the road," he said. "You've gone to University. I haven't studied anything. We're walking. Some child has shit on the road. We both step in it. 'That's shit!' I say. I scrape my foot; it's gone. But educated people have doubts about everything. You say, 'What's this?!' and you rub your foot against the other." Swamiji shot up from his prone position, and placing his feet on the linoleum, stared at them with intensity. He rubbed the right sole against the left ankle. "Then you reach down to feel what it could be," his fingers now explored the ankle. A grin was breaking over his face. "Something sticky! You lift some up and sniff it. Then you say, 'Oh! This is *shit*.'" The hand which had vigorously rubbed his nose was flung out in a gesture of disgust.

Swamiji turned back toward me, cheeks lifted under their white stubble in a toothless and delighted grin. Everyone present in the room was laughing uncontrollably. I managed an uncomfortable smile.

"See how many places it touched in the meantime," Swamiji continued. "Educated people always doubt everything. They lie awake at night thinking, 'What was that? Why did it happen? What is the meaning and the

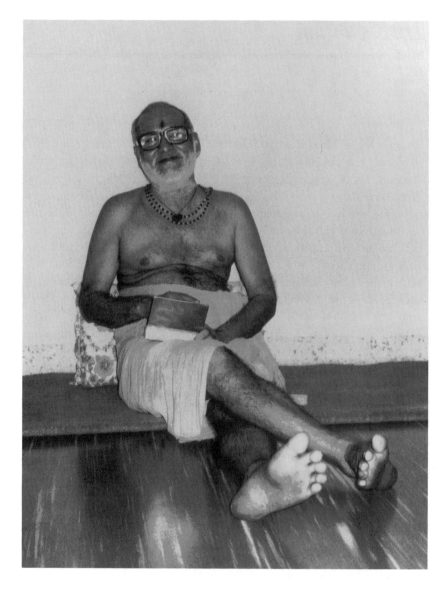

Swamiji sits with a box of *kumkum* waiting to receive visitors.

cause of it?' Uneducated people pass judgment and walk on. They get a good night's sleep."

Others present were educated in varying degrees: Swamiji himself had gone to a village school until the fourth grade, and "Gulelal" from Pittsburgh had once been enrolled in a doctoral program in philosophy. This parable, though, was aimed at me, the half-Indian, half-American graduate student in anthropology at the University of California at Berkeley. I had known Swamiji since I was a child, yet here I now was, armed with a research proposal to study folk narrative as a form of religious teaching. That Swamiji and other Hindu holy people should draw on stories to illustrate religious insights was taken for granted by all who were present. They enjoyed the stories; they learned from them. Yet I brought the weightiness of perpetual enquiry to the enterprise. When Swamiji told stories, I was poised with a tape recorder; whenever he spoke about stories or related themes, I whipped out my notebook, too. I was always asking him and others questions about functions, sources, interpretations. "What was that? Why was it? What is the meaning and the cause of it?" rang in my ears as a parody of my own relentless questioning.

I looked up at Swamiji from my position on the floor and tried to avoid the eyes of the others who still watched me with broad smiles on their faces. I had to agree that among the academics I represented analysis could often become obsessive. But I also felt awkward, even a little hurt. This parable seemed to dismiss all the years that education had dominated my life. It ridiculed my very presence here.

Swamiji must have read the discomfort on my face, for when he settled back into the aluminum deck chair, he turned to me again. "It's not that you shouldn't study," he said, voice low and kind. "You should gain wisdom. But you should realize that in the end this means nothing."

*   *   *

This episode occurred in September 1985, in the pilgrimage town of Nasik where Swamiji lives. In the intervening years, I have often thought back to these moments, and have repeated the story many times to friends. Swamiji's parable has seemed to encapsulate his attitude toward my research: a mixture of amusement, dismissal, and sustained kindness. From the start he was supportive, allowing me to sit beside him and observe his interactions day after day. The very week of my first university-sponsored summer visit in 1983, he had distributed sweets in honor of the book I would one day write, even though at that point I was not considering a dissertation, let alone a book, that involved him. In the intervening two years before I returned for a second term of fieldwork, he had sent letters expressing the hope that Jagadamba, Mother of the Universe, would support me in all my undertakings. Yet while he wished the best for me personally, he seemed uninterested in the outcome of my project. He did not, for example, want his name included, and requested that when I wrote I refer to him by the generic name Swamiji. "What need do I have for publicity?" he asked. "Just write that some 'Swamiji' told you all this." When I returned a third time with a completed dissertation—red-bound for auspiciousness and scrupulously avoiding mention of his name—Swamiji flipped through it upside down, then asked that it be set atop the silver sandals of his Guru (where its cumbrous presence baffled those who tried to bow at the altar). He was not interested in hearing my explanations of what I had written. Rather, he wanted to teach me how to cook a snack made from flattened rice (*pohā*). Finally, when I wrote that the book had been accepted for publication, Swamiji dictated a reply saying that he hoped Bhagavati, the Goddess, would guide me, and that his blessings were with whatever I wrote. So although this book clearly involves Swamiji, he has always viewed it as much more my own affair. I can only hope that I have lived up to this generous trust.

Swamiji was in his late sixties through the years of my research with him. He lived in an apartment adjoining a nursing home run by his doctor. Because of varied health problems—angina, high blood pressure, diabetes—he was not as active as he had been in his questing past. He rarely left his rooms and spent much of each day reclining on the deck chair which was later replaced by a wooden bed. My descriptions of Swamiji span several years, but to better understand him as a storyteller shaping tales around his own concerns I also take stock of the decades before our association. Born into an orthodox Brahman family in Karnataka, south India, he left home first to join the Independence movement and later to wander in search of spiritual wisdom. Celibate, itinerant, and wearing white, for many years he lived like a holy man even though he was not formally initiated into any order. It was not until his forties that he settled in Maharashtra, directed his allegiance to a particular Guru, and became an ochre-wearing *sannyāsī* renouncer. Though he founded an ashram to feed and house tribal children, he has subsequently turned this over to other hands. He now lives apart from any institutional framework. He meets with visitors twice a day, and often in the course of his interactions he will draw upon a story. Some Gurus sing compositions by poet-saints, others chant from Sanskrit scriptures, and yet others instruct through silence. But for Swamiji, as with many other religious men and women in India, folk narrative is a dominant medium for the expression of Hindu insights.[1] As a child in India, I had learned about Hindu gods, Gurus, and morals primarily through stories. Of all the tellers I encountered, Swamiji drew from the largest repertoire and retold traditional narratives[2] with a verve and humor that marked them as his own.

The precedents for religious storytellers, as I knew from growing up in a household steeped in comparative religion, are immense. Christ told parables, Buddha recounted episodes from his past lives, Jewish rabbis use stories, Sufi masters frequently instruct disciples through tales, and even the paradoxical statements of Zen masters often have a narrative form. Furthermore, when I started reading in the domains of anthropology and folklore, I found that for many tribal societies folk narrative was a major vehicle of instruction by elders. Additionally, Burmese Buddhist monks improvised teaching tales based on their folk traditions rather than on the Jataka model.[3] Jamaa prophets in Zaire used traditional Luba tales as allegories to express their Bantu-Christian faith.[4] Hasidic rebbes told legends and were the source of legends, even in New York.[5] Christ, I discovered, was not a lone storyteller: there was a rich Christian tradition in which preachers used exempla or "example-stories" in Europe between the thirteenth and fifteenth centuries.[6] While Christian preachers everywhere continued to sprinkle their sermons with stories, black American preachers in the American South were found in the 1960s to draw on formulaic themes in their impassioned sermons.[7] In many of these cases in which tellers spoke from an institutionalized religious role, their stories featured characters like themselves. Christian exempla abound with priests, nuns, and bishops; Burmese Buddhist monks' tales frequently depict monks; rebbes tell about previous rebbes, and so on. In this context, Swamiji's many stories about *sādhus*—Hindu ascetics—are no surprise.

I now have over seventy of Swamiji's stories on tape, but in this book I reproduce just eight folk narratives that comment directly or obliquely on Hindu ascetics and storytellers. These stories are reflexive; a folklore commentary on the themes with which I am concerned. Viewed together, the stories present a multifaceted image of the Hindu ascetic as simpleton, charlatan, saint, and storyteller. Surrounding these stories are circles of context widening in many dimensions. The interaction amid which stories arose, Swamiji's comments about storytelling, my accounts of fieldwork, his listeners' interpretations, networks of Indian narratives, Hindu ascetic traditions, and the issue of narrative as a form of understanding are among the frames I use to highlight meaning in these tales. Though the frames often criss-cross, the book itself is organized into three sections. In the opening section, I begin with a folktale and then locate Swamiji as a religious storyteller in cultural, historical, and contemporary social contexts. The middle section is exclusively centered around storytelling events and the interpretations gleaned from Swamiji, his listeners, and relevant scholarly literature. The final section looks back over the previous chapters, weaving together themes from within the stories and making explicit their theoretical setting.

I started my research with some questions in mind, and though the questions multiplied as I proceeded, answers gradually came into focus. The central puzzle is: what is it about stories that make them such a compelling vehicle for religious instruction? From here extend related lines of inquiry: why do religious teachers of many persuasions draw on the narrative form if they wish to make a moral or doctrinal point? How might orally transmitted folk narratives differ in their impact from written religious traditions? How are these stories updated by creative tellers, and how do listeners hear tales from the lips of a teller believed to have direct access to spiritual truths? How do such traditional stories throw light on all the assorted paths of listeners? As my readers meet Swamiji, his listeners, and allied scholarly literature, I hope that they will begin to make out the shapes of answers for themselves even though I end with an explicit set of conclusions.

Although the theoretical quest that underlies this ethnography is to comprehend the power of storytelling in religion, there are also other themes that occur in counterpoint through this work. This is secondly a book about the Hindu tradition of renunciation, exploring the cultural concerns that converge in the figure of the *sādhu,* and the nexus of social interaction that forms around a charismatic holy person. An imbedded argument takes issue with what I perceive to be romantic Western misconceptions of Gurus. Third, it is a portrait of one compelling *sādhu*— Swamiji—a person whose intelligence, generosity, humor, and humility cannot fail to impress those who encounter him.

My primary orientation lies in the fields of folklore and anthropology, but in the course of this book I have drawn on a diversity of disciplines. My interest is in lived experience and ways to better understand it, not in any monolithic theoretical framework. I have ended up adopting an eclec-

tic "tool box approach,"[8] choosing from an array of theoretical imple-
ments as different themes demanding intellectual craftsmanship emerged. I
have also drawn liberally on indigenous theories. Swamiji voiced insights
rooted in his own experience when the issue of traditional storytelling and
religion arose. His range of listeners also spoke reflectively on the form,
function, and meaning of stories. Bringing together these varied perspectives from books and people, I hope to avoid a flatness in presentation or a
simplification of issues into a single theoretical cast.

*   *   *

Anthropologists have traditionally studied the Other, setting off for distant jungles and villages where alien ways of life prevail. The task of anthropology has been to translate one culture into the terms of another, and
then to theorize cross-culturally about disjunctures and correspondences
in the way human beings choose to live. Folklorists, on the other hand,
have tended to study their own society. Though the emergent theory took
many directions, the impetus for documenting folk traditions was most
often that of exploring and asserting one's identity. Whether folklore was
assembled from "savages" believed to be at an earlier state of social evolution, from simple peasants thought to preserve a glorious past, or from
compatriots and equals, it has tended to focus on the cultural Self.

My own perspective involves an uneasy balance of both anthropology
and folklore, a shifting between distance and identification. Although I
may be identified with the increasing post-colonial phenomenon of the
"indigenous" or "native" anthropologist,[9] my situation is actually more
complex. I have a Gujarati father and a German-American mother; I was
brought up in India but have lived in the United States since I was sixteen.
Swamiji is someone I have known since I was ten, and my bringing graduate school training to bear on his storytelling is but one phase of a long
and ongoing relationship.

Nasik, the industrialized pilgrimage town where most of these folk narratives were recorded, is also my father's home town. Although I grew up
in Bombay, my grandmother's house in Nasik has remained a center where
the family gathers for any important ritual event. I was regularly recognized as a daughter of a local family when I started fieldwork. I struggled
to conform to this role, behaving with the decorum appropriate for a
young unmarried woman. This position made me sensitive to cultural
nuance, but I often felt powerless and constrained. Again and again during

my research I felt that I lacked the authority to steer a conversation in a particular direction. While this constraint derived partly from my age and gender, it was also a form of patient supplication that I recognize in other ethnographies about religion, sorcery, or witchcraft. When fieldworkers study aspects of knowledge considered esoteric or power-laden in a culture, indigenous experts can decide if and when they might impart this knowledge.[10] I simply could not push Swamiji to be my "informant." It was he who chose whether or not stories were told or religion discussed as my tape recorder whirled ahead.

Although I was partially assimilated as a local woman, I did not altogether "pass." While in Nasik I dressed in a sari, with earrings, bangles, and anklets, my hair in a braid, and *kumkum* on my forehead. But I was a little too fair; a little too tall; my Hindi accent betrayed that English was my first language; and my foreign tape recorder gave away my affiliations with a project that would not concern most local women. Everyone who visited Swamiji sooner or later figured out my ties to another continent. Among his visitors was a handful of Westerners from England, France, the United States, and Australia who stayed for short periods of time. I shared many references with the Westerners present, especially those who had lived in America. But even as I identified with them, I was acutely aware of the cultural faux pas they good-naturedly made and was anxious not to be lumped together with them, the "foreigners." I was perpetually trying to balance these twin sets of identification within myself. Also, I played the outer role of cultural mediator when I translated Swamiji's stories into English for my Western companions, forwarded their questions and comments in colloquial Hindi for him, or explained the activities of both Indians and Westerners to each other.

During my fieldwork in 1983, I lived next door to Swamiji with three women: two were American and one was English. At this time I participated in the demanding daily routine that unfolded around Swamiji, rising at 5 A.M. to chant Sanskrit verses. In 1985, at my family's insistence I stayed with my grandmother, aunt, and cousins, and commuted daily, arriving shortly before 10 A.M. With both my Western roommates and my Indian family, though, I often felt the loneliness of intellectual distance and different goals. My roommates would be meditating while I listened through earphones and transcribed tapes; in the evenings as my cousins gathered together around the television, I tended to be off in a remote corner of the house, writing field notes. The people associated with Swamiji generally thought my project was worthwhile since it related to him, but my family was less sure. Though my own faraway parents were supportive, my cousins clearly thought that spending time with a Guru was old-fashioned, even baffling for someone who lived a "modern" life abroad. As usual my grandmother, Ba, had arrived at her own conclusions. For years she had queried, "I might be illiterate, but does that mean that I have no brains?" I now overheard her boasting to her white-wearing widow friends that I was writing the epic *Rāmāyaṇa*—for her the epitome of a religious story. To me, though, she flicked her hand at a Ph.D., advising that I think of more sensible things for my age, like marriage. Through both fieldwork periods she continually hauled me off to astrologers to ascertain when this craze for studying would lift and I would finally settle down. When I returned with a completed degree, Ba broadcasted, "She's a Doctor now," adding emphatically, "and she *doesn't* poke you with injections!" I was astonished when she retracted her earlier disapproval and gave me a treasured ring to commemorate my gaining more education than any other woman and most men in our caste network.

*   *   *

This is all to say that during my fieldwork India sometimes represented a Self, and that sometimes this Self was to be found among Western elements while India slipped apart as an Other. On occasion, such as when Swamiji aimed humorous arrows at my project, my academic training set me apart from everyone else, marking me as an Other. Then, too, there could be a rich spirit of community and shared participation among all those who together entered the captivating world of Swamiji's tales and religious concerns. At this time, the Self and Other distinctions collapsed and the disparate gathering seemed bonded in an inclusive We.

My shifting identifications worked their way into this text. On one hand I am explicating what is familiar through the prism of my own sensibilities in conjunction with the concepts of academe. On the other hand I am discovering aspects of India and the West, of people and situations, that I probably would have never known without the direction of a research project. Rather than being a discovery of the exotic, this work is in many ways a deepening of the familiar.

Living on a continuum between cultures, I have allowed all the intersections and clashes that increasingly characterize the post-modern world to carry over into my text. Though an ancient and sacred city, Nasik is today replete with the juxtapositions of contemporary India. Walking the back way to Swamiji's apartment, one passes a temple, bangle shops, and then a slew of garishly postered video parlors. A bullock cart is sometimes parked outside the concrete building in which Swamiji is housed. A young Englishman wearing saffron robes sits listening to a story beside a local boy in a nylon shirt and terylene pants. A French woman has the traditional *kumkum* powder on her forehead; a visiting college student wears instead a reusable spot made of sticky plastic and red felt. Swamiji leans back in an aluminum deck chair one could picture beside a swimming pool instead. While there are Hindu deities on his altar, there is a Swiss skiing calendar on the wall. I have not tried to simulate a "pure" Hindu context, but have included all these seemingly discordant details in my account. This is partly to emphasize the historical moment in which this study is set, and partly to dispel lingering Western stereotypes of the mysterious East where holy men only meditate among Himalayan snows or lounge on beds of nails.

Too close to step back and typify people, I have also been reluctant to blur singular voices into generalized ones. When people speak, they are identified rather than being subsumed within categories such as "Hindu Gurus," "Western youth," or "pious middle-class Indians." While I attempt to locate my companions within the framework of cultural patterns, historical shifts, and sociological trends, I have hesitated to undertake psychological analyses that might offend. I do acknowledge the value of incorporating unconscious motivation into the understanding of daily life, but my excursions into the unconscious are largely stated in terms of shared cultural themes rather than a particular individual's experiences.

Familiarity with the situation has also made me aware of complexities that I cannot glibly simplify. I have been acutely conscious that my knowledge is partial, and that Swamiji and his listeners often knew more about what I was trying to research than I did myself. For this reason, I have tried to share my interpretive authority with them. I elicited their comments on storytelling in general and, whenever possible, their exegeses of particular narratives. Admittedly, the arrangement of their views in this text is my own responsibility and forms an order of interpretation. Yet it is an attempt to allow others to speak out, to diverge from my viewpoint, and to critique my project within my own text.

Swamiji, as I have noted, asked that he remain anonymous, so I have referred to him by this generic term for a holy man, blurring certain markers that would identify and locate him. When I reproduce his critiques of prominent contemporary Gurus, in the interest of diplomacy I keep their identity obscure. Otherwise, with the exception of myself and my family, everyone has been given pseudonyms based on the names they were referred to by Swamiji and the others around him. Many older men bore honorific titles that Swamiji—often whimsically—appended to their names: for example, Maharaj (great king), Seth (wealthy proprietor), or Saheb. Swamiji spoke of all women as Mataji or Amma (north and south Indian renditions of "mother"), and sometimes older women had these terms tacked onto their names as a matter of course. Almost all the foreigners sported Indian names which they had received from ashrams they were at previously, or from Swamiji himself. In the following pages, when I refer to a Westerner with an acquired Indian name, I use quotation marks to distinguish him or her from those who were given their names at birth. So "Pagaldas" from Oakland and "Ahalya Amma" from Melbourne are different from Jagadish Seth of Nasik and Chandralekha from Bombay. Swamiji himself is often referred to as Babaji (respected father) or Maharaj; to avoid confusion in presenting others' comments on him, though, I have smoothed over these various terms of address with the single name Swamiji.

*   *   *

Through the arduous process of bringing a book to completion, I have tried at all times to stay close to the advice that J. D. Salinger's Seymour Glass so fervently communicated to his younger brother, Buddy: write what you would most love to read. After leaving Swamiji, I have written—and rewritten—the ethnography I would find most insightful and evocative if handed to read. I have modeled this on other ethnographies which gripped my imagination and which I entered with enjoyment as much as academic duty. These books have shared several features: a vivid sense of people and atmosphere; recourse to stories (whether illustrative anecdotes, case histories, oral histories, or folk narratives); the use of theory as an illumination of people's lives rather than as an end in itself; and the inclusion of the ethnographer as a person rather than a distanced recorder. The importance of the theoretical perspectives underlying such ethnographic writing has been masterfully argued in other texts, and rather than undertaking belabored justifications, I have simply integrated the insights gleaned from these texts into my own work.[11]

While writing the kind of anthropology I would most like to read, I have felt a strong aesthetic obligation to try making my ethnography as lively as the stories it contains. As my friend Champa, who sometimes visits Swamiji, said, "He tells the story with happiness on his face. He laughs a little, he uses actions. Because he tells it laughing and happy [*hansi khushi se*], because he tells it with affection, the story has an effect [*asar*] on people." The folk narratives that I reproduce in the following chapters obviously delight Swamiji; his listeners, leaning forward, have smiles flickering on their faces. I, too, have enjoyed these stories and the lighthearted presence of their teller. I hope that my pleasure is shared with my readers in the pages ahead.

I

Orientations

1. There's Always a Reason

"Come Mataji, come in," Swamiji called through the screen window. It was a morning in September 1985. I had just arrived at the second-floor flat where he stays, and was slipping off my sandals outside the door. The fine netted screen allows Swamiji to see out but blocks the view within. His voice—low, rumbling, rich with the warmth of a grin—had greeted me before I could see him.

When I entered I found Swamiji sitting alone at the end of the narrow room, and he was indeed smiling. After the clamor on the street outside, this room bore an ordered serenity. Instead of sharp sunshine, the rush of vehicles, the calls of vendors, here there was cool and quiet. The walls, linoleum, and curtains were all pale greens, though the altar dominating one wall was ablaze with the colors of various deities. Swamiji sat to the left of the altar. He rested in the aluminum deck chair, legs crossed at the knee.

"You're all alone Swamiji?" I asked, moving toward the altar to lay down my offering of one dozen ripe green bananas. I was surprised, for most mornings when I arrived from across town there were already several people present.

"I'm sitting here with my Mother," said Swamiji, relaxed from his chair. "The Mother of the Universe [*Jagajanani*] is everywhere. She's with me now, keeping me company."

"Yes, Swamiji." This statement, both playful and earnest, set me smiling too. I took a seat by the wall and began to unpack the bag in which I kept my perpetual companions: a pen, a slim notebook, a camera, and a tape recorder. As usual, Swamiji watched my conscientious bustling with amused interest. When I caught that glint of amusement I sometimes wondered if he still saw in me the child with two plaits who, the first time we met, had only briefly interrupted doll-playing to pay him respects.

Swamiji is a Hindu *sādhu,* a holy man. He is a *sannyāsī,* a "renouncer" who has performed his own death ceremonies and taken on a new identity

A view of the riverbank at the Nasik "Ganga."

emphasizing the lack of personal ties and possessions. Like other *sannyāsīs* of the Dashanami Dandi order, he wears ochre robes and sacred *rudrāksh* beads around his neck. Also, like other *sannyāsīs*, he is a Guru, drawing disciples from a variety of backgrounds. Yet, while Gurus often become the center of large ashrams and organizations, Swamiji has resisted institutionalization. The ashram he founded twenty years ago to house and feed tribal children has subsequently been handed over to two other *sādhus*. "Isn't renunciation supposed to be the virtue of a holy man?" he enquires if anyone asks him why he left behind such a fine place. If disciples from elsewhere now wish to spend time with him they must stay with other families in the area. On that morning I had puttered here in a motor rickshaw from the rambling Victorian bungalow my grandfather built. Most other mornings I came this distance along the Nasik roads, crushed among pilgrims and local people in a dusty State Transport bus.

Nasik lies in central Maharashta, northeast of Bombay.[1] By train or by bus it is roughly a four-hour journey from Bombay, rising from sea level up into the Deccan plateau with its misshapen volcanic mountains, scattered villages, and open stretches of forests and paddy fields. A Marathi proverb states that "Nasik is settled on seven hills" (*nāsik nav ṭekāvar vasāvile*), and so the name is often derived from the Sanskrit *navashikhara*, "nine peaks." Folk etymology, however, links Nasik with *nāk*, "nose," for it is here that Lakshman is believed to have cut off the demoness Surpanakha's nose. Lakshman is the brother of Ram, hero of the *Rāmāyaṇa* epic. According to the legend, when Ram was exiled to the forest he wandered here, accompanied by his brother and wife. The landscape is marked by their doings: in this pool, Ram bathed; on that mountain (dented like a pillow on which a head has rested), Ram slept.

Nasik is also sacred because of the presence of the river Godavari. She is considered to be a goddess and sister of the river Ganga (Ganges) which glides through the north Indian plains. When Ganga leapt from the matted locks of Lord Shiva in the Himalayas, one drop remained; later, this drop is said to have spattered across the subcontinent to become the Godavari river, running through the Deccan plateau east to the Indian Ocean. Like the Ganga, the Godavari carries holy water and can wash away sins: in fact, she is known as "Ganga" in Nasik. The banks of the Nasik "Ganga" are crowded with temples and bathing places. Temples also extend beyond the river; all in all, there may be as many as two hundred of them serving different Hindu deities. These include ancient rock-cut temples whose steps have been flattened by many feet and new cement temples with marble floors and inlaid walls.

Pilgrims flock to Nasik at most times of year and especially in March for the Ram Navami festival honoring Ram. Every twelve years, a great fair for bathing, the Kumbha Mela, takes place, drawing *sādhus* and *sādhvis*— holy men and women—from all over the country. Even during normal years, Nasik attracts ascetics from a wide variety of sects. Riding the bus to Swamiji's each day, I often saw many kinds of white or ochre-clad ascetics trudging along roads toward the river. There is an abundance of monasteries, ashrams, rest houses, and independent housing arrangements for these ascetics in Nasik. Swamiji himself now lives in an apartment building that is owned by disciples who are doctors and that also contains their nursing home.

Despite—and also because of—these sacred credentials, Nasik is a city of trade and industry as well. For centuries it has been located on a major highway that links inner Maharashtra with the coast. With the coming of tarred roads and trains, Nasik has continued to lie on crucial trade routes. A variety of industries now flourish in the area around the wood-carved old city and in the new townships built in the vicinity. These industries provide employment for local people and draw immigrants from other regions. Among Swamiji's disciples, for example, there are people from Mysore employed at the Government of India Security Press, which prints paper money and stamps; Maharashtrians from the V.I.P. factory, which makes suitcases; Tamilians from the M.I.G. factory, which manufactures defense aircraft. There are small shopkeepers and Udipi hotel owners (pilgrims and businessmen need places to eat and rest). There are professionals from different urban regions, especially doctors, for through the years Swamiji's bad health has brought him into contact with many general practitioners and specialists from allopathic, ayurvedic, and homeopathic backgrounds. There are rick-shaw drivers and angry, unemployed young men. There are housewives and college students, and hordes of children from the neighborhood. While some of these people visit Swamiji regularly, others only show up for special occasions or in times of difficulty.

The range of disciples drawn to Swamiji also extends beyond those settled in Nasik. Peasants come from villages in the vicinity, disciples whose jobs took them to different towns return to visit. There are also disciples whose ties with Swamiji derive from his trips elsewhere, such as Gujarat, Delhi, or Bombay. And finally, there are foreigners who come predominantly from the United States, England, France, and Australia. Most of these Westerners met Swamiji when he was visiting the multinational ashram of his Guru, or else they had heard of him from other Western followers. The presence of these fair-skinned religious seekers in Indian clothes was a reminder of the historical moment in which Swamiji and his interactions are set. Gurus today travel abroad; the ones who stay home also accept foreign disciples. Hinduism, always flexible and accommodating, has been further stretched to conform to the demands of an overarching world system.

Among the visitors who had gathered around Swamiji that warm September morning were an American physiotherapist, neat in her sari; a French nurse with attentive brown eyes; a retired south Indian journalist; a clerk from the government mint; a novice celibate wearing an orange shirt; the town barber with mud-streaked clothes and a winning bucktoothed smile. We sat there in Swamiji's presence, listening as he spoke, and sometimes entering the conversation ourselves. Incense drifted from the altar, and the conversation took various twists and turns.

In the course of the morning, two small boys slipped in to deposit white flowers at the altar. With their torn khaki shorts and stained white shirts, they appeared to be schoolboys from poor families in the neighborhood who were on their way to class. They pulled the flowers out of a khaki bag, and laid them fragrant at the feet of the bronze Goddess Saptashring Nivasini Devi; before brass Dattatreya, three-headed Guru of the Gods; on top of the silver-plated sandals of Swamiji's Guru; before the stone monkey-faced Hanuman, painted orange. Though currents of conversation were flowing through the room, these two boys performed their act of worship with silent aplomb. Then they bobbed down before Swamiji's feet, accepted a banana apiece, and were out the door with a scamper of skinny legs. They would be back in the evening when a crowd of local children gathered to sing devotional songs and accept—with grinning delight—more fruit and sweets. "If you want to change the world," Swamiji says, "start with the children. With adults it's often too late." Wherever he goes, his affection, stories, and sweets draw children around him.

Swamiji is one of the most garrulous people I have ever met. Leaning back in his chair, shoulders sloping, glasses glinting, body relaxed and still, he will chat for hours at a stretch. He speaks what he called an "*agaṛam bagaṛam bhāshā*"—a "topsy-turvy language"—composed of several different languages he has been exposed to. Born in the southern state of Karnataka, Kannada is his mother tongue. But because he left home at eighteen to wander north, he has picked up Hindi, India's national language. Through reciting sacred texts, he also uses Sanskrit terms. For the last thirty years he has lived primarily in Maharashtra, and so he speaks an approximation of the regional language, Marathi, too. Along the way he also has picked up a smattering of English words, and if there is no translator present he emphatically repeats these words until a visiting foreigner catches on. In Swamiji's idiosyncratic mixture of all these languages, the basic framework is Hindi, while Kannada case endings, Marathi colloquialisms, Sanskrit religious terms, and English words are all thrown in.

Most of Swamiji's visitors appear to have no trouble understanding him (except when there is tobacco wadded in his cheek and words become impossibly slurred). Having grown up in Bombay where several regional languages are thrown together in a collage mocked by outsiders as "Bombay Hindi," it is easy for me to comprehend Swamiji. A north Indian who spoke impeccably literate Hindi, on the other hand, might well be perplexed by his cheerful mixing together of languages. This was illustrated when a friend from Delhi asked to hear a tape of Swamiji's stories. After several sentences, his discomfort could not be contained. As he confessed, "It's hard to dissociate what he says from the crude language, Bombay Hindi. You know for me, it conjures up associations of a villain in Hindi films. . . ."

The colorful, earthy texture of Swamiji's speech that so disarms the refined literati is, as I reflected daily, impossible to transfer into an English translation, because by translating it into one language I am smoothing out the different languages that sprang to his lips. A linguist would have a field day sorting out the ways in which he mixes and matches the dialects at his disposal. Though varied sociological resonances permeate words that are drawn from different languages and specialized vocabularies within each language,[2] I believe that Swamiji's listeners do not consciously busy themselves with a taxonomy of linguistic elements in each story even if it directs their interpretations. As I have transformed tapes into written English translations, I have tried to capture the flavors I discern in Swamiji's varied use of languages, but I only separate out English itself. English words are all distinguished with an asterisk—for example, "photo,*" "procession,*" "income tax,*" and so on. Sometimes, trying to speak English, Swamiji drolly enunciates wrong words. When he had a bad bout of arthritis, for example, I heard him informing people, "I myself am happy, but this body* is suffering. What to do, it's an old body.* It got arithmetic.*"

A Story

Swamiji has a love for spinning stories—whether folk narratives, reminiscences, or bemused accounts of other lives. That morning, we had spoken about a number of issues: my brother who was ill far off in America; the shine that comes onto people's faces when they worship; the trick of rotating a coconut between two coins; the power of the dollar over the rupee; terrorism in the Punjab. Then Swamiji began telling us stories about a couple, Govindbhai and his wife, who had stopped by the previous night. Govindbhai was an industrialist from Gujarat. Swamiji spoke with affection of the family's simplicity despite their wealth. He described Govindbhai's meticulous work, the air-conditioned house, the simple food, the garden filled with fruit trees, the birds that flew among the flowers, the warmth and hospitality the family extended. Some of us present had met them; I had not. At the crack of dawn, before I arrived from my home, they had set off for Ellora to visit the great Shiva temple. I listened as Swamiji spoke, thinking that though I was learning more than I ever wanted to about these unknown people, this was not a good morning for taping folk narratives.

Shortly before noon, to everyone's surprise, Govindbhai and his wife were back. They came in through the door looking badly shaken. One of the trucks that terrorizes the Indian highways had run right into their Mercedes. The front of the car had been smashed. They could have been killed, and yet here they were: both fine. "It was your blessings that protected us," Govindbhai bowed before Swamiji. "Your blessings," his wife agreed, adjusting her sari over her bent head. They were both small people, delicate featured, fair, wearing simple but obviously expensive clothes.

Swamiji listened to the account of their accident with concern. He asked question after question, as though he too wanted to enter the experience: "Did you see the truck coming?" "How did you get back?" "Will you stay over now?" Govindbhai asked Swamiji if he thought they should make another attempt to get to the temple, procuring another car or hiring a taxi. Swamiji considered the plan, asked more questions to make sure they were not hurt, then agreed it might be a good thing if they returned.

"Today is Thursday," Swamiji said, "so there will be a crowd there. If you go in the evening, the crowd will have thinned. You can have *darshan* in peace."

Darshan, "to view," is the act of obtaining audience from a more powerful being, whether a respected elder, holy person, or image of a deity.[3]

Swamiji, as he spoke, was "giving *darshan*"; soon Govindbhai and his wife would "take *darshan*" at the Shiva temple. The weeks and months, in Swamiji's conception of time, are patterned with traditional Hindu meanings. As a day sacred to the Guru, Thursday (*guruvār*) would mean a fairly large crowd during this sacred month of Shravan. (However, on Monday, sacred to Shiva, the crowds would be at their peak.)

Govindbhai and his wife nodded: yes, they would set off once again. On the wall above us, the clock neared noon. It was a square plastic clock mounted with an image of elephant-headed Ganesh, and inscribed with the names of the people who had given Swamiji this gift linking modern practicality with an ancient deity. Orange Ganesh looked on benignly as the hands moved forward reminding us that it was time for Swamiji to withdraw inside for lunch and a rest. Those of us who had been interjecting occasional comments and exclamations in the background now prepared to leave.

"Maybe God wants to meet you alone," Swamiji continued, oblivious of the time. His face was serious, his voice low and comforting. "There must be some reason [*kāran*] for this happening. There's always a reason."

Then, without warning, he began a story.

*   *   *

There was a King. He had a Minister. Whenever the King said anything—whatever he said—the Minister would say, "That's good!" [*acchā huā*]. Whatever happened, he would say, "It was good that it occurred."

["You might have heard this story," Swamiji looks up at Govindbhai standing at the foot of his chair, "to say that whatever happens is good?" Govindbhai smiles, nodding. In fact, most of the rest of us have heard this story, too, for it is one of Swamiji's favorites.]

One day the King went to hunt somewhere. One of his toes was cut* off. In his assembly, he said, "One of my toes was cut* off."

"That's good," said the Minister.

"What kind of idiot is this?" said the King. "He's my Minister and when I tell him my toe was cut off he says that's good! I'll dismiss* him," he said. "You're sacked from your job," he said.

"Very good," said the Minister.

"Go home!" he said [loud and abrupt].

"That's very good." [Swamiji agreeably rolls his head, voice level and resigned.] He went home.

The King remained silent. He had sent the Minister home. Things continued like this, and then in a few days the King went out hunting. The Minister wasn't around so he took the army [*senā*] with him. Night came. The King went off in one direction, the army went off in the other. The tribal people [*janglī log*] there captured the King. They captured him, and they have a custom for what they catch: the custom of offering sacrifice. "We've found a nice goat," they thought. They were going to offer him to their god. They have a tribal god [*janglī devatā*]. They look out for a good day, those people. After finding this day, all the people of the jungle get together for a big function.* They play all kinds of instruments, then they slaughter something. After slaughtering it, everyone takes away a little consecrated food [*prasād*].

They planned this celebration [*utsav*]: "Just today we found him." They planned to slaughter him. They decorated him, they played instruments. They said, "You're going to be slaughtered and offered as a sacrifice. We will offer you to our god."

There was nobody to free him. Just as goats are taken [for sacrifice], he was being led forward, with a garland around his neck and instruments playing. He was weeping. But who would free him? He was King only in his own house. Now tribals were taking him.

There, from inside the priest [*pūjārī*] was coming forward, dancing like this:

[Swamiji sits upright to wave his right arm above his head, torso swaying.]

There was a big sword in his hand. He came and looked at the King. "So this is the animal!"

["You understand what I mean by 'animal,' don't you?" Swamiji laughs, "Goat!" Govindbhai nods, smiling.]

He walked round* the King three times, holding the sword. The garland had already been put on. He was sprinkling water on the King. He looked at the King from top to bottom. He saw that on his foot, one toe had been cut off.

"Where did you get him from?" he asked [tone indignant and eyes fierce behind spectacles].

Those people asked [voice dropping into surprise], "Why? We brought him from just over there."

"This won't do!" he said [loud again]. "He's been cut once before. Something that's already been cut won't do for our god. It can't be offered to Bhagavan. He's already been cut once. Let him go!" he said.

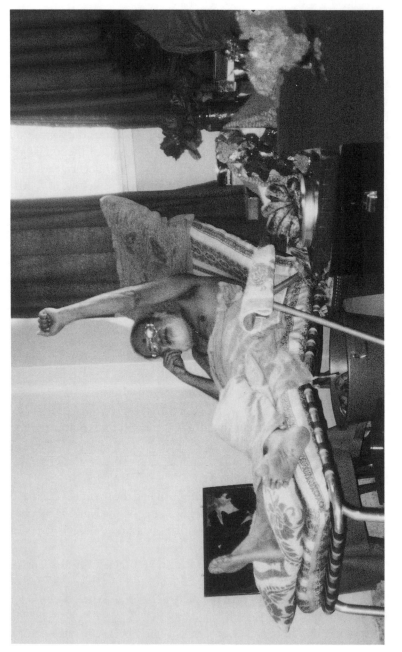

Telling "That's Good, Very Good," Swamiji demonstrates how the tribal priest lifted his sword over the king.

Once he said the King should be released he couldn't be offered. So they set him free.

When the King was freed he thought, "My life was saved!"

[Swamiji is laughing, and the rest of us join, relieved.]

He went and sat on his throne. After he sat there, he called for his Minister. He had been saved because his toe was cut off, right? So he remembered the Minister. He called that same Minister who had said that before. He gave the job back to him. "Come brother, what you said was very good. You said it was good that my toe was cut off. This and that happened to me, and it really was good that the toe had been cut off. My life was saved. Yes? This was good. And you said it was good."

[Govindbhai is called next door for a long distance call from Bombay. "I'll be right back," he tells Swamiji. Swamiji looks after him hurrying out the door. Then after a pause, Swamiji continues for the rest of us present. He fixes his eyes on Govindbhai's wife. She sits on the women's side of the room, nodding her head.]

"You said it was good, and it was good. Then when I dismissed you from your job you said it was very good. What was very good for you in that? You were sent home. You said it was good that my toe was cut* off; you said it was very good that you were dismissed* from work. What's very good about losing a job? What was very good about that?"

The Minister said, "Maharaj, what happened is this: I said it was very good because you and I were always together. Your toe was cut* off. We would have wandered there together. Those people let you go because your toe was cut* off. But my toe isn't cut* off. They would have let you go but caught hold of me. I would have been offered as the sacrifice. Because you let me go, my life was saved too. That's why I said it was very good."

[A pleased murmur of laughter rises through the room.]

Both of them were saved! [Swamiji beams.] It's good, it's very good. Whatever Bhagavan does, there's always some reason or the other.

*   *   *

Emerging from the frame[4] of the story, Swamiji returned to his earlier conjecture that this accident would allow the couple to peacefully visit the temple in the evening when there were no crowds. When Govindbhai returned from the telephone, Swamiji quickly summarized the end of the story for him. Swamiji had scooted forward to the foot of his armchair and lifted a tray of bananas into his lap. Like the tribals who expected their "goat" to be distributed, each of us now stepped forward to receive a banana as consecrated food (*prasād*).[5] Since visitors rarely came in empty-handed, the bunch from which Swamiji wrenched the bananas might have been brought by any one of us present.

"It's all the Lord's will," Govindbhai agreed, receiving a banana and bowing deeply. Then we all trooped out to leave Swamiji alone for his lunch and afternoon rest.

Versions

Folklore, in its very nature, displays multiple existence and variation. Passed along from person to person, memory and improvisation come into play to recast folklore forms which are not rigorously fixed. A folktale like "That's Good, Very Good" (a title Swamiji uses) can be retold in many ways, both by the same teller and by tellers separated in time and space. The version Swamiji told the couple was by no means an authoritative text. Rather, it was just one among many retellings, using a hodge-podge language and narrative details shaped in performance to a particular set of circumstances.[6]

A month earlier, for example, Swamiji had launched into the story when Dr. Hans, a homeopathic doctor from Albuquerque, arrived. Hans had made plans to come visit Swamiji a good deal earlier, but had experienced many frustrating delays. When Hans eventually flew into Bombay, he stopped at his friend Raj Seth's house and learned that it was his birthday. Raj Seth was also a disciple of Swamiji's and, like many followers of a Guru who desire blessings on a special occasion, had been planning to visit Swamiji on this day. So rather than negotiating his trip to Nasik alone, Hans rode the clattering train with Raj Seth.

They arrived in the early afternoon. Swamiji greeted them with warmth. He offered them bananas and advised that they go next door and drink tea to wash away the exhaustion of their trip. As these two broad-shouldered friends, American and Indian, were standing to go, Swamiji looked up at Hans. "You were worried about the delay," he said, "but look how well it turned out! You had a companion to come here with." Then he proceeded to tell this story as Raj Seth translated it into English. Raj Seth came from a minor royal family in the North, and whenever Swamiji mentioned the actions of the King, Raj Seth looked both sheepish and pleased. When

Swamiji prefaced the King's expedition to the jungle with, "Now, it's the habit of kings to go hunting," Raj Seth beamed outright.

Isabel, the French nurse, was present on this occasion. She was also present the next month when Swamiji retold the tale. Later she commented on the somber mood that had pervaded the retelling for Govindbhai in contrast to the spirit of fun that rippled through the retelling for Hans and Raj Seth. There had been a female ascetic visiting Swamiji that day whose Guru was known to inspire explosive spiritual awakenings. With bright-eyed verve, Swamiji had described the tribal priest as undergoing a "spiritual awakening" which made him dance in an ecstatic frenzy. Swamiji elaborated on the scene before the tribal deity with animation. He spoke of the roll of drums, and, sitting upright in his chair, he fluttered his eyes and swayed recklessly from side to side. Everyone present in the audience was grinning, chuckling, or unrestrainedly laughing at this dramatization. The visiting ascetic smiled too, though a little wanly; perhaps she caught on that this might be a parody of what happened to disciples of her own Guru. Yet for Govindbhai and his wife, no mention was made of spiritual awakening. As Isabel observed in her French-accented English, "It is very interesting to see how he tells the same story differently on different occasions."

While in Nasik, I was exclusively concerned with Swamiji's retellings, but on my return to Berkeley I began to place these within the vast Indian tradition of folk narratives. I learned that this is a popular folktale[7] belonging to a larger tradition of stories featuring exchanges between a king and a sharp-witted courtier: in the North, there are cycles of stories involving King Akbar and his courtier Birbal, while in the South, King Krishna Deva Raya and his courtier Tenaliraman are well-known. In Berkeley alone, I encountered several Indians who recognized the story. A woman from the Punjab remembered reading this in a Hindi reader as a child; a man from Madhya Pradesh recalled having heard a variant in which a man whose finger had been cut off was later freed by thugs who wished to sacrifice him before the Goddess Kali. Among printed collections, however, I have came across just one variant.[8] This is from Pandit S. M. Natesa Sastri's *Indian Folk Tales*.

Natesa Sastri (1859–1906) was a learned man from Madras who published widely in both Tamil and English. His collections of folktales were based on Tamil versions drawn from his own memory and then translated into English. His retellings are obviously addressed to a non-Indian audience since he feels called upon to explicate Hindu beliefs. To show how a story changes across regions, through time, between tellers, and even among translators, I reproduce the quaintly worded story that appeared in his *Indian Folk Tales*.[9]

It Is for the Best

In a certain country there lived a king who had a peculiar minister, and whatever the minister consulted him about he always replied, "It is for the best." In a word, this minister was what would now be called an optimist.

One day the king lost one of his fingers in handling a sharp instrument, and, sending for the minister, he showed him his hand and said, sorrowfully, "See what a calamity has happened to me; I have lost one of my fingers."

The minister coolly replied, "It is for the best."

Greatly was the monarch enraged. "Vile wretch! Do you dare to say that the loss of a finger is for the best? You shall see the result of your stupid motto. You shall live in prison for scores of years," said the king. But again the minister merely replied, "It is for the best."

"What impertinence!" said the king, and sent the minister off to jail; and so our hero had to undergo imprisonment.

The day after this affair the king went to the forest to hunt, to which amusement he was in the habit of taking the minister along with him. But as he had imprisoned him he had to go all alone, and after a long tiring hunt, he rested under a tree for a short sleep. Before long he heard the roar of a lion and considered himself as good as dead, for the lord of the beasts had seen the lord of men and had marked him down for his prey. The king went off into a dead faint. Now, it is a belief among the Hindus, that lions do not eat a man who is deformed or who sleeps. And so when the lion examined the fainting king and came to the mutilated hand he went away, spurning the monarch as useless for his prey as long as a finger was wanting.

When the king awoke, he thought within himself, "The words of my good minister have proved to be true when I showed him my deformed hand yesterday and he said, 'It is for the best'; but I, in the love of my own self, took his words in a wrong sense and imprisoned him. Now, had it not been for my lost finger I would have fallen a prey to the lion. So my loss has worked for my good. But what good can possibly result from the imprisonment of my minister? He said it was for the best, and I shall ascertain from his own mouth what he meant."

So thinking the king returned, and at once ordered the minister to be released and to be brought before him. He came and stood before his lord accordingly, and the king explained to him all about the lion and how his words had proved to be true so far. "But how can my sending you to jail be for the best?" said the king.

Replied the minister, "My most noble lord! Had it not been for my imprisonment in the jail I would have accompanied you to the forest and fallen a prey to the lion. After rejecting you for being deformed he would have

taken me away for his feast. So I should have died. Therefore even my having lived in jail for a day was for the best."

The king was extremely pleased with the reply and received his minister
into still greater confidence.

This is obviously the same story, even if the details are different. It is at
the same level of what Vladímir Propp has called "functions," or the actions of the characters in a folktale. Alan Dundes has suggested that the
term "function" be replaced by "motifeme" and that the varying details
which fill the slot of a motifeme be termed "allomotifs." As Dundes has
demonstrated, allomotifs are generally symbolically equivalent.[10] Indeed,
applying this structural framework to the story of "That's Good, Very
Good," the details that vary between Swamiji's and Natesa Sastri's versions
can be seen as equivalent. The King loses a toe in one case, a finger in another; both are extremities, the loss of which, though painful, is not greatly
debilitating. The Minister is sent home in one case and to jail in the other;
both tales involve a dismissal from court. The King goes to the forest to
hunt and ends up alone. Tribal people capture him in one case, and he falls
asleep in another; both being captured and falling asleep involve a vulnera-
bility, a loss of control. The King is prepared for sacrifice to a tribal deity
in one case and is about to be eaten by a lion in the other; both the tribal
deity and the lion represent a powerful, dangerous figure associated with
the forest as an area beyond the King's domain.

Although the thrust of meaning remains much the same between Natesa Sastri's and Swamiji's versions, Natesa Sastri presents the view that
everything that happens is for the best as an example of a Pangloss-like
optimism. Swamiji, on the other hand, locates this proposition within a
religious perspective: it happens for the best because this is Bhagavan's
will. Here, then, is a concrete example of how a single story can be told as
entertainment or charged with religious meaning, depending on the views
of the teller. Every *sādhu*, after all, was once an uninitiated child who listened to stories told by relatives and friends. What was once told by a
mother may later be retold by a Guru to rapt disciples. But since stories are
reshaped by a teller's creativity and concerns, a *sādhu's* version is likely to
highlight religion.

If this is a traditional story, what then are the cultural categories contained in it? As is the case with most other Indian stories featuring kings
and ministers, the King represents willfulness and force, while the Minister stands for a considered wisdom that corrects and contains the King's

brash actions. Although caste is not explicitly mentioned, the King is probably a hot-blooded warrior while the Minister is a restrained Brahman. The folk tradition has charged the relationship between Kings and Ministers, Kshatriyas and Brahmans, with a proverbial quality, to which Swamiji had alluded in situations extending beyond this particular story. Two years earlier, for example, I had heard him admonish Prakash Seth, who had been entrusted with the responsibility for distributing specially prepared sweets to visitors. Prakash Seth had followed Swamiji's instructions too literally, and problems had ensued. "Even if a King is an idiot," Swamiji chided, "the Minister should be smart. You should think things through for yourself." Later the same summer, Swamiji told the legend of the Nose-Cutter sect in which a Prime Minister's grandfather saves a kingdom. "Now a Prime Minister," Swamiji said, "is always smarter than a King." Standing by the King's side with a detached wisdom, the Minister is structurally equivalent to the holy man who stands to the side of the world, setting events in a cosmic perspective. By assuring Govindbhai—a man of wealth and power, a king in Indian industry—that it was a good thing he had met with an accident, Swamiji was paralleling the Minister's assurances to the King. Like the Minister, he had transformed the account of an accident into a narrative of God's grace. Similarly with Dr. Hans, he had replaced a story of frustrating mishaps with one in which inconveniences made sense. Experience became redefined.

The jungle, where indigenous tribal people live, is a "heart of darkness" for the caste Hindu imagination: here, *adharma,* the forces of chaos opposing the ordered social world, holds sway.[11] It is here, presumably, that the King first lost his little toe while hunting; it is here that he is captured and in danger of losing his life. Though a King in his own domain, in this dangerous territory he is little better than a goat. The story indicates that tribals are cannibalistic "savages" with a bloodthirsty god. Yet many Hindu village deities, particularly goddesses, also have cults involving sacrifice and possession. On the mountain where Swamiji lived for many years, goats were sometimes sacrificed on the rock stairway to the Goddess's temple, until the steps were slippery and red. Animal sacrifice is now outlawed there, but when Swamiji described the King as a goat garlanded with flowers and sprinkled with purifying water, it is likely that he was drawing on images he himself had witnessed.

This story emphasizes that suffering may carry consequences that are positive in a larger picture. Swamiji's chosen deity (*ishta devatā*) is the

Mother Goddess, and when people bring him their troubles he often says, "Pray to Her; She is compassionate [*dayālu*]." Suffering, he explains, can be her way of teaching. Just as a mother may slap her child and pour bitter worm medicine down his throat before she takes him in her lap and feeds him sweets, so, explains Swamiji, the Mother doles out suffering to cure people of their imperfections and to make them wise. Another analogy he often uses is that of a bit of metal lying by the road. Only after being hammered and pounded with many blows does this piece of junk become a valuable object such as a watch; in the same way, a person should view the blows of fate as a means of self-improvement.

The extent to which some of Swamiji's listeners accept the view put forward in this story was illustrated by Nathu Maharaj, the barber, who later told me as we sat in his garret crowded with children and grandchildren, "This world is a good place, even when there are difficulties. One should understand that it's a good place. Otherwise you become sad. What's meant to happen will happen." Or, as both Mr. Karnad, the south Indian journalist, and "Prabhu," the Jewish American hypnotherapist, said at different times—collapsing this story into an English adage much as a fan is slapped slim—"Everything is for the best."

When Swamiji so triumphantly said, "Both of them were saved!" he seemed to express relief for all of us shaken by the Gujarati couple's near escape from death. He often uses stories like this one to calm and counsel people at times of crisis. He could just extend a summary assurance that everything will turn out to be fine, but by telling a story, he evokes the emotions of loss, fear, and hope and binds people in suspense. Relating people's experience to a traditional tale, Swamiji reaffirms that the apparently arbitrary, often tragic events that occur in the course of everyday life make sense within an overarching framework of meaning. People do not just lose toes; they lose jobs (like the Minister), cars (like Govindbhai and his wife), time (like Dr. Hans). They lose health, loved ones, confidence, and even faith. Swamiji accepts all these losses when they are reported to him. He empathizes with the person concerned. But he also stresses that while the meaning may not immediately be apparent, it may later be discovered through hindsight and reflection. This attitude extends comfort, encouraging people not to grieve over the past but to scan events for any possible positive consequences. By finding an emotional resolution for disappointment or tragedy, people can continue with the life that stretches on ahead.

Bhagavan

When Swamiji speaks of Bhagavan, he means God, yet "Bhagavan" has penumbra of Hindu associations that become altogether eclipsed by monotheistic Christian meanings when translated directly into English. Bhagavan is a term of male gender that can be used generally for abstract God, or in association with particular deities, as in Ram Bhagavan, Krishna Bhagavan, and so on.[12] Sometimes Swamiji refers to the divine principle as Bhagavati—Goddess. She is Jagajanani—Mother of all Beings, in whose presence Swamiji always sits; She is Jagadamba, Mother of the Universe, in whose name he greets each person who bows before him. Swamiji cheerfully moves between male and female references to the divine principle: both are complementary, Shiva and Shakti, Vishnu and Lakshmi, and so forth. This nonchalance about attributing a particular identity to a divine principle is shared by many Hindus and has often bemused Western observers. Classical Hindu doctrine phrases this multiplicity in terms of one supreme Brahman, transcendent and formless, who manifests in myriad forms. Among these forms are 33 million deities (*deva*), a figure that Swamiji is fond of citing, his eyes enormous: "Thirty-three MILLION!"

One afternoon, two years before this story was told, Swamiji had explained Hindu polytheism to me in terms of the believers who projected forms onto the formless. He was lying on the cool, green linoleum, resting on one side with a hand under his chin. I sat cross-legged at some distance, a tape twirling in the recorder. Prakash Seth, a farmer and disciple from a nearby village, was massaging Swamiji's feet. I had asked Swamiji what he thought of visions during meditation, and he had answered, "More than seeing Bhagavan, you should *become* Bhagavan." Then the followng conversation took place:

> SWAMIJI: The way we are is how we describe our deity [*deva*]. Take a pig . . . or else a buffalo. It too probably thinks, "There's a Bhagavan just like me. He has two horns, four legs, a little tail. . . ."
> [Kirin explodes into laughter at this droll image of a buffalo contemplating its God. Swamiji grins and continues.]
> SWAMIJI: Yes? Buffalos also probably think about what kind of Bhagavan they have. Goats probably think about it, dogs probably think about it, too. That's why, in our Hindu religion [*dharma*] everything has been made into Bhagavan. Buffalos are Bhagavan, dogs are Bhagavan. Someone might say, "In your *dharma*, in the Hindu *dharma* there are *so many* deities!" We call

dogs Bhagavan, we call buffalos Bhagavan too. Cows, fish, then trees. Trees have life, too, don't they?

KIRIN (murmurs): Yes.

SWAMIJI: They too probably think [in a low, marveling voice], "There's a tree, with many branches, with lots of fruit." Our scriptures [*shāstra*], you know, are ve-r-ry deep. Look, a peepul tree, it's very big, it stays alive for a thousand years. The tree folk have made this a Bhagavan. Yes? What do you think, Prakash Seth, isn't that so?

PRAKASH SETH: Yes, Baba. On full moon, we worship the *vār,* the *pīpal* . . . [kinds of trees].

SWAMIJI: We say there are 33 million [*tethīs kotī*] Bhagavan. There are 33 million kinds of life, and there are as many Bhagavan as there are kinds of life.

[Kirin's tape snaps to a halt; she fumbles to insert another. Swamiji looks on, indulgent and nearsighted, for his spectacles are off. He waits, sticking a wad of tobacco in his mouth, until the new tape is in place. Then he continues.]

SWAMIJI: A person, you know, can't directly arrive at the attributeless [*nirguṇ*], to the formless [*nirākār*]. Bhagavan has no form [*ākār*]. If you want to reach the formless, you can only go from what has form [*sākār*] to what has no form. First form, then the formless. Only by staying with a form will you slowly, slowly, come to the formless.

Why? Because all this is formless. Take a flower: some people practice this. Stare and stare at the flower, and it will disappear. You went from form to the formless. I'm telling the truth. If you look and look at a person, too, you no longer see the person. Through form you come to the formless. Actually, a person has no form and is formless. But we create forms: "This is this, that is that." Now if you say this, does it mean everything is false [*jhūṭ*]? No, it's not false. Form didn't exist before, and it won't exist afterwards. But now it's here. [Swamiji raises himself on an elbow, to ask Kirin intently:] When you look back, were you sitting here a month ago?

KIRIN (shaking her head): No.

SWAMIJI: Is there any guarantee* that you'll be sitting here tomorrow at this time? Or in four months? You're here now. . . . [Someone knocks at the door, and Swamiji calls out, "Who's there, *jī*?" So this conversation abruptly ends and another, involving greetings and questions about a family, flows into form.]

The concept of God as Bhagavan, then, is broad enough to include a stupendous array of forms. Swamiji's acceptance of relative points of view exemplifies the Hindu perspective at its most tolerant: each to his or her own God. He enjoyed citing the Marathi proverb, "Where the feeling, there the God" (*ticche bhāv tikṛe dev*). This acceptance of multiplicity and the position that all forms are in flux express the classical Hindu view of the phenomenal world as illusion (*māyā*) and the Hindu conception of vast cycles of mythological time in which this universe, one among millions, is placed. Since forms are representations of the formless, it is acceptable for Hindus to worship a lively collection of different deities depending on family and regional traditions, as well as personal choice. As in Swamiji's altar, homes of religious Hindus have many different gods present. And even the tribals, as this story shows, have their own "jungle god."

Hindu *Dharma*

Just as when Bhagavan is equated with God, when *dharma* is translated as "religion" its meaning overlaps only partially with religion as a Western category.[13] *Dharma* means religion but also stands for duty, role, function, righteousness, and law. Deriving from the Sanskrit root *dhri*, "to hold together," "to support," *dharma* is that which aligns the individual with the group and eventually the workings of the universe. Swami R., a young renouncer close to Swamiji, drew on a quote from Sanskrit to elucidate this concept: "*Dhārayati yāh sāh dharma,*" or "Dharma is that which supports." Depending on context—the locale (*desh*) and the time (*kal*)—*dharma* varies; it is recognized that what is *dharma* in one place and moment can be its opposite, *adharma,* in another. Similarly, *dharma* differs from person to person and group to group. The ultimate aim of *dharma* is to direct an individual toward salvation while living in society, though the final step toward *moksha,* liberation, may involve renunciation of the social world.

Dharma is the closest indigenous equivalent for religion, and what we refer to today as Hinduism is a clumping together of a great diversity of sects and doctrinal positions, a number of coexisting and sometimes rival *dharmas.* The term "Hindu" was first used by Muslims to describe Indians who had not converted to Islam; it was next adopted by British colonizers and has finally come to be accepted by Indians themselves. Hinduism has emerged through the interaction between indigenous religions, the formation of dissenting sects, and the encounters with first Islam and subsequently Christianity. Contemporary Hinduism, then, is a historical accretion, with layers of earlier visions coexisting in doctrine and practice.[14]

Because believers tend to seek ultimate truths rather than historically shaped practices, I suspect that neither Swamiji nor his visitors are interested in the historical dimension of the religion he advocates. Yet history underlies their belief and practice. When Swamiji tells people to perform fire ceremonies (*yajna* or *havan*), he is echoing ancient Vedic practices. Advising others to meditate, he is playing upon themes elaborated in the *Upanishads*. He revels in the complexities of Puranic mythologies. He emphasizes the importance of *bhakti*, devotion, advising that deep love is a simple means of union with divinity. He is also concerned with social responsibility as an aspect of religion. Following the example of nineteenth-century reformers like Vivekananda, he has striven to arrange meals for the poor, facilitate education for tribal children, find jobs for widows, and so on. Though not active in politics, he is interested in current affairs and listens to the news on the radio each day. When visitors gather, the conversation often establishes a bridge between political events and a religious world view. The message that Swamiji repeats runs counter to the alarming contemporary wave of Hindu chauvinism and religious separatism. "Look after other people," he says. "Treat them as your own, whatever caste or country they are from. The same divine Self [*ātman*] in them is in you, too."

Although Hinduism has changed through history, it also exhibits considerable geographic variation at any particular moment in time. While there are certain common elements unifying Hinduism through the subcontinent, it lacks a centralized, monitoring authority. From region to region, caste to caste, sect to sect, and even family to family, there is a staggering diversity in practice and belief. How to make sense of any unity amid all the differences has been a bewildering issue for students of Hinduism. Can patterns of unity be found in the "spread" of elements across regions and between castes?[15] Does unity emerge in the interactions between Sanskritic and folk traditions?[16] Does unity lie at the level of "images" of the world which are recombined in different ways?[17] Or is unity manifested in "cultural performances"—observable units of cultural behavior such as dance performances, storytelling sequences, or gatherings for devotional songs which surface in villages and cities throughout the subcontinent?[18] Given the subject of my research, I find this last approach of cultural performances, formulated by Milton Singer, to be the most helpful in connecting the specificity of what I studied with Hinduism in the widest sense.

When Swamiji tells stories he is involved in an informal cultural performance; informal, because these stories are not demarcated as predictable events but arise spontaneously in the flow of ongoing activities. Drawn from both Sanskritic texts and folk traditions, his folk narratives are connected historically and geographically, through texts and performances, to other versions. When he tells portions of the *Mahābhārata,* for example, his rendition is one link in a chain of oral storytelling by *sādhus,* professional storytellers, *paṇḍits* and lay people. It is also related to dance or drama productions of the story (including Peter Brook's); to Sanskrit, vernacular, and English texts; to paintings and posters; and possibly even to a television production or two. Although each storytelling session is unique because it is shaped around a particular situation, all the folk narratives that Swamiji uses express themes integral to a Hindu world view that remains recognizable despite historical and regional variation. Following the bright strands of meaning in his folk narratives out into the Hindu tradition, one sees patterns that are repeated through the entire fabric. Multi-formed, many-hued, this fabric spun through stories extends through time and space without any clear edges.

2. Lives and Stories

"It's hardly that *I* make up the stories," said Swamiji one morning. He had just enquired whether I liked the story I had taped, and I had replied that it was beautiful like all the stories he told. "I only tell what has come to us from the past," Swamiji said, redirecting my compliment. "This happened, then that happened. I don't make anything up. I just tell what's already there."

"But as you tell a story don't you change it?" I asked, straining forward. As soon as Swamiji mentioned stories, I had switched on the tape recorder beside me. "Like you—"

"A person tells stories according to the feelings [*bhāvanā*] he has," said Swamiji. I murmured assent, and Swamiji paused. "What were you saying just now?" he asked. "I interrupted you."

Fumbling for expression as I translated into Hindi concepts that I had previously understood only in English, I said, "I was just thinking, it seems to me that every time you tell a story you change it a little, so it includes the people sitting there."

"Their feelings!" said Swamiji, extending a hand to the assembled group: a young *brahmachārī* wearing orange, two slim French women in saris, a college student in tight trousers, a hotel keeper with a white dhoti hooped between his legs, an American with a ponytail at the back of his balding head, a little girl with a nosering and bright red ribbons in her hair. Though for a moment the conversation was just between Swamiji and me, everyone else was looking on with interest. "Yes, I tell stories so they fit their feelings," Swamiji acknowledged.

"When you tell a story," he began again after a moment's reflection, "you should look at the situation and tell it. Then it turns out well. If you tell just any story any time, it's not really good. You must consider the time and shape the story so it's right. All stories are told for some purpose."

At this point Nathu Maharaj, the barber who visited daily, shuffled in, grinning from ear to ear. "Now Nathu Maharaj has come," said Swamiji. "He's reminded me of a story." "Tell it!" exclaimed Nathu Maharaj. "I'll tell a story that's been told before," said Swamiji. "A story should be told well. Understand?" He adjusted his spectacles and added, "Take it as a joke.*"

The story was about a Barber, attached to King Akbar's court, who had tried to oust a Brahman but was apprehended by the shrewd minister, Birbal, and ended up dying himself. Legends about Birbal are favorites among children, and Satish, a twelve-year-old boy who had also just arrived, seemed to know the story well. As Swamiji proceeded in a leisurely way through the plot, Satish raced ahead foreshadowing events with excitement. Each time Satish interrupted Swamiji, Nathu Maharaj tried to hush him with a poke in the back. Finally Nathu Maharaj issued a stern "Shut up!" The story cast the Barber as a sly and unsavory character, but this did not seem to offend Nathu Maharaj. He was used to being teased by Swamiji. At comic moments in the plot, he laughed hardest, his betel-stained buck teeth splaying straight out.

Having been steeped in theories of performance, I was exhilarated to find that Swamiji acknowledged that stories emerged in particular contexts to make particular points and were shaped by the interaction between teller and audience. Concepts learned in graduate school, I thought, did indeed hold up in everyday life! I was anxious to pursue this line of talk, but was reluctant to divert public conversations toward my own interests. I had to wait until Swamiji himself spoke directly about stories again. He had just told the story of "That's Good, Very Good" to Dr. Hans. On finishing, he noticed that I clicked my tape recorder off. "I've told you this story before, haven't I?" he asked. "Why did you tape it then?"

"Because each time you tell it differently," I replied.

Swamiji agreed, reiterating that he changed stories with each retelling. "It depends on what the person who's listening is like. Stories, you know, are about people."

I went on to ask where Swamiji had learned "That's Good, Very Good." "How can I say where?" Swamiji waved aside the question. "Someone like you told it, I listened. Someone tells, another hears. Whatever is needed in the heart [dil] will settle in the mind [man]. Isn't that so? Do you remember everything you hear? Just sometimes you remember a story and you can tell it in a flash."

"Like a computer,*" put in a troll-like man who worked for the railways and sat hunched on the floor, staring intently at Swamiji.

"I hear a lot," Swamiji continued, acknowledging the man's comment with a nod, "but I don't understand or remember everything. At a certain time you recall a story, and then you make a link* to whatever is happening. So far I must have heard so many stories. This is why I say the Lord is within you and is the one who teaches you. We think, 'I learned this! I have value*!' But we are nothing. It's all the Lord."

This comment juxtaposed storytelling and religion but at a different angle from the one that I had envisaged. Focusing on how stories serve as vehicles for morals, it had not occurred to me that a religious storyteller might see his stories as divinely inspired. One afternoon soon afterward, Swamiji reiterated this position in a different way. He had unexpectedly launched into a folktale about two friends, a Prince and a Prime Minister's son, and their various adventures. It was a gripping tale, but I could not understand why Swamiji had decided to tell it. When I asked him, Swamiji said, "I told it spontaneously. There was no reason. I'm not the one who tells the stories. The teller is Bhagavan." Once again he brushed aside my desire to pinpoint personal sources and motivations, speaking instead in terms of the overarching divine will.

While on the subject of stories, I questioned Swamiji about how he delineated different genres of tales. There were four words that I had heard him use for stories: *kathā*, *kahānī*, *drishṭānt*, and *upamā*. I started by asking about *kathā* and *kahānī*. In other parts of India, I knew, a difference is recognized between *kathā* as a religious story believed to be true and often accompanying a ritual, and *kahānī* as a purely fictional and secular tale. Yet Swamiji seemed to use the two words interchangeably. In response to my question, he said, "They're the same thing." This statement could indicate that from his perspective, both kinds of stories can be used to illuminate religious principles acting in the world. Whether or not a story is light entertainment in other contexts, it can be transformed in retelling to convey religious teaching. It is also possible that in his view both kinds of narratives are grouped together as fictions of illusion (*māyā*), since the highest reality cannot be represented through arrangements of words.

I went on to ask about the other two terms, *drishṭānt* and *upamā*. Swamiji made me repeat my question, his face solemn as he leaned forward to listen. "A *drishṭānt*," he said, "means how something came to pass. It can also be something that you see in the future, something that will happen to you. When you sit to worship, you see that something will happen. When it happens, it's a *drishṭānt*." In this definition, Swamiji used the word in terms of a vision or narrative of future events. Yet in the course of conversation he sometimes used *drishṭānt* differently, as "illustration." While discoursing on the nature of the universe, for example, Swamiji would often say, "There's a *drishṭānt*," and then build a metaphorical analogy that often emerged as a short narrative.

As for *upamā*, Swamiji said, "This is used to properly explain what something is, to give an example. This is something, this is how it happens. Something happens to someone, and you look at the reason that it happened. . . . What was the cause? This is an *upamā*." He went on to cite the example of "That's Good, Very Good" that he had told Govindbhai the previous day as an *upamā*. The term *upamā*, then, applies when a story is brought out as a mirror that reflects certain aspects of a situation; an *upamā* is a parable (from the Greek *parabola*—"to compare").

Whenever I systematically questioned Swamiji, I worried later about having been impertinent in twisting his conversations to my own ends. After this exchange I let general theories of storytelling rest and focused on taping, transcribing, and talking about particular tales. Several weeks and many tapes later, we returned by chance to the theme of storytelling as religious teaching. Swamiji had just told a story about a naive celibate novice (*brahmachārī*) who saw a married couple and mistook them for gods. As Swamiji described the boy leaving the mountain where his Guru lived to visit the town I thought I recognized the settings of the story. Surely, I reasoned, this must be a story drawn from Swamiji's own experience that he now retold in the style of a folktale. The place where the Guru lived seemed much like the mountain village where Swamiji had stayed in the past, and the town could well have been Nasik. I asked Swamiji whether this tale had actually occurred and if it was about these places.

"No, it's not about Saptashring and Nasik," Swamiji looked at me with surprise. "It's a traditional story [*pauranic kathā*]. But as I tell stories, I put in things. Whatever the story is, I tell it my own way."

"Yes, yes," I said. As he spoke, I was linking back his words to theoretical perspectives in anthropology. He seemed to emphasize the extent to which received culture is recreated in performance; that even the most "traditional" arenas of culture are in dynamic process, improvised on by individuals. I thought of an article by Walter Benjamin in which there was a passage that echoed what Swamiji had just said about telling stories his own way.[1]

> [A story] does not aim to convey the pure essence of the thing, like information or a report. It sinks the thing into the life of the storyteller, in order to bring it out of him again. Thus traces of the storyteller cling to the story the way handprints of the potter cling to the clay vessel.

Swamiji went on: "In many *Purāṇas*, the Mahatmas [Great Souls] tell stories as examples [*upamā*]. To give an example, they put one story into another. This is while they're giving instruction. To make things stick in people's heads, as they speak Mahatmas put in stories as examples." He paused, rubbing his chin as he looked out of the screen door. "When I tell stories," he turned back toward me to reiterate, "I never make them up. They're all traditional."

"Where did you hear all these traditional stories?" I asked, absurdly hoping that he might review his life with a systematic catalogue of the places and people that were the sources of his narratives. But Swamiji just smiled and shook his head.

"Mataji, look at my age: sixty-eight! I must have heard *so many* stories."

"So many," I agreed.

"I don't go anywhere now, but just think how much I wandered in the past! I went to many different places. I heard stories told in different styles, by different kinds of people. And all these stories probably got lodged in my head. I heard many in discourses. You don't need to read something to remember it. Things that you've heard stick in your head. It's easier to re-member things you hear than what you read. When you hear something, the action* makes it stick in your mind. When you read, there's no ac-tion,* but when you hear something, the acting* makes it stick imme-diately. It's not the same when you read; to remember something you have to reread it many times. Then it sticks in your head. But what you've heard you can immediately recall: I heard it on that particular day, in that par-ticular place. You remember what the person said. Does this happen when you read? No. You would have to reread it many times and make an effort to memorize it."

This comment revealed Swamiji's alignment to an oral tradition, al-though before he lost his vision he could read and write. Writing has been present in India for over three millennia, yet large portions of the popula-tion remain illiterate, and much cultural knowledge continues to be orally transmitted. Swamiji's description of associating sound with gesture, and of words being entangled in concrete human situations, points to the attri-butes of an oral culture.[2] My own dependence on tapes and notebooks to store memories was a source of perpetual amusement to him. "Through writing," he once said, "you learn to forget."

All these comments were addressed to me, in direct dialogue with Swam-iji's understanding of my project. They indicate that he has a conscious, sophisticated understanding of the way stories are used and reshaped, how they are assimilated into his repertoire, and how his storytelling carries forward past traditions. I wondered how much my presence had caused

Swamiji to systematize incipient theories, but I heard him speak about stories even when he wasn't addressing me. Additionally, other people reported on comments he had made when I was not present.

For example, when he was told that a young man had been killed in an accident, Swamiji mused to a cluster of white-haired visitors that perhaps this wasn't such a bad thing after all. "If just we old people died, Bhagavan would get fed up. Some young people should die, too! Otherwise, Bhagavan will say, 'What use is this old storyteller?' When you choose vegetables, don't you prefer the fresh ones to the old and rotten? If only old people died, they'd just sit around in heaven swapping stories. There should be someone strong to serve Bhagavan. Maybe that's why many good young people die." White-haired Purshottam Seth nodded, lips twisting in an expression that was reflective, sad, and amused at the same time. An elderly couple from Poona smiled. With this comment, Swamiji had lifted the somberness that accompanied the news of death.

On another occasion, Swamiji had linked stories with the young rather than the old. Dr. Mukund reported an exchange that had occurred between my two field trips: English "Dattatreya" apparently had asked Swamiji why he told stories with talking animals. "You know animals don't speak to human beings like that," "Dattatreya" had said. "The Western mind likes things logical, like two plus two is four, you know." Swamiji responded, "When you were a child didn't you read stories like that?" "Yes," "Dattatreya" replied. "In kindergarten books didn't lions talk?" "Yes." "Well, I tell these stories because in the eyes of Bhagavan we are always children. We are Her children. We have to approach Her like a child."

The Hindu Narrative Tradition

Many of Swamiji's comments about storytelling emphasize his grounding in a tradition of religious stories and storytellers. These other texts and tellers surround his own use in a gentle penumbra of presence. I accepted what Swamiji said, and thought I understood the sources he alluded to in vague terms. Yet when I started to write my dissertation, I found that my implicit knowledge needed organization, revision, and further precision. Circling around Swamiji into the tradition to which he aligns himself, I found that the sources for his stories could be organized into four major groups, even though many stories seeped between categories.

STORIES IN HINDU SCRIPTURE

The Hindu sacred texts can be divided into two categories: *shruti* and *smriti*. *Shruti,* "what is heard," is a core set of texts which contain the fundamental tenets of Hinduism. These texts include the *Vedas,* the *Brāhmaṇas,* and the *Upanishads,* and they are believed to have emerged from direct spiritual revelation. The earliest Vedic text, the *Rig Veda,* may be as old as 1200 B.C.[3] The latest major *Upanishad* (and there are many minor ones) dates from roughly the fifth century B.C. This cluster of texts contains narratives that range from accounts of creation to stories backing ritual and parables told by religious teachers to their students. *Upanishad* means "sitting beneath" and, indeed, most of the *Upanishads* relate the teachings gleaned at the feet of various teachers. R. Mookerji, describing the *Upanishads* in his *Ancient Indian Education,* observes, "In these discourses are found utilized all the familiar devices of oral teaching such as apt illustrations . . . stories . . . and parables."[4] Clearly, the use of storytelling as a medium for religious instruction extends far back into Indian history.

While the *shruti* set of texts are fixed, the *smriti* set are open-ended. Texts grouped under *smriti,* "what is remembered," include the great *Rāmāyaṇa* and *Mahābhārata* epics, eighteen main *Purāṇas* and many subsidiary ones, and law books like the *Dharma Shāstras.* Since *smriti* can be added to and elaborated upon, various sectarian traditions have their own interpretations of what constitutes *smriti* scripture. Stories are important in this group as well. The narratives in the *Mahābhārata* (300 B.C. to A.D. 300) and the *Rāmāyaṇa* (200 B.C. to A.D. 200) have powerfully shaped the Hindu imagination: they are told, performed, rewritten, parodied, and often alluded to in the course of ongoing life. Both have a primary narrative that often branches off into other stories as well as metaphysical musings (the *Bhagavad Gītā,* part of the *Mahābhārata,* is a celebrated example of an excursion into philosophy at a gripping moment in a plot). The eighteen major *Purāṇas,* which were composed between A.D. 300–1500, are also replete with stories; depending on the sect to which a particular *Purāṇa* was sacred, the central personae vary between different deities in the Hindu pantheon. A *Purāṇa* that is particularly popular for performance by professional storytellers is the *Bhāgavata,* starring Krishna, incarnation of Vishnu the Preserver.[5]

This distinction between *shruti* and *smriti* is one I learned when still in India. While tracking down readings that might help me comprehend

Swamiji's storytelling, however, I discovered an article by Thomas Coburn which critiques the prevailing conceptions of Hindu scripture. Coburn points out that the definition of what constitutes Hindu "scripture" is Christian-biased and literary. Written texts, he argues, should really be considered as a subset of holy verbal phenomenon in Hinduism, because in actual practice mystical experience and the oral transmission of religious concepts are emphasized over what is written down. To a disciple, the words of a Guru may achieve the status of revealed *shruti,* and so, instead of being fixed in a distant past, *shruti* "must be seen as an ongoing and experientially based feature of the Hindu religious tradition."[6] Coburn also points out that the sacredness accorded to a particular text is histori-cally contingent. The *Bhagavad Gītā,* for example, is considered so holy that it could be grouped among the *shruti* texts; yet the *Bhagavad Gītā's* status springs from the colonial interest in isolating one representative scripture or "Hindu Bible."[7] Coburn breaks down the rigid *shruti/smriti* distinction, arguing that while certain portions of "scripture" are immu-table and sacred, other portions are continually changing as they are re-told, rewritten, and improvised.

Swamiji would agree with Coburn's assertion that a Guru's words are sacred, revealed wisdom. Shortly after his own Guru died, Swamiji re-flected, "The Guru is absorbed in the Absolute [*brahman*]. That's why his speech is the Absolute: it is everywhere in this universe. For this reason, the Guru's words should be worshipped. This, I think, is what we should understand."

"I don't know how to speak properly," Swamiji continued as his rapt disciples listened. As usual, even though he backed the authority of the Guru as an abstract principle which could surface in many beings, he ducked an ascription of wisdom to himself. "I think that the Guru's words will never be destroyed; they will always remain, they are immortal. This body has shit, urine, and all kinds of other impurities in it. It has good qualities and bad qualities. We don't want the bad qualities, we want the good ones. This is what I think."

Swamiji went on to fondly describe some idiosyncrasies of his Guru. Then he said, "We shouldn't imitate his actions but his teachings. That's the service of the Guru. What he's said, the words we have listened to, will endure. Even if the body goes, these are still with us. We worship his words. We follow them though his body went. Our bodies will go, too; no one stops over."

As Swamiji mused about the power of the Guru's words, tears had come into the eyes of the retired journalist, Mr. Karnad. He later asked me for the transcription so he could write it down for himself. For me this was a concrete and moving illustration of how a disciple can treasure a Guru's words as "scripture."

STORY COLLECTIONS

Though Hindu scriptures contain many narratives, there is also a cluster of Buddhist, Jain, and Hindu story collections known as the "*Kathā* literature." These collections are not watertight compartments, and often motifs, themes, and entire tales have seeped between them. Of particular importance are the Buddhist *Jātaka* tales, a collection of stories attributed to the Buddha who, on confronting particular situations, lapsed into reminiscences of his past lives. These "birth stories," dating from about the fourth century B.C., are often echoed in other story collections. In addition, there are the *Panchatantra* fables (which inspired Aesop), the *Hitopadesha,* the *Sukasaptati,* the *Kathāsaritsāgara,* and the *Brihatkathāmanjarī.*[8]

The *Kathā* literature can be self-conscious about the use of narrative in religious and moral instruction. The *Panchatantra* fables, for example, are framed within a story of a king who wanted his three sons to receive a fine education; he entrusted them to a Brahman called Vishnusharman who composed fables to edify the princes in the art of intelligent living. An introductory passage confidently asserts that acquaintance with the stories in this work will equip a person for the vicissitudes of life.[9]

> Whoever learns the work by heart
> Or through the storyteller's art
>   Becomes acquainted,
> His life by sad defeat—although
> The king of heaven be his foe—
>   is never tainted.

Although stories are brought together in written collections, they continue to circulate orally in versions that often diverge from the written form. The great Sanskritist W. Norman Brown, for example, painstakingly compared stories from the *Panchatantra* with the folk narratives collected through the nineteenth and early twentieth centuries and found that over half of the oral tales had a written correlate.[10] Brown emphasized the role of written literature in carrying stories through the subcontinent, but since stories also circulate orally and even bounce back into collections, written versions cannot be viewed as a central source. Rather, they represent particular crystallizations amid a flow across generations and through centuries.

KATHĀ PERFORMANCES

Distinct from the *Kathā* literature are the religious stories, also called *kathā*, whose performances constitute a demarcated ritual event. These performances are closely tied to the sacred calendar and cluster around nodes of sacred geography.[11] The narratives told are from the epics, the *Purāṇas*, and regional religious traditions. While they are often enshrined in books or pamphlets that are read aloud, they also may be drawn out of memory in performance. Even if they are read aloud, an expositor's asides can invoke folk narratives; furthermore, the listeners who appropriate the narrative as it is told may become "active bearers," retelling the stories on other occasions.

Kathā are told in villages, towns, and cities alike. Some *kathā* are informally organized and take place in homes. Among these domestic *kathā* are the *vrat kathā*, which explain why a particular practice like fasting (*vrat*) is observed to honor a particular deity (mostly, these fasts are observed by women).[12] Other *kathā* have a more collective orientation. In villages, a local temple or some other communal place may be used; in towns and cities, the performances may even be held in large halls or auditoriums. Sponsors may be a particular individual or an association. For a *kathā* that involves a *paṇḍit* or professional storyteller, it is customary that he be paid by the sponsor and that the audience also make small donations after the performance.

The tellers of *kathā*, then, fall into four categories: first, the non-specialists, who may sometimes read aloud from a printed pamphlet; second, Brahman *paṇḍits* are called upon for ritual occasions; third, professional storytellers (*kathākār, paurāṇika*) assemble audiences; and fourth, *sādhus* while discoursing read aloud from a sacred text such as the *Rāmāyaṇa* or *Bhāgavata*, and then digress in asides that can involve illustrative parables. Through history, itinerant *sādhus* traveling through regions of India have played a vital role in popularizing the epic and *Purāṇa* literature as "a living force to guide the people in their day-to-day life."[13]

OTHER STORIES TOLD BY *SĀDHUS*

Although Swamiji tells stories, these are not formalized *kathā* sessions, but arise in the flow of other activities. Similarly, other *sādhus* frequently draw on parables in the course of conversations, not intending these stories as demarcated events but as a means of illuminating certain religious themes. While some *sādhus* are learned scholars and can spout Sanskrit with ease, as much as three-quarters of the ascetic population are illiterate or semi-literate,[14] so the sources for their stories are most often in the oral tradition. John Campbell Oman, a colonial observer of *sādhus,* reported as much at the turn of this century: [15]

> Nearly every *sadhu,* however ignorant he may be of letters, or however regardless in practice of what are usually held as the essentials of a moral life, is aware of, and, on occasion, can parade wise maxims, instructive stories, and pithy parables intended to point the way to virtue or dissuade from vice.

When *sādhus* are also Gurus, their disciples may treasure their stories and collect them in books. I was unable to trace the exact sources of many of Swamiji's stories, but at least two in this collection also appear in the published discourses of revered Gurus. In both cases Swamiji has read their books, and as he retells their versions of tales, words enshrined in writing pass back into the oral tradition. With my recording, they return to written form in yet another strand in the long and complex chain of relations between literacy and orality in India.

Swamiji's Life and Repertoire

When Swamiji said, "Mataji, look at my age, Mataji: sixty-eight!" and then referred to his past wanderings, he knew that I had some knowledge of what he meant. This was because two summers earlier I had recorded his reminiscences of the contours of his past. The Hindu narrative tradition forms a backdrop for Swamiji stories, but his knowledge of this tradition is partial and selective, shaped by his life experience. His past determined not only stories he was exposed to but also those he remembers and retells. As he said, "What is needed by the heart will settle in the mind."[16] To better understand Swamiji's stories and why they so often feature *sādhus,* I brought out the old transcription of his life history.

This transcription runs to about sixty typewritten pages and was mostly taped during sessions of about two hours each over the course of three days. I had explained to Swamiji that my university had funded me to document the life history of a *sādhu,* and when I arrived he promptly sat me down to tape what he had to say. I started out by questioning him but soon realized that he had a form worked out for telling of his life, and while he answered my questions, he treated them as asides before returning to his own course. Swamiji must have been well used to sharing yarns of his past: comparing what I recorded with an account my mother had written down several years before, I found that large portions were of a common mold that had become set through many retellings. Summarizing his accounts here, I refer to Swamiji by this name for clarity, although he actually adopted the title of Swami only when he was initiated into *sannyās* at the age of forty-five. Since he performed death rites for his previous identity when being initiated, the name he received at birth is now defunct.

"From childhood, were you a devotee of the Goddess?" was my opening question. Swamiji was leaning against the wall on his bed, legs resting on a stool before him. A pink mosquito net was hooped over his head. I sat on the floor at his feet. He looked past me to the altar on the opposite wall where there was a color picture of Saptashring Nivasini Devi, silver sandals belonging to his Guru, a picture of his Guru, a silver square inscribed with a geometrical *shrī yantra* (representing the Goddess)—and with Swamiji's flair for improvisation, a globe and clouded mirror. Bowing to the altar, my head had grazed Africa and then I had confronted myself through a pearly haze.

"*Hān?* What?" My question took a moment to sink in. "No, nothing like that," Swamiji said as he waved a palm. "Does a man become a *bābā* [holy man] from childhood? I didn't revere the Goddess from childhood, though, so to speak, everyone reveres Her since She is everywhere. I wasn't Her devotee to begin with. At first I was a devotee of Datta [Guru of the Gods]."

The story began where my question coaxed it. In my mother's transcription, the account began with his leaving home. Both beginnings, the vision of the Goddess and the act of cutting ties with his family, are important to Swamiji's identity as *sādhu*. Swamiji looked down at me as he spoke, but as he entered the realm of the story, his eyes focused at a point beyond the altar he faced.

> I saw the Goddess in my childhood. In my childhood, when I was about eight years old. I was lying down. It could have been about eight at night. This was a village; people went to sleep at eight o'clock. I wasn't asleep, but I had my eyes closed. It was a habit of mine to close my eyes though I wasn't

doing any kind of meditation. What kind of worship can an eight-year-old child do? . . . My grandmother slept on one side of me. Not beside me, at some distance away. I closed my eyes, ready to sleep. Then I saw something behind my closed lids. "I see something," I said. "What do you see?" she asked. I said, "Some large face." Now in our parts there is one caste that puts on masks around Divali [festival of lights]. With these large faces, they come to the houses and dance. They're given alms. "You must have seen one of these masks," said my grandmother. These are terrifying masks. They're known as Balindra. "You've seen Bali's sister and remembered it. That's what you're seeing now." I said, "No, it's not that. What I see has many arms." She said, "You're just making something up." I saw this for a minute* or two. Then it went away.

He had been born in November 1917 to an orthodox Madhava Brahman family in Karnataka. He was the second child and had an elder sister as well as a younger brother and sister. His formal education had been patchy because the rituals emphasized at home interfered with the village school routine. Yet he picked up many stories at school, particularly animal fables with sources in the *Panchatantra*. *Kathā* were told from time to time in the village temple, and at these events his fund of myths, legends, and folktales was further enriched.

When he was nine his mother died, and all the children were sent to their maternal uncle's house. Here their grandmother brought them up. Swamiji was very attached to her, and when she died in his late teens he felt unmoored from his family. He left home for the town Mysore in the mid-1930s, planning to join the Independence movement that would free India from British rule. An ardent follower of Mahatma Gandhi, he took to spinning ("even a ninety count thread!") and would only wear cloth he had spun himself. He attended rallies and participated in marches. Yet amid this life of political activism a curiosity about spirituality remained:

I used to think Gandhiji was Bhagavan. I thought people who wore ochre clothes [*bhagvā kaprā*] had nothing else to do but to thieve, that they lived free off other people's earnings. This is what I thought. I respected Viveka- nanda [a nineteenth-century socially active *sannyāsī*]. But I saw all the other ochre-robed people as thieves. Really! That's what I thought!

There was a man who used to call Gandhiji "Strife." This man said Gan- dhiji was wrecking the country. He'd throw curses at Gandhi; I'd say he was Bhagavan. We'd argue. We were friends. Every day we'd argue.

Then, one day I thought, "There's this Bhagavan that people talk about. Where is he? Where does one meet him? Bhagavan is in so many places," I thought, "Kashi and elsewhere." So I decided, "I'll go." [Swamiji rolls his head to one side, then straight up, the gesture of a young man ready to take on anything.] "I'll go!"

Swamiji proceeded first to the adjoining state, Maharashtra, where he pawned his gold watch. Next he went on to the Hindu sacred center, Kashi (Benares). He intended to do a tour of various temples and perform commemorative rites (*shrāddh*) for the soul of his dead mother. Young, naive, and with little knowledge of Hindi, he ended up being fleeced by the local ritual specialists (*pāṇḍās*). He visited the local temples, and went to the ashram of a Guru of the Bharati order. Here, for the first time he was offered *sannyās*.

> "Anyone can take *sannyās*" he [the Guru] said, "and they must do this: I have 300 devotees. They have to live for six months in the fields. You'd go with them, serving here and there. And the rest of the time, you'd do service [*sevā*] in this ashram."
> "What do you mean, 'service'?"
> "Doing the work here: scrubbing dishes, throwing out garbage, sweeping, begging alms, then bringing them back to the Guru."
> "And don't you worship Bhagavan?"
> "Yes, we do all that and worship Bhagavan too."
> Then I said, "I don't want to do all this. Just give me a *mantra*. Don't give me anything to drink, anything to eat. Just give me a place to stay, any old place. I won't eat, I won't drink. I won't go out, I won't wander around. Let's see if I find Bhagavan. I'll continue this as long as it takes to find Bhagavan. Just give me your blessing."
> "This can't be done," he said.
> "Why not? Have *you* seen Bhagavan?" I asked. "There are some who have. Have you seen Bhagavan?" [in a brisk, lawyerly tone].
> "No, I haven't seen Him" [regretful and embarrassed].
> "If you haven't seen Him, how are you going to show Him to me? Only through experience can you really know. You haven't seen anything; what can you show me then?" I was a Congress-minded man. My head was turned.

From here this headstrong young man went on to Allahabad to visit Congress workers at the Nehru residence, Anand Bhavan. As he started back to Mysore, he was arrested by the police who hauled him off the train for interrogation, mistaking him for a volunteer of the revolutionary Subhaschandra Bose, suspected of carrying a bomb to Bombay. He ended up stranded in central India without money or food. A *sādhu* fed him. Somehow he found his way back to Maharashtra, where he worked in a hotel. Then once more he set off in his wanderings, this time down south by foot. He considered enlisting in the army, but "Gandhi had preached that one shouldn't join the army, so I refused to go."

At the temple of Madurai Meenakshi, Swamiji met an old *sādhu* who gave him the initiation he had been seeking. At this time Swamiji had no money at all and was watching from a distance as a crowd of *sādhus* scrabbled to receive the coupons that would entitle them to free meals.

I was sitting in one place. At some distance, a shopkeeper was handing out coupons—six or ten of them. For these, at least a hundred men wearing ochre robes were shoving each other. "I want a coupon, I want a coupon!" I was watching [chin in hand] from afar, watching and laughing in my mind. An old Maharaj came up. He came up right beside me. "Did you get a coupon?" he asked.

"What? A coupon? What for?" I said.

He said, "A coupon for food."

I said, "I have no need for food."

"Why have you no need? Don't you eat anything?" he asked.

I said, "If I didn't eat anything, would I have got so big?" I was a haughty person from the beginning! [Swamiji flicks a hand and grins.]

He said [gently], "Not like that. Looking at your face it shows that you haven't eaten for many days. Why don't you take a coupon? Why don't you eat?"

I said, "You're right. It's been many days since I ate. It's my wish to see Bhagavan and then to eat."

He said, "Where have you been?"

I told him everything. "I've gone to Kashi. I've gone here and there."

"And no one was able to show you Bhagavan in these places?"

I said, "No, till now, no one could show me Bhagavan. In Kashi there were a *lot* of rascals."

I told him of all the places I'd been. In a little while he said [in a low, confidential voice], "I'll show you what no one else has shown you."

I said [loud and forthright], "First you show me Bhagavan, then I'll eat."

He said, "Not like that. Look, there's a question. Does the seed come from the tree or the tree from the seed? Is the tree first or the seed?"

[A silence. Swamiji strokes his stubbly chin as though he is once again a perplexed young man standing outside the temple.]

He continued, "Does a tree have seeds? Yes. If fruit doesn't appear, if the seeds don't appear, what should be done? It should be nourished. And if you stop giving the tree manure, if you stop giving it water, it will die. In some days, after it's dead, do you have a tree?"

"No."

"Do you have any fruit?"

"No."

"Why do you plant a tree? To receive fruits, you plant a tree. Understand?"

[Swamiji pauses, and Kirin, unsure whether this question is part of the story or aimed at her, nods a hasty "Yes, yes."]

"What is your body for? To see Bhagavan. In your very body, there's Bhagavan. . . . If you haven't achieved Bhagavan and you destroy your body, is there any Bhagavan? No. Is there even a body? . . . If you want to see Bhagavan you must look after your body. Give it food regularly, give it water regularly. Bhagavan is in your body. You can go to Kashi or anywhere else, but all that isn't Bhagavan. Bhagavan is in your body itself. To see Bhagavan you can take a *mantra* from a true Guru and keep repeating it.

"You might think [petulantly], 'I want to meet Bhagavan right away!' But who is Bhagavan, your servant or something? When the right time comes you can meet Him. Until fruit is ripe on a tree, you can't receive it. If you pick it when it's still unripe, it won't be sweet. When fruit ripens, you receive it of its own accord. Then, what is our Bhagavan like? Brahma [the creator], Vishnu [the preserver], Maheshvar [the destroyer]; all three are in your body." He sat down and told me all this in a fine and thorough fashion. Then he took me and fed me. I went and ate. After this he took me into the temple, and gave me a *mantra*.

Swamiji wandered for some time with this old holy man; the teachings gleaned from him surface in many of the stories Swamiji now tells. He then began to earn through manual work: filling water, grinding barrels of flour. He explains that possibly his strength attracted the evil eye (*nazar*), for he came down with acute dysentery and had to be shipped home. After several months he left again for Mysore, to participate further in the freedom-fighting activities. He was about thirty years old by then, and though not yet an initiated ascetic, with his white garments and habit of living alone and feeding others, he was known as "Swamiji." He organized marches, defied curfews, and was imprisoned with all his friends for what he describes as a happy vacation. They had daily shaves from the jail barber, swapped stories, apportioned ministries in the future government among themselves, organized protests, were shifted between jails, and eventually were released. With time, though, a disenchantment with politics set in.

I saw that in Mysore, everyone was fighting over power. We had certainly done *satyāgraha* ["grasping the truth"; Gandhian freedom-fighting] together. But now, we all fought over power. I thought, "We did so much for the government but there's no substance to this." This is what entered my mind. No one was helping the poor. This is what I realized. I saw this, and because of it, I left the movement.* Gandhiji had also said, "I'm not in the Congress!" Yes, at the time of his death, Gandhiji was not in the Congress

Party. He had said that when India became independent there should no longer be any Congress.

Leaving Mysore, Swamiji went to live in Goa. Here, in a temple on a mountain, he worshipped Dattatreya, Guru of the Gods. He made a living through folk medicine, soothsaying, and astrology. His reputation spread, and he was soon earning enough to establish a new pattern of spending three months in one place and then traveling for the next three. He went as far north as Mount Kailash and as far east as the Temple of Kamakshi (where he was present for the Goddess's yearly 'menstruation,' and even brought back a piece of silk stained with the sacred blood). He visited various renowned Gurus, staying in their ashrams for some time. The discourses of all these holy men must have further enriched his repertoire of stories. He remained fiercely independent and would not stay in any institution for long. Then a friend he had made in Maharashtra advised him to settle on the mountain Saptashring, "Seven Horns," which is sacred to the goddess Saptashring Nivasini Devi.

> "I don't want to soothsay for anybody," I said. "Whatever is meant to happen, happens. You can't avert it. No one can change the course of fate. This profession is just lies. I don't want to practice it anymore. I just want to remember Bhagavan's name, sitting in one place. That's why I wish to settle somewhere."
> "Go stay in Saptashring," he said. "It's the Goddess's mountain. It's very nice there. No one comes. It's cool there."

In 1956, Swamiji moved to this mountain, having arranged that his friend send him five rupees a month. A photograph from this time (hanging today in some disciples' homes) shows a man with deeply set black eyes, a long beard, and oiled hair snaking below his shoulders. He wore a Brahman's sacred thread but also the *rudrāksh* beads of someone involved in spiritual practices. He was thirty-nine years old, still a bachelor, and had more or less detached himself from his family and roots in Mysore state.

> I went to Saptashring at the same time of year that there had been the festival in my house [in honor of a saintly ancestor]. It was the same month: Dhanurmas. There's an *āratī* at the Devi's temple at dawn. Not too many people attended this. . . . At eight, I bathed and went straight to the Devi. I went there and sat, reciting the Hymn to Narayani and looking at Her. Sandalwood paste is applied to Her. As I sat reciting, a piece fell down—

phat!—the sandalwood fell. It struck me that Bhagavati had given me *prasād.*

I kept looking at Her, thinking, "I've seen Her somewhere. I've seen this image [*mūrti*] somewhere before." I stared and stared at Her, and then I remembered that I had seen Her in my childhood. My eyes filled. I felt like weeping. I thought, "How compassionate the Mother is. I wandered in so many places, but saw no image like Her. Even then, You were always with me." [Swamiji gazes at the image of this Goddess on his altar, and for a moment is silent.]

Here then, he recognized the mysterious face he had described to his grandmother as they lay together, drifting off to sleep. Here, too, was a divine extension of the mother he had lost as a child. The Devi emerging large-eyed from the cliff face became the center of his devotion. He stayed on the mountainside for many months, engaging in various spiritual practices. Then he was taken by some friends to a village in central Maharashtra where the man who was to become his Guru then lived. Just as others often call Swamiji himself "Babaji," or respected father, Swamiji affectionately refers to his own Guru in this way.

After the others had left, Babaji sat down with me inside and we talked. "Where are you from? What are you doing?"

I told him it's like this, it's like that. "I live in such an such a place," I said. "I haven't made anyone my Guru so far. I wish to make a Guru. If you stay in one place, you need one Guru. Anyone might come up and ask, 'Who's your Guru?' You should be able to reply, 'Such and such a person is my Guru.' Can I give them your name? Can I make you my Guru? So to speak, I've had four or five Gurus, but I've never formally accepted anyone. Can I give your name?"

[Kirin pipes up from the floor, "How come you trusted him so soon? How did you choose him so fast?" Swamiji answers, "I had thought previously that I needed someone. What's a Guru, after all? What is a Guru? Our heart chooses a Guru. A man doesn't make a Guru." Then he returns to his story.]

Babaji said, "Yes, you can give my name." We sat there. It was dusk. Then he should give some *mantra,* shouldn't he? He pressed my eyeballs, too. Someone else had also done this to me before, saying, "I'm showing you Bhagavan." When Babaji did this, I saw a brilliant flame. He said, "Om Namah Shivaya" [a *mantra* sacred to Shiva]. I had learned this *mantra* at my sacred thread initiation. Babaji said, "Keep reciting this." And I kept reciting it.

I had a rupee and a quarter [*savā rūpyā,* an auspicious sum] with me. The next day I set it before him. He refused. "Why?" he asked. I said, "It won't do to take a *mantra* and give nothing. This is all I have and I want to offer it to you."

Babaji said, "Don't do that." Instead, he took out money and gave it to me. "You're younger than me," he said. "Take this. You don't have acquaintances here. People bring me money. Later, when I visit this place, I'll write to you and then you should come."

Following this initiation, Swamiji would visit his Guru from time to time though he remained based in Saptashring. He planned to travel north to an ice-bound Himalayan region and stay for six months, but his Guru urged him not to do so. Having accepted a Guru, Swamiji, as a disciple, had to heed his commands. Soon his Guru advised him to formally become a *sannyāsī* renouncer.

Then he said, "You take *sannyās*."

I said, "Maharaj, *sannyās* . . . what's there in clothes?" I disliked *sannyās*. I didn't think much of ochre clothes. "What does *sannyās* have to do with Bhagavan? It's not as though you find Bhagavan if you shave your head."

Maharaj said, "That's not so. This is a lineage [*paramparā*]. Shankaracharya founded this lineage and it continues."

I said, "No Maharaj, not like this." I put it off for three years saying, "I don't have time for this." But every year, Babaji would remind me.

In the end his Guru prevailed and Swamiji was initiated at Nasik into the order of Dashanami *sannyāsīs* in 1962. It was then that he received his name Swami —— Saraswati that he carries today. In the years that followed, the feeding of children that Swamiji had informally undertaken became more systematized. Other people brought ingredients; some made donations. Soon an ashram was built with the prime objective of housing the Adivasi "aboriginal" children so they could attend a government-sponsored school nearby. Through the years Swamiji regularly visited his Guru's ashram but always declined a long stay. His Guru was a compelling public speaker who had wandered for decades; listening to his discourses no doubt enriched Swamiji's folk narrative repertoire. This ashram grew in the 1970s to cross-continental proportions with many foreign disciples. Secretaries around the Guru often translated stories from other religious traditions—fables of Mulla Nasruddin, parables of Christ or the Rabbis—and these, retold in the public speeches, perhaps influenced Swamiji. It was also at his Guru's ashram that foreign disciples first encountered Swamiji.

By the late 1970s Swamiji began to visit a house that a disciple had built for him in Nasik. After the many years of wandering and irregular eating habits his health had begun to fail. Nearly blind, he had a cataract operation and was given the heavy spectacles he now wears. All his teeth, rotted by years of chewing tobacco, needed to be pulled out; though he was given false teeth, these were set aside in a box. He had a heart attack and was advised to reduce travel and the hours he was available to visitors. He was discovered to have severe diabetes and was put on a restricted diet. As his health failed, Swamiji stayed on the mountain less and in town more. He handed over his ashram to two other *sādhus*. In 1983 he moved from the disciple's house to the apartment adjoining his doctor's small hospital. It was here that I arrived as a graduate student bearing tapes.

The Story of Fieldwork

Just as Swamiji's acquaintance with a narrative tradition follows the contours of his life, so my understanding of Swamiji is shaped by years of association with him. He speaks of seeing my mother, a young white woman in a sari, in the Nasik bazaar in the early 1950s before he took *sannyās*. My mother in turn was able to dig through trunks and unearth an undated diary entry recording their wordless encounter:

> I saw a Sadhu who wears white robes, one wound as a skirt, one thrown over his strong shoulders, his hair growing to his shoulders, his medium beard the strength of his erect and dignified bearing, the hair, the beard, the costume, the regular elongated face with a prominent nose and piercing eyes, reminded me of Jesus, who must have indeed been just such a man as this, barefoot, standing somewhat aside and radiating assurance and inner poise.

It was almost twenty years later that we were drawn into more direct contact with Swamiji. When I was ten, in 1970, my elder brother, Rahoul, had stupefied my family by dropping out of high school and announcing that he would renounce the world to become a *sannyāsī*. He went to the ashram of Swamiji's Guru, and from there to Swamiji's own ashram at Saptashring. For several months, he stayed there helping out with the feeding and schooling of the local children. Rahoul subsequently dropped the idea of *sannyās* and went on to college in the United States. But while he was at Saptashring he wrote us letters, and when he stopped in at home he was brimming with vivid stories. My family also visited Rahoul, climbing several hours by foot up the mountain. My memory of Swamiji from those days is dim: I was shy and did not fully understand the long stories he told, but I enjoyed the sweets he cooked and dispensed. My connection with him was through my family: I recall tugging at my mother's sari, sitting beside my brother, standing behind my aunt and hoping that when I followed her in making the ritual gesture of touching a *sādhu's* feet, I would not make a fool of myself. No one in the family was Swamiji's disciple, but we all looked up to him with affection and respect. Since we often visited our Nasik house we would see Swamiji from time to time at his own ashram, or at his Guru's. After hearing a few of Swamiji's stories, he was established in my mind as a Scheherazade among *sādhus*.

In 1980, after I graduated from Sarah Lawrence College, I was visiting my father in Nasik. We went to see Swamiji at the house in town where he then lived. That year, a Kumbha Mela (an occasion when ascetics gather from many parts of India for a ceremonial dip) was being held at Tryambakeshwar, near Nasik. Swamiji offered to take me along. For me this was a spectacular adventure. Swamiji was turned out in his full ascetic regalia—a staff in one hand, a gourd waterpot (*kamaṇḍalū*) in the other. A hotel-owner from Swamiji's native Karnataka and his family came along; so did a priest with diamond earrings from a temple of the Goddess in the South. We crammed into two cars to Tryambakeshwar, the Shiva temple that was the center of these celebrations. It was on this trip that for the first time Swamiji made a powerful personal impression on me, apart from my family. Nearly blind himself, he was always peering through his heavy spectacles to make sure everyone was still along. As a *sādhu* he could have gone directly into the sanctum sanctorum of the Shiva temple we visited for *darshan* after our dips in the temple pond. But he refused special treatment and stood with the rest of us in the snaking line as the sun set and the stars appeared. Driving back through the darkness, Swamiji chatted about this and that, and as often happens when he chats, he lapsed into stories: folktales, legends, myths. My imagination was fired. I found him to be a kind man with a hearty sense of humor; a man who, beneath his unassuming exterior, carried a vast stock of folklore, spiritual insight, and life experience. As so often happens when my imagination is sparked, I was inspired to write. I wrote accounts in my journal and letters to my mother and friends. I also started keeping notes on what Swamiji said.

For the remainder of my stay in Nasik, whenever I visited I had a notebook in hand. The first morning I began to write, a large spot of *kumkum* landed on my page. I looked around, wondering whether it had fallen from my forehead or from one of the pictures nearby. "Where do you think this came from?" I asked, frankly puzzled. "Maybe Bhagavati is pleased with you," Swamiji said. "This could be her *prasād*." Much later when he told me about the blob of sandalwood that had fallen from the image in the temple, I wondered if he had seen an analogy of grace. Perhaps this was among the reasons that he supported my future project.

By 1982 I had finished my first year in graduate school and was aching for any excuse that would take me back to India. I had dimly formulated a project involving the documentation of Swamiji's life history and interactions as a *sādhu*. During the summer I was in the Himalayan foothills but stopped briefly in at Nasik to visit my cousins. At this time I asked Swamiji if I could come spend a few months with him the following year. He agreed. In June 1983 I returned to live near him.

Swamiji received me with a kindness that was overwhelming. He seemed amused that a foreign university would actually sponsor my visit to record what he referred to as his "topsy-turvy" (*agaram-bagaram*) and "any-which-way" (*ultā-sultā*) words. He shared information freely. He answered whatever I asked him, volunteered stories he thought might be helpful, and allowed me to tape his public conversations. Yet he did not see my project as associated with me alone, or even the university from which I came. "You might think that you came here for your own benefit," he said in the course of a disquisition on divine will, "but it was for Himself that the Lord sent you here."

Swamiji occasionally drew on my presence to illustrate whatever point he was making. For example, one day when he was talking about anger, he said, "Anger comes when desires are not fulfilled. I'll give you an illustration. Now, suppose I tell you 'write my story' or if I say, 'sit in this way.' And if you don't sit and listen properly and write my story, and if I try to make you understand and even then you don't . . . yes? Then to make you understand could be called a wish of mine. An obstinacy enters my mind. 'She *will* understand,' I think. . . . 'I *must* teach her something.' To teach you is my resolution, but when you don't learn, obstinacy enters. Because of your destiny this won't settle in your brain. Anger arises. I try to make you understand, but you don't. Then I begin to scold you, to hurl abuses. '*Now* she will understand,' I think. But you don't. Then I'll be *very* angry. What happens to me?"

Swamiji went on to describe how harmful the effects of anger are: "With anger, your wisdom burns, and your ignorance burns, too. Anger arises from ignorance, never from wisdom. A wise one is never enraged. Laughing inside, the wise person walks on, thinking, 'Who am I to teach this person a lesson? Bhagavan is the one who teaches.'" Still, the hypothetical description of how he might get angry at me left its mark. I consistently tried to listen with complete attentiveness whenever he was addressing me.

Cataloguing my recordings at the end of the summer, I found I had taped thirty-two folk narratives. Gradually, the idea of doing a dissertation on storytelling as religious teaching began to take form. The materials I had previously collected were so rich that they could have been approached from a number of angles, but I chose this project not only because it involved an intersection between two areas of academic interest—religion and folklore—but also because I sensed that it would be least offensive to Swamiji and all those around him. If I had focused primarily on his life history, for example, I would have had to hazard psychological interpretations that may have delighted scholars but alienated me from those whom I cared about in Nasik. I corresponded with Swamiji through the two-year interval before my return so he knew of and endorsed my research plans.

Because of the benevolence and amused assistance that Swamiji had extended to my work so far, I was badly shaken during my second trip when Swamiji began to critique my project. One September morning, in the course of a disquisition on the current dark age (*kali-yug*), Swamiji observed that people today were generally interested in Bhagavan more for worldly status and material profit than inner growth. Several other visitors were gathered in the room, and as usual a tape recorder was poised by my knee. I was serenely listening to this flow of general comments and was startled when they became redirected toward me.

"You're taking this on tape," Swamiji said, turning toward me. "You'll take this and do a business.* Understand? Everyone's going to ask you, 'What is Bhagavan? What is Bhagavan?' You'll go there and do a business.* In your university* you'll say, 'I saw this, I saw that. This is what Bhagavan is.'" Swamiji paused, eyes enormous behind his heavy spectacles, "That's why you learn this; not to understand it."

I squirmed as Swamiji spoke. "I'm also trying to understand your words . . . ," I weakly protested. But even as I said this, I realized that Swamiji was partly right. What I was taping of his words would become, for me, a form of academic currency. I did not exactly intend to start a "business" selling his stories and teachings, but it was inherent to my enterprise that I would exchange what I learned from him to gain a degree, lectures, grants, publications, jobs. What I was taking from him would buy me academic credibility for years ahead.

"Some people, I say," Swamiji continued evasively. "Not just you. It's best to first talk about oneself, though. Wherever there's a space in a temple, there's a priest [*pūjārī*] to make money. This is the dark age; people have no sense of Bhagavan inside them."

He went on to describe how divinity cannot be expressed or communicated through words alone. "Can you tell someone what the smell of a flower is?" Swamiji asked. Nathu Maharaj said no, you could not. Swamiji continued: "You can't. You can keep describing it, but still only someone who has smelled it will understand. You can just keep lecturing: it's like this, it's like that. But only the heart knows. This is what the Lord's form is. This is love. You can't ask questions about it. It must be revealed from inside. You can't write about it. You can't sell it either, Mataji. . . ."

I continued to listen, my ears burning red. Sitting among people with whom I felt a comfortable sense of solidarity, I had suddenly been thrust apart as an academic outsider. While others were here for spiritual reasons, Swamiji indicated that I was here not to experience but to appropriate; not to feel from my heart, but to bind up in words and take away. I had the acute sense of being split down the middle: the Western academic had to agree, the local woman cried out that she did indeed care. I felt nervous and uncertain, thrown off-kilter and out of sync. It was with difficulty that I continued to sit in the room. When noon came and we visitors stood to leave, Swamiji reiterated more gently, "Don't just take these stories; understand them."

It was partly my own fault that I had become identified with an academic community. While recording wedding songs in Kangra,[17] I had discovered that one way of gathering authority which the culture did not automatically dispense to a young unmarried woman was to back myself with the prestige of Western academics. I would explain projects in terms of my "professor's" interests and would phrase delicate questions with the preface, "my professors want to know. . . ." When I invoked my professors it was not individuals I meant, but a blanket category that served as my metonym for anthropology and academic enterprise. I tried to hide behind my "professors" with Swamiji as well, occasionally establishing the worth of a question through a discreet reference to their interests. But Swamiji was not taken in. The day after he had rebuked me for wanting to do a "business," he ended a discussion of meditation techniques by standing up, moving toward the door, and abruptly addressing me: "What are your professors* going to to with this?"

I was already uncomfortable over not having clarified my position the day before. Once again I was being challenged about the outcome of my research. I knew that my professors were not about to settle down cross-legged if I reappeared in their offices with instructions for meditation. Nor would they write about or retell Swamiji's stories. As the mixed group in the room looked on, I started to mumble something about document-ing Indian culture. "But what will your *professors** do with it?" Swamiji repeated.

"They won't do anything with it," I had to confess. "It's for me." Swamiji questioningly looked down at me. I took a deep breath, tried to steady my voice, and continued to use his own idiom of the will of the Divine Mother, reiterating what I had already explained in letters. "If it's the Goddess's wish I'll write a book," I said. "One can write a Ph.D. disser-tation on anything, and I've chosen this. Many *sādhus* tell stories and you tell these stories, too. Your stories contain your teachings; your stories and your spiritual teachings are the same thing."

"*Hān hān hān. . . .*" Swamiji let out a stream of assent. After he had spit his tobacco, he returned to ask, "Do you know why the elephant has a trunk? There are so many stories in India that you must have heard. You must have heard the story of Ganga [river Ganges], you must have heard the story of Pandavas [in the *Mahābhārata* epic]. Haven't you heard Chandrahasa's story. No? What are you saying? You haven't heard about Chandrahasa?! There was a King in the past. You're taping this, aren't you? You can tape this one, it's very good. . . ."

The tension was released; Swamiji's grin returned. I had been taping Swamiji's stories as they emerged in the context of dispensing advice to people, but over the next few weeks it seemed as though he was telling stories to illustrate every twist in the conversation, amusement flickering on his face as I unwrapped, inserted, switched, labeled tapes. My presence seemed to have brought on a storytelling spree. When I asked a housewife who visited in the afternoons why she thought Swamiji told stories, she replied without hesitation, speaking Hindi, "He tells these stories out of love for you. These are his gift to you. He tells them so you can take them on a tape and make a name for yourself in America."

Of course Swamiji also tells many stories when I am not present. Most of the forty-six stories he told in 1985 were not even addressed to me. But with his willingness to help people—whatever their interests or prob-lems—I suspect that he made it a point to tell extra stories while I strained forward, adjusting my tape recorder. Even if ethnographers fit into a social situation without the alibi of their discipline, they cannot help but enter the process of creating what they study. Reading the stories that are reproduced here, my presence as occasional translator and tape recorder–bearing ethnographer should be kept in mind as factors that possibly influenced Swamiji's style, rendition, and choice of stories told.

All these jocular or critical comments that Swamiji directed to my research are etched deeply into my approach to this work. In accusing me of starting a "business," Swamiji had struck a raw nerve for every fieldworker: the ethical dilemma involved in appropriating fragments from others' lives. While this appropriation serves the ends of academic careers, the uncomfortable question remains as to how the people concerned, who provided hospitality, time, and insights, might gain. Furthermore, Swamiji had hit upon the issue of how the materials gleaned through fieldwork affect one's own attitudes and choices of how to live. Swamiji's concern that I strive to understand the meanings embedded in these stories was a direct reminder that intellectual issues are hollow without accompanying praxis. To study storytelling as religious teaching, Swamiji reminded me, I had to think over how these teachings might relate to me personally. I spare my readers extended soul-searching on these pages. But I do acknowledge that as I have written this, I have consistently tried to keep sight of the ways any wisdom that Swamiji or his listeners shared with me might apply to my own ongoing life.

A related issue that plagues all fieldworkers is reciprocity.[18] If the people one works with are as unstintingly generous as Swamiji, how can one even begin to reciprocate for the materials they share? These materials, after all, are the building blocks of academic careers; they help shape the very quality of a researcher's life. Throughout my research, I brought small offerings to Swamiji, but the most symbolic of my gifts to him was the tape recorder that had been my omnipresent companion, allowing me to "take" his words. He had always been intrigued by this recorder and had once even listened to his own words through headphones with a broad and toothless grin (the picture I took of this event makes an advertisement for Sony matched only by one of my grandmother with headphones under her sari, dancing to Bob Marley!). The day before I left, I presented the recorder to him. "I'll call this 'Kirin,'" said Swamiji. "I won't give it away. I'll listen to *bhajans* [devotional songs] in my room and when I go on pilgrimage." He paused, and an impish smile came over his face. "Maybe I'll tape other people's stories," he said.

3. Sādhus

"A *sādhu* is dressed up and put on show," said Swamiji one morning after three busloads of pilgrims from Gujarat had descended for his *darshan*. From bent old grandparents to babies in arms, they filed through the room in what seemed like a never-ending procession. *"Jai jagadambā mātājī kī jai, jai jagadambā mātājī kī jai."* Swamiji kept up a steady stream of blessings as he doled out sugar balls as *prasād*. When the waves of people engulfing the room had finally withdrawn and once more there were just a few of us sitting against the walls, Swamiji reclined with relief in his chair. This seemed to have been a moment when he felt "on show," called upon to perform to unknown people's expectations. "If he dances well," Swamiji continued, "the world approves. If he can't dance, he's criticized."

Sādhus do not exactly "dance," but there is a bundle of cultural expectations weighing down their everyday interactions. The definition of a holy person in India has shifted through history, and at any particular moment in time displays variation between different ascetic orders as well as different segments of the lay population. Yet certain general statements can be made about what a *sādhu* is and has been to Hindus. It might seem audacious to summarize an ancient and complex tradition in the space of a single chapter, but an overview is necessary to understand both Swamiji's niche in society as well as the culturally constructed, historically shaped images of *sādhus* present in his folk narratives.

The term *sādhu* is commonly translated as "holy man" or "ascetic." *Sādhu* denotes a male; a holy woman would be a *sādhvī*, and so in some ways I find the word "ascetic" preferable since it is gender-free. Yet as a Christian category, the word "ascetic" misleads even as it communicates. Asceticism conjures up images of hair shirts, flagellation, and deprivations of all bodily appetites. While some *sādhus* do undergo severe austerities, this is certainly not the case for all of them. The British colonial obsession with documenting beds of nails, chains and spikes, arms raised until withered, is, I suspect, a distorted emphasis stemming from expectations about ascetics from within the Christian tradition, even as it reflects an urge to exoticize cultural difference. It seems unfortunate that the scholarly literature on *sādhus* describes them as "ascetics." How is Swamiji an ascetic? one might ask. He wears clothes, he sleeps on a bed, he eats at least once a day, he switches on a fan if it is too hot. I find the translation troublesome, but would answer that he is a Hindu ascetic simply because this is the shorthand term commonly used for a *sādhu*. He is also an ascetic because like most other *sādhus* he is celibate, detached from the material objects around him, and devoted to a spiritual life over one emphasizing bodily fulfillment.

Most broadly, *sādhu* means "good man" or "virtuous man." Among its fan of Sanskrit meanings, *sādhu* denotes "straight" and "to hit the goal": a *sādhu* is someone who aims for the goal of salvation. More specifically, *sādhu* stands for someone who has been initiated into an ascetic sect to devote himself to achieving release from the cycle of death and rebirth. *Sādhus* are ideally celibate. They do not work for wages but are rather dependent on alms and donations. They do not identify with ties of blood or caste. *Sādhus,* then, are seen as fundamentally different from lay householders (*grahasthī*) caught up in the world of social enterprise (*samsār*). This difference is also dramatized in the use of the term *sādhu* for lay people who do not behave in conventionally expected ways, such as those who are powerful, selfless, or celibate at an inappropriate stage of life.[1]

Swamiji refers to himself as a *sādhu*, but more specifically he says that he is a *sannyāsī*, or "renouncer." This means that he has been initiated into *sannyās*, "renunciation," joining the Saraswati branch of the ten (Dashanami) monastic orders established by the charismatic young Shankaracharya in the eighth century A.D. His ochre robes, *rudrāksh* beads, and name (Swami —— Saraswati) all represent his affiliation to this order. This, at least, is the institutional aspect of his *sannyās*, but following an interpretation he ascribes to the *Bhagavad Gītā,* Swamiji often refers to *sannyās* as more an inner state of renunciation than a matter of externals. For example, one afternoon in July 1983, "Dattatreya," a young Englishman dressed in ochre who was contemplating a formal initiation, asked Swamiji if he could explain how one became a *sannyāsī*.

> SWAMIJI (propped up against an orange pillow and addressing "Dattatreya" with earnest intensity): To begin with, there's no question of giving or taking *sannyās*. You can't just GIVE *sannyās* to someone. In the *Gītā*, too, Bhagavan says that you can't GIVE it. That's what he said. You must BECOME a *sannyāsī*. Did you understand? You didn't understand?
>
> "DATTATREYA" (nodding agreement): You must become—

SWAMIJI: It's not a matter of giving or taking. Your soul [*ātmā*] must become a *sannyāsī*, you see, not the body. It's not a matter of shaving a beard or growing a beard. *Sannyās* is a kind of action [*vritti*]. The way a person lives is *sannyās*. A lot of people who have put on the robes and shaved their heads say, "Now we're *sannyāsīs*." They aren't really *sannyāsīs*. They just look like them. It's openly stated in the *Gītā*: *sannyās* is very difficult, it's something that you have to become. You can't give it, you can't take it. You must become it. Then, if you look into the matter, say you want to become a *sannyāsī*, to be fully awake: that is the supreme *sannyās*. Harbor no grudges, remain indifferent, control the senses: this is what's called *sannyās*. It's not the beard, not the clothes; it's in the heart [*dil*].

Now, if a *sannyāsī* shaves his head but enjoys pleasure with a woman, what kind of *sannyāsī* is that? I'm telling the truth! This is called a Ravana *sannyāsī*. Ravana disguised himself as a *sannyāsī*—just so he could carry off Sita.

[Swamiji surveys "Dattatreya" as though to gauge what he is making of this novel event. Ravana, the villain of the *Rāmāyaṇa*, managed to abduct Sita, Ram's wife, after visiting her in ascetic costume and begging alms. "Dattatreya," who has been assenting to all that Swamiji says, lets out another "yes" with a nod.]

It's there in all our stories, who took *sannyās* and why. People trust in a *sannyāsī*. Women come and sit beside him. A *sannyāsī* can be like a tiger with the face of a cow. A tiger poses as a cow. All the cows think he's one of them. And then, what the tiger does is catch each one and eat it up! [Swamiji laughs.] I'm telling the truth!

Sannyās happens from inside, not without. It doesn't matter what people call you—they could call you an idiot as easily as a *sannyāsī*. It doesn't matter if they bow before you.

Built into Swamiji's perception of how a *sannyāsī* should internally be, then, was a recognition of possible outer abuses of this role. Holy people are venerated as divinities in human form by traditional Hindus; the detached *sannyāsī* is a cultural ideal. Wandering ascetics are fed by lay Hindus and showered with offerings. When an ascetic is chosen as a Guru, disciples will fully submit to his or her will. It is not surprising then that a role charged with such power is tempting to those with less than honest motives. Through history, false ascetics have devised elaborate scams. Swamiji could even have used the scandals surrounding contemporary ascetics to make his point about false *sannyāsīs*, but he chose instead to refer to the authority of folk narratives.

Shankaracharya, the founder of Swamiji's order, himself recognized the possibility that ascetics could be fake. Hearing of my project, Swami R. directed me to a rollicking Sanskrit couplet from one of Shankaracharya's hymns, *Bhaja Govindam*, or "Worship the Lord." As Swami R. pointed out, this was a pithy description of deluded men who adopted ascetic attire not for salvation but to be parasitic on disciples: [2]

> The ascetic with matted locks, the one with his head shaven,
>   the one with his hairs pulled out one by one,
> The one who disguises himself variously with the ochre-colored
>   robes—
> Such a one is a fool, who though seeing, does not see.
> Indeed, this varied disguise is for the sake of the belly.

As this couplet suggests, there are many different kinds of ascetics. *Sannyāsīs* are but a subset of the wider category of *sādhu* which embraces a profusion of orders with all their variation in life-styles, insignia, and spiritual practices.[3] There is no overarching structure to monitor all these kinds of ascetics spread through the subcontinent, and even within the same sect or monastery *sādhus* may display a marked individuality. There are naked *sādhus* and ochre-clad *sādhus; sādhus* with matted hair, and those with shining bare scalps; poor, wandering *sādhus* and jet-set, Rolls Royce–transported *sādhus; sādhus* who interact with a handful of Indian villagers, and *sādhus* who hold forth to audiences of thousands in New York or Switzerland. Swamiji often characterized himself as "just a topsy-turvy" (*agaṛam bagaṛam*) *sādhu,* which seemed to express his informality, playfulness, and distrust of institutional structures.

Though most ascetics are men, there are some women *sādhvīs* or *sannyāsinīs,* too, perhaps as many as 15% of the entire ascetic population.[4] This imbalance in numbers springs from the cultural expectation that women be defined relationally to men; as daughters, wives, and mothers. Women who cut all social ties to embark on the solitary ascetic life are an anomaly in this scheme. The women who do become *sādhvīs* or *sannyāsinīs* tend to have never married because of unusual circumstances, to have been married to a man who became deeply involved in religious practices, or to be older widows. When they are appended to the male orders, they live separately from the men. Occasionally they are formed into orders of their own.

When a woman is recognized as a Guru, the devaluation of single women is overshadowed by the cultural idealization of motherhood. As holy mother—Mataji, Amma, Gurumai—she is likely to gain a large following. Through history, there have been many revered Hindu women saints (even though some, like the poet Mira Bai, were not formally initiated into an ascetic order). When I use the male pronoun to describe *sādhus,* I do not mean to underestimate the women involved. Rather, it is because Swamiji and most other initiated ascetics do happen to be male. Additionally, the images of ascetics in folklore tend to emphasize men who shrink from women as sexual beings.

History

When Swamiji receives visitors during the 1980s, his behavior occurs on a continuum with an ascetic tradition that stretches back several thousand years.[5] Through this time, the category of Hindu holy person has shifted in meaning. The identity of a *sādhu* today has emerged not just from within the Hindu tradition but also in dialogue with other religions such as Buddhism, Jainism, Islam, and Christianity. Ascetic practices may date back as far as the Indus Valley civilization in the third millenium B.C. The *Vedas* mention ascetics with shamanistic attributes: they drink poison, they fly on the wind (*Rig Veda* 10.136.1–7). The *Upanishads* and *Aranyakās* also carry ascetic strands in that they advocate the practice of world rejection and techniques of concentration in order to realize the indwelling divine Self. But it was only in the middle of the first millennium B.C. that asceticism became a powerful social force countering Brahmanical authority. This outbreak of asceticism through the Ganges Valley has been ascribed to disorientation stemming from the breakdown of tribal society, and rapid social change.[6] Among the ascetic sects were the Jain and Buddhist ones, which became religions in their own right.

Through Vedic times, Brahman ritual specialists had been central religious authorities. Though it can be argued that the values of renunciation may be incipient within the Brahmanical world view evident in Vedic ritual texts,[7] there is no doubt that asceticism, representing an alternative form of religious authority based on experience rather than learning, posed a powerful challenge to Brahman hegemony. In an effort to assimilate and contain asceticism within the framework of Brahmanical authority, renunciation became associated with the fourth and last stage of a "twice-born" or upper-caste man's life. In the idealized conception of the life course, a twice-born man would progress from the stage of celibate student (*brahmacharya*) to married householder maintaining society through production and reproduction (*grahastha*). With middle age he would begin to withdraw from the social arena, moving to the forest in the company of his wife (*vanaprastha*) and eventually renouncing the world (*sannyāsa*).[8]

Sannyās involves a symbolic social death: renouncing all personal ties and possessions, the *sannyāsī* must devote himself to contemplating the Inner Self. The *Laws of Manu,* a handbook of Brahmanical social life which was formalized between A.D. 100 and 300, describes the sparse life-style of a renouncer at length:

> Departing from his house . . . let him wander about absolutely silent, and caring nothing for enjoyments that may be offered. Let him always wander alone without any companion in order to attain (final liberation), fully understanding that the solitary (man, who) neither forsakes nor is forsaken, gains his end. He shall neither possess a fire nor a dwelling, he may go to a village for his food, (he shall be) indifferent to everything, firm of purpose, meditating (and) concentrating his mind on Brahman. A potsherd (instead of an almsbowl), the roots of trees (for a dwelling), coarse worn-out garments, life in solitude and indifference towards everything are the marks of one who has attained liberation. (*Manu* VI:41–44)

Though a Brahmanical ideal, it is questionable how many old men actually took to wandering about in tattered garments, begging for food, and meditating on the Absolute. Today it is a rare individual who takes *sannyās* after his children have grown up. Yet the conception of the detached elder continues to orient many Hindus' lives. If not a time to put on ochre robes, old age is seen by many as a time to relinquish household authority to the younger generation, to find a spiritual teacher, and to devote oneself to religious concerns.[9] Even around Swamiji, many of the people who found the time to visit daily were older or retired.

Despite Brahmanical attempts to contain asceticism to the last stage of life, a multitude of ascetic sects continued to flourish through the early centuries of the common era. While Hindu ascetics were disorganized in their variety, Buddhism had a unified monastic structure and was drawing Hindus into its fold. In the ninth century A.D., Shankaracharya responded to the Buddhist challenge by shaping *sannyās* into a monastic order. He laid out a monastic framework with four centers at different ends of India, four elected Shankaracharyas, and ten orders. Though Shankaracharya's formalization could not contain all the existent orders of ascetics or the new orders that continued to spring up, the pan-Indian organization he established was a landmark in the development of Hindu asceticism, and continues to the present day.[10]

Shankaracharya's monastic tradition is Shaiva—that is, it emphasizes worship of the deity Shiva, destroyer of the universe. Those who worship Vishnu, preserver of the universe, or his incarnations such as Ram or

Krishna, are known instead as Vaishnava.[11] Vaishnava asceticism is thought to have developed after the Shaiva and to be centrally linked to the *bhakti* movement. In the eleventh or twelfth century A.D., Ramanuja—who like Shankaracharya was from the South—reacted against Shankaracharya's nondualism and articulated a dissident theology that emphasized devotion to a personal God. Ramanuja's Srivaishnava sect included both house-holders and ascetics. While Shankara had restricted ascetic membership to Brahmans, Ramanuja also allowed low-caste Shudras to enter the sect.[12] As *bhakti* movements stressing devotion and frequently incorporating Islamic elements later blazed through the northern part of India, the ascetic groups that emerged tended to follow this Vaishnava orientation and to allow open caste membership.[13]

From the early eleventh century, there began Islamic invasions in northern India; by the thirteenth century large portions had fallen under Muslim control. Though it is likely that there were militant *sādhus* before this time, "fighting ascetic" orders were mobilized in direct repose to Islam. Naked Naga *sannyāsīs* who carried arms became appended to the Dashanami orders, reputedly in order to protect the monastic institutions from harassment by Mohammedan *fakīrs*. While explaining the Dashanami organization to "Dattatreya," Swamiji referred to the Nagas as "militree" *sādhus* who could be non-Brahmans, as opposed to the three orders of Saraswati, Giri, and Puri, who traditionally accepted only Brahmans.[14] By the late seventeenth century, Vaishnavas also incorporated militant ascetics into their ranks. Since then, sectarian rivalry has sparked occasional skirmishes between the Shaiva and Vaishnava armed groups. Who bathes first at the great ascetic gathering, the Kumbha Mela, has been a particularly fraught issue, and Nasik itself has seen some violent confrontations.

The monasteries to which these armed ascetics belonged often owned tracts of land, receiving rent from tenants and donations from disciples. In the political upheaval of the eighteenth and nineteenth centuries, a group of armed Shaiva ascetics known as Gosains also emerged as important traders in the North.[15] They had ample capital from their assets (which through monastic succession did not become divided as when passed from father to sons); they had a preexisting trading network based on pilgrimage routes and linked by monasteries; they traveled in large, armed bodies; and because of their religious role they were treated with respect. So while lay merchants encountered difficulties, these ascetic traders transported cargos with ease, gaining wealth, power, and prestige.

These ascetics also alarmed officials of the East India Company by plundering temples, peasants, landholders, and even British revenue collectors in Bengal. Following a severe famine in 1770, raiding escalated. The British responded by mobilizing troops and issuing directives designed to expel the bands of ascetics. Local people were asked to report on the movements of *sannyāsīs* and *fakīrs* they came across; local rulers were instructed not to give them asylum. By the early nineteenth century, they were forced to withdraw.[16] Though no longer active traders or raiders, these orders continue to flourish in their "gymnasiums" (*akhāṛā*, as opposed to monastery, *maṭh*).

While the carrying of arms contradicted the ascetic ideal of peaceful detachment from worldly affairs, the control of property ran counter to the ideal of the *sannyāsī* who lacked possessions. Robert Gross, who preceded me in writing a dissertation about *sādhus,* brings together evidence suggesting that the militant ascetic orders decisively transformed the popular image of the *sādhu.* Far from being austere figures meditating in isolation or in monasteries, ascetics now moved aggressively in the thick of social life.[17]

British colonial representations of *sādhus* range from portraying them as misguided pagans to romanticizing them as representative of "the mystical mind of the East."[18] This bifurcated image corresponds to the two Indias that had emerged in Western accounts. One was the India of the administrators, an India rife with what were perceived to be barbarous customs like widow-burning, worship of Kali with human sacrifice, and so on. The other was the India popularized by scholars working with ancient texts, an India of lofty spirituality that set Western materialism to shame.[19] The colorful *sādhu* could serve as a metonym for whichever India was being presented. For example, if bizarre customs were being stressed, then *sādhus,* with their range of ascetic practices, were rich material. In many accounts asceticism sounds like a freak show. As Alexander Dow of the East India Company wrote in the late eighteenth century:[20]

> These fellows sometimes hold up one arm in a fixed position till it becomes stiff and remains in that situation during the rest of their lives. Some clench their fists very hard, and keep them so till their nails grow into their palms and appear through the back of their hands. Others turn their faces over one shoulder and keep them in that situation till they fix for ever their heads looking backward. Many turn their eyes to the point of their nose, till they have lost the power of looking in any other direction.

European lithographs and picture postcards of ascetics tended to present them in precisely such postures. The bed of nails—another form of austerity—was also a popular theme. This image is still alive, and Westerners who know little else about Hindu ascetics are aware of at least this allegedly endemic practice. In 1985, shortly after I returned from India, I was amused to find an advertisement for running shoes in *The New York Times* featuring a *sādhu*. Ash-smeared, scantily clothed, and grinning, he squatted on a bed of nails; the accompanying copy compared the shoes' comfort to his seat.

The second view of the *sādhu* as wise sage rather than freak was fostered by the discovery of Hindu scriptures by German romanticism and American transcendentalism. It was backed by the Theosophical Society, founded in 1875 to recover Western occult thought but which soon shifted its interests to India and Tibet. Finally, the stunning debut of Swami Vivekananda at the World Parliament of Religions held at Chicago in 1893 made it clear that the tradition of Hindu Gurus was by no means buried in scripture but was a vital force in the present.[21]

By the early part of the twentieth century, British and American travel writers were depicting *sādhus* in a way that mixed sensationalism with grudging respect. In British accounts, though, the colonial setting of the encounter with Hinduism was rarely forgotten. J. C. Oman went so far as to argue that asceticism had made India vulnerable to colonial rule.[22]

> The *detachment* from human affairs which *sadhuism* demands must have been at all times adverse to patriotism in any form, and there can be no doubt that it is largely due to the subtle effects of the spirit of *sadhuism* upon the character of the people of India that the country is so easily governed by a handful of foreign officials and a few thousand white soldiers.

The colonial presence also caused educated Indians to adopt a critical stance toward their own traditions, and the *sādhu* in particular came under attack. The *sādhu* was presented as an idler who lacked social responsibility and stood in the way of progress. Examples of these indigenous critiques abound, but here is a fiery sample: "Every fellow who is too worthless to be a good citizen shirks his civil duties and forthwith dons the ochre colored robe, thus becoming *mukta* ('free')—free to live in luxury and vice at the expense of his better and more credulous fellow citizens."[23]

Not only did lay Hindus criticize *sādhus,* but among ascetics themselves the British colonial presence brought about a reevaluation of the role. The twin colonial images of India were mirrored in the two faces of indigenous response; while one stressed the revival of a glorious past, the other, inseparable side, emphasized reform of the fallen present.[24] These movements of the late nineteenth century were formulated in direct dialogue with British values and ushered in the image of the socially involved renouncer. Swami Vivekananda, the energetic disciple of the Bengali saint Sri Ramakrishna, is especially responsible for popularizing a vision of the ideal ascetic who would uplift the country. In a letter to a fellow Swami written in 1893, Vivekananda described his hopes for such a modern *sannyāsī*. The program he outlined, stressing education and a lack of caste distinctions, continues to be fulfilled by the Ramakrishna Mission today.[25]

> We are so many *Sannyasins* wandering about and teaching our people metaphysics—it is all madness. . . . Suppose some disinterested *Sannyasins* bent on doing good to others go from village to village, disseminating education and seeking in various ways to better the condition of all down to the Chandala [Untouchable], through oral teachings and by means of maps, cameras, globes.

For the modern *sādhu,* then, selflessness is seen to manifest less in detachment from social affairs than in active service of humanity. This image coupled with the older association between asceticism and social protest has in this century allowed ascetics to become influential leaders in such movements as the battle against Untouchability.[26] Swamiji's own orientation is more toward service than active reform, yet he too aligns himself with Vivekananda. As he said in the course of relating his life, he initially distrusted all *sādhus* except Vivekananda. "There's a difference," he often repeated, "between a *sādhu* and a *svādhu* [selfish person]." One afternoon after he had been reeling off recipes to me he concluded, "Make everything, but make it for the world [*duniyā*], not just for yourself." "Yes," I nodded. "Then think about doing something to better the world," Swamiji went on. "One should think about the welfare of the world." I rolled my head, wondering how the conversation had slipped from the intricacies of spiced rice to the service of humanity. Swamiji's voice had grown far away. "This is the *dharma* of a *sādhu*," he said.

Vivekananda was also the first *sannyāsī* to attract a significant following of Western disciples. After his appearance in Chicago in 1893, he stayed on in the United States lecturing until 1896. Many Americans accepted him as their Guru and a few were even initiated into *sannyās*. Since Vivekananda, many other Gurus have also traveled to the West, establishing institutions and attracting disciples. Additionally, Westerners have trekked to India to find Gurus there. Active Western interest in Hinduism had its heyday in the 1960s and early 1970s. Even cultural heroes like the Beatles found themselves a Guru, and Jimi Hendrix put out an infamous album cover featuring himself as a Hindu deity. My own hospitable home was swarming with young Westerners en route to ashrams in those days; coining "Urug" as the Western inversion of "Guru," my father chanted about this mass invasion: "The Urugs are coming, ah-ha, ah-ha, the Urugs are coming. . . ."[27]

Though there had been satellite centers of a few Gurus' ashrams already established in America and Europe, it was after the 1960s that the phenomenon of Hindu asceticism became more entrenched in different parts of the world, especially in metropolitan areas already known for cultural eclecticism. During my graduate school years in Berkeley, I learned that one could attend Sunday services performed by a Swami at the local chapter of the Vedanta Society, or attend concerts of the Hare Krishna temple while an eerie mannequin of their deceased Guru Swami Prabhupada looked on. Walking to the campus one might encounter a pale troupe of Hare Krishnas dancing to the accompaniment of drums and tambourines, joined by an occasional excited dog or bum. Slipping down to get milk from a corner grocery, one might see followers of the Maharishi Mahesh Yogi proceeding to a lesson in levitation. At one time the "neo-*sannyāsīs*" initiated by the self-styled "Bhagavan" Rajneesh contributed deep maroons to the local color as they stopped en route to Oregon. Campus bulletin boards perpetually advertised lectures by an array of different visiting Gurus. Yet Berkeley was just one link in a larger global network associated with the travels, organizations, and disciples of these different Gurus. Hinduism today, it would seem, has spilled beyond India and is perhaps best viewed in terms of an interlinked, intercontinental world system.

Sādhus and Householders

Why have there been ascetics present in India for such an enormous span of time? What is the relationship of *sādhus* to society in India? How can the institutional structure of asceticism be conceptualized? These are the kinds of questions asked by the anthropologists whose works I have rounded up in order to connect Swamiji with the issues that he shares with *sādhus* in the different corners of India. The precedents for this anthropological literature lie in the writings of colonial commentators, and so colonial biases—particularly a preoccupation with caste[28]—have carried over into the conceptual framework through which *sādhus* are viewed.

Fieldwork in India traditionally involved studying tribes, villages, and castes. Itinerant *sādhus,* who are generally unaffiliated with a caste, slipped clear of anthropology's guiding categories. In the 1950s, though, two groundbreaking works demonstrated the importance of *sādhus.* The first was Govind Sadashiv Ghurye's *Indian Sadhus* (1953), which provides an overview of various ascetic sects in a historical and scriptural framework. The second, more theoretical work was an essay by Louis Dumont, first published in French (1959) and then translated into English as "World Renunciation in Indian Religions" (1960). Since the 1960s the interest in Hindu religion prevalent in the Western world inspired a growing number of foreign and Indian anthropologists to study *sādhus* and Gurus: to live with them, travel with them, and even be initiated by them. In addition, theorists of caste have increasingly included renunciation of caste by *sannyāsīs* in their discussions.

In the Hindu caste hierarchy, the most pure Brahmans stand supreme. Brahmans represent established religion; they carry a form of authority that is birth-ascribed. Ascetics, however, stand conceptually apart from the caste system, and their role is achieved. With initiation, an ascetic dies to the world, renouncing the previous identity defined by kinship and caste. Through spiritual practices a *sādhu* gains a religious authority that surpasses even the Brahman's. And so, the austere ascetic role carries such prestige that the Brahmanical life-style has been modeled upon it, and from the perspective of other castes, Brahmans may be closely allied with ascetics.[29]

Louis Dumont has popularized a view of renunciation as the dialectical opposition to caste society: the renouncer, he argues, is an individual outside the world in an otherwise relationally oriented hierarchy.[30] In this scheme, because the renouncer negates caste, the caste system achieves a balance which allows it to continue. Hinduism itself derives its vitality from the dialogue between renouncers, who have stepped outside the world, and the people who have remained within it. Emulated by high-castes, inspiring devotion across castes, and surrounded by disciples in sects, renouncers become the dynamic center of religious development and change:[31]

> Is it really too adventurous to say that the agent of development in Indian religion and speculation, the "creator of values," has been the renouncer? The Brahman, as a scholar, has mainly preserved, aggregated, and combined; he may well have created and developed special branches of knowledge. Not only the founding of sects and their maintenance, but the major

ideas, the "inventions" are due to the renouncer whose unique position gave him a sort of monopoly for putting everything into question.

This standing aside from the world is reminiscent of Victor Turner's conception of liminality as a state in which an individual or group leaves society to be suspended "betwixt and between" social categories.[32] The *sannyāsī* does indeed appear to be in a permanent state of liminality, standing on the threshold between humans and deities, between caste society and the religious transcendence of society, between the living and the dead.[33] Robert Gross, linking both Dumont and Turner to his own field-work, argues that just as lapses into liminality or "anti-structure" can strengthen and renew structure, so renunciation can be conceptualized as a safety valve for the endemic stress of caste society. Socially, renunciation allows individuals to transcend birth-ascribed positions in the caste hierarchy. Economically, surplus population is supported by the pious. Psychologically, marginal individuals who are at odds with the caste system are allowed an arena in which they can choose to redefine their identity.[34]

This opposition between renunciation and caste is compelling in its elegance. Yet like all simplistic divisions, it illuminates broad patterns even as it obscures the messy variations in lived behavior. Before showing how the opposition breaks down under scrutiny, though, it is useful to mull over why it has had such a powerful hold over anthropological theories of renunciation. The foremost reason, as I see it, is that indigenous Brahmanical theory itself depicts renunciation as the antithesis of caste society. The ascetic seeking salvation is distinguished from householders caught up in the world. Householders viewing *sādhus* from the outside acknowledge the difference as much as *sādhus* do in their own self-definition.[35]

Second, *sādhus,* having renounced caste with initiation, will often negate caste in their interactions as well. Many *bhakti* sects were founded by Gurus who were low-caste and accepted people of all castes. To this day, many *sādhus* accept disciples from a cross-section of castes, living out a compelling egalitarian ideal. As Swamiji said, "To accept all castes [*jātī*] as your own is a *sannyāsī's dharma*. The same Bhagavan is in all of them as in you."

Yet caste is not the only dimension of social difference that *sādhus* should ideally ignore, a point which is lost sight of in discussions that place caste at center stage. At other times Swamiji stated that *sādhus* should accept people whether they are rich or poor, powerful or powerless; that visitors should be greeted with love even if they are of a different religion or nationality. Similarly, a number of Swamiji's visitors who commented on his egalitarianism did not necessarily focus on caste. For example, when I asked Meena Gupta why she thought people visited Swamiji, she answered in Hindi: "His love, that's the main reason. He sees everyone equally. There's no question of great or lowly. If people are poor, he loves them all the more. Even dark and fair. He sees white people as the same as black ones!"

I was never sure whether Meena was amazed that naive foreigners were treated with warmth, or whether she found it more remarkable that these foreigners were not given more privileged treatment than Indians. While she mentioned power, wealth, and nationality (phrased in terms of color, which is also an entrenched Indian status symbol), Colonel Khanna mentioned religion, too. With his grey moustache quivering, he spoke to me in brisk English.

> He's really a great man, there's no doubt about it. He doesn't make any distinction, whether a person is poor or rich: he has no attachment whether a person is rich. For example, the other day when I brought that old man [who was clearly poor, with a hennaed beard and lungi], I quietly asked him, "Babaji, he wants to see you, and all this." And he immediately left everything. He went inside and talked with the man. The old man was so happy, he wants to come every day now. He's a Muslim. That is why I told him: Babaji has no particular religion. With a Muslim he's a Muslim, with a Hindu he's a Hindu, with a Christian he's a Christian. That's what my feeling is. The old man came out of the room fully satisfied and said, "You have introduced me to a very, very, great man."

Westerners also remarked on Swamiji's attentive respect for the variety of people who visited him. My impression was that the Westerners, less attuned to nuances of social differences in India, saw Swamiji's egalitarianism more in terms of a general humanistic attitude than in terms of the specific kinds of cultural categories he ignored. Yet here, too, the disciple's vision was trained on the Guru's personality. Swamiji was seen as egalitarian not just because he was a *sādhu* but because of his own character. "Dattatreya," for example, told me how he had met Swamiji about ten years earlier at the ashram of Swamiji's Guru, who at that time was absent. Eager to receive initiation, he followed Swamiji to his own ashram.

> Let's check him out, I thought. So I went up to Saptashring. I went up for a week. And in that week, I saw a little of how he was. The way he treated everyone just the same: a small child, a great man, all the same. I was fasci-

nated. And the way he moved! He had a strong body in those days, with those massive legs. There was something about him that was really, really complete. A complete man. One doesn't meet people quite like that everyday. Complete. Sort of all there, you know.

All these comments from Swamiji and his visitors, then, point to the fact that ignoring caste is but one dimension of a *sādhu*'s indifference to social categories. The neat dichotomy of caste and renunciation also breaks down in another direction when one looks more closely at socialization and ascetic organization. All Indian *sādhus* were, after all, born into a particular caste, and the indoctrination of upbringing does not altogether vanish with initiation. Swami R., for example, acknowledged that he felt an affinity with Swamiji's values since they were both Brahmans, though from different parts of India. Watching Swamiji, it struck me that in certain arenas of interaction he did indeed continue to act like a Brahman concerned with purity: his small kitchen was always scrupulously cleaned, and though he welcomed people from low castes he nonetheless saw menstruation as polluting and asked that women not touch him, his food, or his altar when they "sat apart" (a common euphemism for menstruation).

Scrutinizing ascetic organization, one also finds the values of caste. The variety of ascetic orders can be ranked in terms of relative purity, mirroring the caste order: the negrophagous Aghoris for example, can be compared to Untouchables, while the militant Nagas and Gosains can be likened to the warrior Kshatriyas.[36] Even within a particular grouping of *sannyāsīs,* distinctions based on caste continue to operate. Among the Dashanamis, for example, three orders of *sannyāsī* (Giri, Puri, and Saraswati) will only admit Brahmans. In certain monasteries the *sādhus* of different castes sit in separate lines for feasts.[37] Among the itinerant Ramanandi *sādhus,* caste is ignored only while in the jungles, but distinctions are resumed when they enter a village or pilgrimage site. And the settled Ramanandi *sādhus* who preside over the worship of images in temples are Brahmans who only allow other twice-born *sādhus* into the inner sanctum.[38] Finally, according to the research by B. D. Tripathi, many *sādhus* of different orders continue to maintain links with their families and so do not sever caste ties at all.[39] What distinguishes *sādhus* from other people, then, is not an outright rejection of the values of caste so much as an alternative life-style pivoting around spiritual concerns.

A preoccupation with opposing renunciation to caste also obscures differences between and within ascetic orders, a point most forcefully argued by Richard Burghart who researched itinerant Ramanandi *sādhus* in north India. Burghart points out that Dumont theorizes about Brahmanical theories that oppose the ascetic to caste society rather than working from the views of ascetics themselves. Burghart argues instead that *sādhus* exist in a different conceptual world from those remaining in caste society (an assertion which, though ideally true, probably does not always hold) and so to view ascetics solely from the outsiders' perspective necessarily involves a distortion. To householders, for example, *sādhus* are first and foremost not householders. Yet the identity of *sādhus* themselves does not arise just in the interaction with householders, but also *between* the different sects of *sādhus* and also *within* their sects: they locate themselves within a framework of internal differentiation.[40] Considering Swamiji's stories about *sādhus,* it is important not to lose sight of Burghart's point. The folk narratives that Swamiji tells depict a generalized *sādhu* without sectarian affiliation, and in the comments explicating these stories to householders Swamiji speaks in the same broad terms. Yet this does not mean that Swamiji ignores his own location within the Saraswati order of Dashanamis, or that he does not acknowledge the differences between all the other kinds of orders.

Apart from caste, another plane of difference between householders and *sādhus* is that householders tend to be settled, whereas *sādhus* are ideally wanderers. Itinerancy, deterring the accumulation of property and personal ties, is thought to promote the spirit of renunciation.[41] Many *sādhus* spend much of their time traveling through India by foot, elephants, bus, train, or airplane. Although some *sādhus* live in the monasteries of their order or in a Guru's ashram, they generally continue to make pilgrimages. Swamiji himself hardly travels now, but he has moved through the length and breadth of India visiting pilgrimage sites and renowned religious teachers (who through the power of their presence create centers of pilgrimage).[42] *Sādhus'* routes through the subcontinent can be viewed as a network extending between temples and Gurus, with the rhythms of movement dictated by a sacred calendar marked with festivals that are celebrated in different locales. On the move through the country, *sādhus* interact with each other and with householders as they proceed. This is why historically *sādhus* have played an important role in the dissemination of religious teachings and folk traditions through the different regions of India. In the days before mass communication, there is no doubt that *sādhus* served as vital agents of cultural integration.

Swami R. once told me, dimples deepening as he spoke, "Though we leave our families, look what happens, the entire world becomes our family!" Ironically, the act of renunciation may in fact push an ascetic into more extensive social involvement than if he or she remained a layperson. *Sādhus* and householders are in fact dependent on each other. Householders make the ascetic enterprise possible by providing material support. A *sādhu* receives offerings such as food, cloth, and cash from lay visitors. Some of these goods many be redistributed: the food as consecrated *prasād;* the cloth and cash as gifts to the needy. But more important, from the householders' point of view, *sādhus* dispense blessings, teachings, and advice. Acting as religious teachers, ascetics give lay followers initiation (*dīkshā*) in a particular spiritual practice. They are consulted on a range of mundane matters as well, ranging from sexual dysfunction to economic decisions. Many are folk healers and astrologers. As impartial third parties they may be asked to settle disputes. A *sādhu,* in short, is someone who may be turned to in times of need, and who serves as spiritual advisor, doctor, lawyer, political commentator, councillor, entertainer, and psychotherapist all rolled into one.

Sitting with Swamiji as visitors came and went, I observed a kaleidoscope of such activities each day. What took place emerged in the interaction between Swamiji's current interests and the preoccupations of his visitors. I was continually impressed by the accepting way in which Swamiji participated in others' concerns. With the Tamil children who stopped in after school, he chatted about geometry or asked riddles. With mothers of growing children he commiserated about the price of milk. With the Udipi hotel owners who came from the same part of the country as he did, he lapsed into their own language but it was clear that he was discussing the availability of vegetables; during a time when coins were in short supply, he also gave whatever change had been offered on his altar. When a person edged forward with a horoscope Swamiji brought out a magnifying glass to pore over it and then suggested ritual practices that might alleviate the effects of malevolent planetary configurations. If a college student asked about mystical experience Swamiji talked about the various methods through which this could be obtained, discussing in particular the hum (*nād*) underlying all other sound until we could practically hear it ringing in our ears. Hearing that a visiting American suffered from asthma, Swamiji prescribed powdered blossoms from the milkweed plant. When a family wanting advice for a pilgrimage stopped in, Swamiji unearthed train timetables, charted alternate routes, and told legends associated with different sites. If I filled a conversational lull with questions about story-telling, Swamiji not only answered my questions but also often threw in a story or two. In short, he met people at their own level, establishing a plane of similarity.

The range of subjects on which people wanted guidance seemed occa-sionally to irk Swamiji. After a day crowded with visitors, Swamiji once reflected, "All I wish is the welfare [*kalyāṇ*] of others. People want to come sit, so we have times for them to do so. Often people want to talk about worldly matters; my husband won't eat, my business isn't doing well. These are hardly my interests! I'm a *sādhu*. If people ask me how to wor-ship, yes, I can tell them something. Not according to the scriptures, but according to my own mind I can tell them something."

Swamiji's solution to having to talk about the varied matters of *saṃsār* was to lead the conversation toward a pervasive divine will. For example, I recorded an exchange one morning when a stout and toothless man came in with a friend. Swamiji asked where they were from and what they did. The stout man confessed that he had persistent chest pains and that he de-sired Swamiji's blessings.

> SWAMIJI: Go to a doctor.
> MAN: I've done that. It didn't help.
> SWAMIJI (asks about medicines, then proceeds): I have chest pains, too. You smoke *beedis,* right? I eat tobacco. You don't have any teeth; neither do I. What? Yours fell out? Mine were pulled out. Then, you're retired, right? He's retired, too [indicating the friend], the man at the back [Mr. Karnad] is retired. I'm retired. We're all retired here.
> [The man grins, toothless gums exposed. The rest of us smile, too, though Kirin is inwardly forming objections to what Swamiji just said. She is cer-tainly not retired.]
> SWAMIJI: This is how it is. A sick person attracts other sick people, just like children go to other children and women talk to women. Like attracts like. There is no remedy I can give you but to say that taking Bhagavan's name brings you peace.

As with any *sādhu,* many of the people who approach Swamiji are not just in casual search of advice but are suffering. Like this man, they may be physically unwell. Or they may be financially unstable, grieving over a re-cent death, at odds with their families, undergoing a crisis in identity. As with this man, Swamiji listens when people unburden themselves. Then by tracing lines of similarity between himself and them, or between them and the generalized human condition, Swamiji extends sympathy for suffering even as he emphasizes that it is a precondition for life in this world. "Life is such that you always have troubles," Swamiji often said. "It's part of living. But you needn't be upset by the troubles. If you hold to Bhagavan, you can have peace of mind. The troubles come and go, but you remain calm and happy."[43]

Apart from psychological assurance, a Guru like Swamiji may have the power to help in material terms. Occasionally when talking with people I would learn that Swamiji had helped them get a job by an introduction to another disciple, or had outright given them money to eat or start a venture. One of the most moving testimonies of the material rather than spiritual effect of Swamiji's presence was from Gangabai, a widow in her forties who came to sweep his apartment each day and also did odd jobs for other disciples in the area. Her account of meeting Swamiji was intertwined with the tale of her struggles to find work once her husband died. Money was central to all she said, making real to me the helpless terror of her poverty. As she spoke Marathi, she began to weep, wiping tears with the rim of her sari.

It's been about ten years now that I've known him. I was in very bad circumstances. Nothing to eat and just one sari. That too, a torn one . . . [she got a job]. One day the Bai [her employer] was going somewhere. "Bai, where are you going?" I asked. "To Saptashring, to meet my Guru." "Which one?" I asked. She said, "There's one there." It was Divali time. She asked me to cook something to take along. She said she wanted to take food for a holiday. I said, "Won't you take me with you? This is your car, you're going free in it. Take me, too." She said, "If there's space you can come." Then she said to the Seth that Gangabai wanted to come. "Come," he said. And they took me. We had *darshan* there and took a photo, too. I'm in that photo, you can see it at the bungalow [now used by other disciples since the couple is now dead].

And from that time I touched his feet, I held on to them up till now. If he asks me to do anything, I do it, I can't say no. He can give me five annas, four annas, ten rupees, or five rupees. Whatever he wants and I never say, "Maharaj I want so much pay." He gives me extra bonuses, gives me saris, clothes, and five, ten, twenty-five rupees above what he said he would pay me. . . .

It's just like this. Once I held Swamiji's feet, after that there was a big change in my life. Now at least I eat well once a day. Before, when I ate, I never knew what my situation would be the next morning, would I eat or not? Because of him I don't have that worry anymore. That's how things have happened with me.

Gurus and Sects

While "Guru" may be used for teachers of all sorts—I have called dancing teachers and Hindi teachers "Guruji"—it is as spiritual teacher that the term carries the greatest weight and has passed over into English usage. The terms *sādhu* and Guru intersect but do not fully overlap. All *sādhus* do not attract disciples to become Gurus; conversely, all Gurus are not *sādhus*. They may be lay people who have achieved mystical insights and who will pass these on outside the structure of ascetic organization. Still, whether they are initiated into a particular order or not, most Gurus are expected, in popular opinion, to maintain the detached perspective of an ascetic.

Just as with a *sādhu*, the meaning and expected behavior of a Guru has varied historically and between sects.[44] Yet certain generalizations can be drawn. Guru derives from "weighty"—a person who commands uncommon prestige. The *Guru Gītā*, or "Song to the Guru" from the *Skanda Purāṇa* chanted every morning beside Swamiji's altar, also states that *gu* means darkness and *ru* means light; a Guru is someone who can guide a disciple from darkness of ignorance to the bright light of understanding. The Guru, then, acts as mediator between the world of illusions and the ultimate reality.

Though some Gurus are inherited through family allegiance, often they are chosen by individuals. Initiation (*dīkshā*) may take many forms: a look, a touch, receipt of a *mantra*, or even, in the realm of folklore, the cutting of a nose. The relationship with a Guru is intense and personal. Once initiated, a disciple is expected to obey the Guru's commands and to honor this bond over the ties of kinship, caste, or in the case of an ascetic the concerns of the larger order. Disciples who gather around a Guru define themselves in terms of fictive kinship: they are "Guru-brothers" (*gurubhāi*) and "Guru-sisters" (*gurubahen*). Following the same logic, the Guru's own relationships become the source for spiritual uncles, aunts, and grandfathers. Disciples may be of two kinds: the lay and the ascetics. Both may advertise their allegiance to a Guru through particular insignia, such as a ring or a string of beads bearing a picture of the Guru. In the structure of the ashram (which literally means "without toil"—a place of rest), ascetic disciples may receive special rights or duties in relation to the lay disciples.

For disciples, a Guru is a divinity in human form, addressed as "Gurudev" or "Guru-God," and worshipped like an image in a temple. In particular, the feet of a Guru are a locus of worship. Throughout India, inferiors often touch superiors' feet as a means of expressing respect; children may

Swamiji's feet are worshipped at Guru Purnima, the full moon sacred to the Guru in July.

be instructed to bob before the feet of elderly relatives, and adults showing deference for each other may do the same. Blessings are extended by the person whose feet are touched. With a Guru, this act of prostration acquires the added resonance of being a channel for potent spiritual power (*shakti*). By grasping the feet of Guru a disciple may absorb some of this power, even as he or she expresses respect, submission, and a plea for blessings.

A Guru gives people hope: that their lives can change, that suffering has meaning, that spiritual illumination can actually be achieved. Around every Guru I have known, including Swamiji, tales of miracles are in constant circulation.[45] People are warned in dreams of forthcoming catastrophes; they are healed with an ease that bewilders their doctors; the Guru appears in meditations, benevolent and smiling, to issue blessings and reassurance. It would appear that the Guru becomes an internalized touchstone of hope and goodness. Watching disciples during Swamiji's *darshan* hours, the heightened emotion shining from their faces seemed not only directed outward toward the man in the armchair but also within, to the best and highest of their own beliefs.

A vital aspect of the relationship with a Guru is the acquisition of techniques to transform consciousness. Mystical experience often has a defined physiological component[46] and there are various time-honored practices used as a means for breaking out of habitual patterns of thought: reciting a sacred group of words (*mantra*), staring at an object until it dissolves, listening until one hears an underlying hum, and so on. Depending on a Guru's expertise, there are several different paths of *yoga*, "union," which may be followed.[47] This esoteric mystical knowledge is the Guru's speciality, but as Swamiji ruefully commented, all disciples may not be interested in it, seeking blessings for worldly gratification instead.

As the group gathered around a Guru grows, it generally acquires a name and an institutional structure with codified positions of responsibility and rules of succession. The term "sect" is problematic when applied to the Hindu context, for sect as a Christian concept carries the implication of dissenting communities formed in opposition to the orthodox church.[48] Yet while Brahmans can be viewed as the orthodoxy, they are neither organized into one church nor the sole locus of authority. Since there is no single overarching Hindu institutional structure to monitor faith, the gathering of people around a novel mode of belief or worship cannot be viewed as a sect based on heterodoxy. Instead, the central defining characteristic of a Hindu sect (*sampradāya, panth*) is that it is a tradition founded by a Guru.

The role of Guru is open to anyone who can convince disciples to follow him or her, and so there are potentially thousands of sects within the Hindu fold. Sects rise; they splinter apart; they are incorporated into the caste hierarchy as yet another caste; they lose credibility and vanish; they are sustained and changed through all the vicissitudes of history. The Guru-disciple relationship, then, is the potent source of historical and regional transformations in Hinduism.[49]

The lack of monitoring devices in Hinduism allows for a rich multi-plicity of religious perspectives, but it can also lead to abuses of the ascetic role. If a fake ascetic becomes a Guru, the repercussions in the lives of dis-ciples are likely to be disastrous. The profession of false Guru—an out-growth of the false *sādhu*—is an appealing one, for the rewards are great. As a caustic Hindu commentator puts it:[50]

> The profession does not require much preliminary training or expenditure of capital. It is unattended with most of the risks that beset the secular poli-tician, and to those who possess the necessary tact, steadiness, histrionic skills, debating power, and genius for inventing unexplodable legends, it brings not only power, money, fame and honour, but everything else that the most wicked lust of the most depraved of human beings can have a crav-ing for.

Sex, of course, is among the items craved by "the most depraved of hu-man beings." Recurring charges against Gurus suspected of fraud pivot around two themes: money and sexuality, both of which outrage the tradi-tional ideal of a holy person as possessionless and celibate. Since a Guru is hoped to be a perfected person devoid of human failings, these transgres-sions are especially disappointing. This is why Swamiji often warned the people who came to him that it was important not to idolize a Guru but to maintain one's discrimination (*vivek*). "Just as every burning lamp has smoke, so every person has failings," he said, a view that stands in contrast to the notion of the Guru as a fully perfected being. "As long as a person eats, there are imperfections. You must distinguish between the wisdom [*jnān*] and the person [*vyakti*]."

The gullible abound in all times and places, prey for a rapacious false Guru. Within India, there are inbuilt cultural mechanisms to limit abuses of this powerful role. The scoundrel ascetics that abound in folklore, for example, remind people that a Guru can be a dangerous fraud. If a Guru is found to be openly transgressing the popular ideal of ascetic behavior, he may be driven out of a place. So people are most likely to bring a respect tinged with suspicion to a strange Guru, rather than to accept him as a saint straightaway. With the transportation of Gurus abroad, though, the context fostering cynicism is often lost. As I will later argue, the enduring trope of Indian spirituality versus Western materialism can blind foreign devotees to the commercial aspects of ashrams and the human foibles of their teachers.

Gurus have grown increasingly important in contemporary urban India, particularly among the middle classes. This trend derives from a number of factors. First, the image of the *sādhu*, and in particular the socially aware "modern" *sādhu*, has played a central role in modern redefinitions of Hinduism,[51] and so urban Indians wishing to rediscover their past may end up at the feet of a Guru. Second, a Guru embodying spiritual wisdom brings an immediacy to religion as opposed to the slow-moving ancient rituals presided over by Brahmans.[52] Third, individuals unmoored from a system of village relationships by emigration to cities turn to the group formed around a Guru as a form of community.[53] Disciples are bonded by their shared feeling, and in many cases a Guru's egalitarian acceptance allows a disciple to come into contact with classes of people which everyday life might not otherwise allow for. Often a Guru bears an aura of glamour: rich, famous, and best of all, a perfected being, a Guru can become the focus for a disciple's fantasies even as a disciple feels virtuous in this identification.

Having described the Guru in broad cultural terms, I will finish with Swamiji's words. His own interpretation of what a Guru truly is detaches the role from an individual, making it a relationship that can arise in any context for the sincere seeker of wisdom.[54] So after this wandering through history, across the subcontinent, and into the ashrams of various Gurus, let us return to Nasik, on a July afternoon in 1983. Swamiji's doors were not yet officially open for *darshan* and he sat in his room. He leaned against the wall, legs resting on a stool placed in front of his bed, the pink mosquito net like a canopy over his head. Light fell through the window on the left side of his face. I sat on the floor, tape recorder by my side. Leaning against the door frame, Prakash Seth listened too. Swamiji spoke slowly, solemnly.

> SWAMIJI: The entire universe is the Guru. Wherever you tread, you should continue to find the Guru. Every second. Whatever you do, find a Guru in it. When you think over something, "Why is it like that?" that act of reflection is the Guru. You can gain some wisdom from everything, so the entire uni-

verse is the Guru. We learn each thing from this universe, don't we? That's why it should be saluted as the Guru.

KIRIN: So the Guru is not one person?

SWAMIJI: That's what I think. Dattatreya [Guru of the Gods] made twenty-four Gurus. He learned something from each one of them. He even made a prostitute his Guru, a dog his Guru. Look how honest and faithful a dog is—if you feed it just a bit of bread it doesn't forget you. A human being should be like this, too. That's why Dattatreya made a dog one of his Gurus. Even if you strike a dog after you've fed it, it won't bite you; it rolls at your feet.

He made a python a Guru, too. Why? Because it keeps lying in one place. It doesn't go out in search of food. It just leaves its mouth open trusting that whatever is destined will come its way. When it feels hungry, it inhales deeply and something or the other enters its mouth. At the most it will move ten feet away from where it lives. That's why the python was made a Guru: it's so peaceful, just lying there. . . .

4. The Listeners

"How can she understand *sādhus* in just a few months?" Madan asked Jagadish Seth in Marathi. We were out for a walk on the breathtaking expanse of the Saptashring plateau, and I had lagged behind the two men. Madan had just left home to live near Swamiji as a celibate *brahmachārī* preparing for *sannyās*. Jagadish Seth was from Swamiji's region of India and now worked at Nasik Road for the government mint. Madan must have thought that I was out of earshot or that I didn't understand Marathi since mostly I spoke Hindi. He was obviously talking about me. "We spend our whole lifetime trying to understand their teachings," he continued in an exasperated tone. "Just how is she going to write something?"

My heart beat faster as I heard these words. All the fears of incompetence, partial knowledge, and shoddy scholarship that flap around any research seemed to have come down and alighted with a musty stench on my head. I struggled for the immediacy of mountain air, reminding myself that I was doing my best, that no amount of research would ever unearth every facet of *sādhus* or stories. I could live with Swamiji for twelve years and still not fully understand him; I could follow each listener through his or her daily routine and never gauge the extent to which the stories affected values or choices. Yet even as I formed these defenses I knew that he was partly right. Amid the welter of feeling, there was also emerging a grin of triumph: when I wrote my ethnography, I thought, I could couch my doubts in his very words.

Jagadish Seth had a solid, placid presence, and he was unperturbed by what Madan said. "Swamiji explains everything to her," he assured.

To Jagadish Seth and many others around Swamiji, my standing was as simple as that: Swamiji had endorsed my project and so it was respectable. Whatever my imperfections in understanding, Swamiji would remedy them. Indians were often pleased that Swamiji's words would be carried abroad through my efforts; Westerners seemed happy about the forthcoming translations. Yet my book and whatever it might contain remained marginal to the central issue of their own relationships with Swamiji.

Listening intently from the women's side of the room. The bag and camera cover mark my presence.

I could have pretended that I had not heard anything, but I made a quick decision to confront Madan directly. Hitching up my sari to walk faster and catch up with the two men, I said in a flurry, "When I write, I'll explain that I'm writing as much as my limited understanding permits, but that there are always more meanings. This is why I ask for your views, too."

"Yes, yes," said the genial Jagadish Seth. Madan nodded; I never learned if he was at all convinced.

I had in fact been collecting commentaries from Swamiji's visitors throughout my research. The summer that I was interested in his life history, I had hoped that reminiscences gathered from people around him would set him in a social field where lives were intertwined, shaping each other as they grew. Speaking of Swamiji, people sometimes also brought up his storytelling. When I returned to Nasik with an explicit interest in folk narratives, though, people knew of this research and so they often spontaneously issued comments on Swamiji's stories, even if I hadn't prompted them with questions.

My original intention to elicit audience responses to Swamiji's stories stemmed from an acute sense that I did not have any privileged authority as interpreter. I was aware that other people had views on Swamiji's stories and that the interpretations I ferreted out from texts were ultimately no better or worse than what anyone else who listened to Swamiji might think. By including the views of other listeners I hoped to democratize interpretive authority. I knew that in the field of literary criticism attention had shifted from authors' intention to readers' responses,[1] and I was exhilarated when I found that my intention also had a niche in folklore scholarship. Alan Dundes, my advisor, had called for "oral literary criticism" in 1966 and a decade later he wrote:[2]

> There has been little concrete discussion in the folkloristics literature on precisely what different members of the audience understand by a given item of folklore even though it is clear that the same item of folklore may mean very different things to different listeners . . . One would think that the investigation of audiences and their different understandings (and misunderstandings) of folklore communication events is a likely area for further research.

In folklore, the most notable precedent of attention to audience response lies in Melville Jacobs's studies of Clackamas Chinook narratives. In *The Content and Style of an Oral Literature* (1959), Jacobs points out that it is extremely difficult to appreciate the folk narratives of other cultures, as the texts are mere outlines filled in by the cultural associations of listeners. While the brevity of a text may be mystifying to members of an alien culture, for those familiar with the allusions contained in a body of oral literature, the brevity is a source of imaginative creativity that triggers a range of images and feelings. Folk narratives, Jacobs argues, are not just told; they are *performed* to audiences, and so they act as a form of theater. If a text is to be understood in terms of what it means to listeners, it must be supplemented with an exegesis of cultural meaning, as well as notes on audience participation in performance. Unfortunately, Jacobs himself did not have an opportunity to put his rich ideas into practice in anything but the most hypothetical way. Just one acculturated woman was dictating texts to him, and there was no Chinook audience present. His reconstructions of how people participated in and perceived these stories turns out to be a feat in imaginative conjecture. With Swamiji's listeners, I hoped, I could fulfill Jacobs's mission in a live setting.[3]

Before returning to Nasik a second time, then, I was aware of what I wanted to record on tape, in notebooks, and in my mind when Swamiji told stories. I wanted to be alert to how stories came to be told, to Swamiji's actions and asides, and to how listeners responded. I had even worked out a format I would use to write up the stories: a prose (not poetry) style that captured Swamiji's garrulous, flowing manner, and the use of brackets for notes on the situation in which the story emerged.[4] Yet in the actual storytelling situation I was often called upon to serve as translator and would become more absorbed in capturing accurate shades of meaning than in noting the expressions on the faces of my friends. I tried to transcribe stories from tape the same evening that they were told, so images from the setting would still be fresh. Yet even several years later, when I listen through headphones to Swamiji's voice, the input of listeners, the rattle of traffic, I can once more see and feel the atmosphere and activity surrounding any storytelling session. Heightened attention had engraved these moments in my mind.

I had also planned to elicit interpretations of particular stories just after the story was told. Yet like many systematic plans designed from afar, this crumbled in the actual fieldwork situation. I found it simply impossible to round up listeners after every story. Though a story finished, *darshan* hours often continued, and people slipped away at intervals while I remained sitting inside with Swamiji. When *darshan* formally ended, people quickly dispersed for a return to their routines. I was reluctant to waylay them if they seemed busy, and I preferred to wait until there was a clear indication that they were at leisure and ready to chat. I sometimes gleaned

comments while we were waiting for Swamiji inside his room or just outside the door. Many conversations unfolded in Nasik over hot, sweet tea
in people's homes. Later I made contact with disciples in Berkeley and
New Mexico.

Possibly because my interviews were not tied to particular storytelling
situations, almost everyone I approached tended to speak in generalities. I
would try to push the conversation toward particular stories and could
sometimes evoke a passing exegesis or even a retelling of a favorite folk
narrative. But then the flow of general comments would resume. Indians
and Westerners alike preferred to speak in broad terms of what the stories
as a group meant to them in the context of their relationship with Swamiji.
But before I introduce these comments, I want to make some qualifica-
tions about my sampling.

The composition of the group clustered around Swamiji on any given
day was extremely variable. Visitors from the neighborhood fell into three
groups: those who dropped in once in a while, those who went through
phases during which they came regularly (often coinciding with periods of
personal crisis), and those who were dedicated regulars. There were also
disciples who came from various parts of India and abroad. Occasionally
sādhus or novice *brahmachārīs* stopped by and seated themselves closest to
Swamiji. In gathering commentaries, I sought out the people in whose
company I had listened to stories several times: the "regulars," whether
from the neighborhood or abroad. Obviously this is just a small fraction of
all the people who listen to and are affected by these stories, particularly
since there is an invisible mass of disciples who live at a distance and regard
Swamiji as their Guru even if they only see him once or twice a year.

In my selection of people to interview, I also left out the children, who
did not attend daily *darshan* sessions but came in hordes to chant every
evening. These seventy-odd children lived in the neighborhood and were
mostly from poor and middle-class families. Their clothes ranged from
rags to frilly nylon frocks. Some had snot caked on their faces, dishevelled
hair, a younger brother or sister in tow; others were paragons of clean-
liness, with their hair oiled and combed and every last button in place.
Dr. Mukund had arranged a space for them to assemble and with his wife
supervised half an hour of chanting and a short talk before Swamiji shuffled in. Then there was more chanting and the ceremonial waving of lights
(*āratī*) to pictures of Swamiji's Guru and Guru's Guru. The children
seemed fascinated by Swamiji, who sometimes grinned at them and set
them giggling, and at other times was serious and indrawn. They scrambled
for the fruit, sweets, and snacks he provided. Occasionally Swamiji trans-

formed the cash offerings he had received into clothes, lunch-boxes, books, and other presents: on such days, the children were at a feverish pitch of excitement and delight.

In omitting the children I am underplaying a vital aspect of Swamiji's sense of responsibility to society. "These children are our future," he would say, going on to explain that if you wanted to change the world you had to start with people's attitudes, and since attitudes were most often set in adults, children were the place to begin. Swamiji's interaction with the children was above all loving: he did not seem to be overtly teaching them except through the example of his actions. Occasionally, though, he would entertain them with a folktale. My own role as collector of stories prompted Dr. Mukund to ask if I would tell the children a story one afternoon. When I conferred with Swamiji, he suggested a pithy animal fable about a tiger and a mouse. A baby mouse was scampering about in the forest, and disturbed a tiger who threatened to crush him. The mouse pleaded that he be released, and though the tiger laughed when the mouse suggested that he would forever after help him out, later the tiger was trapped and the mouse chewed through ropes to set him free.[5] The moral of the story, Swamiji said, was that even the small and powerless could help people with clout. He wanted to let the children know that they, too, were important. (It turned out, though, that this story was in a school textbook so almost everyone knew it. I was somewhat nonplussed when this telling became a collaborative venture, with the children animatedly prompting me on what came next!)

In emphasizing stories in my conversations with adults, I am also placing Swamiji's verbal interactions at center stage although many people actually stressed the nonverbal power of his presence. Swamiji's visitors said they experienced peace when they came to him; this peacefulness permeated the space within which words were exchanged and stories spun. English "Dattatreya" (one of the few Westerners whom Swamiji allowed to stay for extended periods of time) described this setting in a journal he allowed me to read and cite:

> When sitting with Swamiji, an invisible current seems to be at work which consoles and pacifies the heart, and eases worries and strain. When Swamiji laughs, everyone in the room will have to laugh, so similarly if Swamiji's mood is serious the room will be hushed and silent.

This "invisible current" that "Dattatreya" describes was called *shakti*, power, by Indians and also Westerners who had picked up the vocabulary.[6]

Shakti is the female energy that pervades this universe, a charge that flows especially from nodes of sacredness. When people spoke of *shakti* and peacefulness in Swamiji's presence, I reflected that these are not just forces emerging from Swamiji but are also rooted in his physical setting and interactions. To begin with, the space in which Swamiji sits forms a peaceful enclave amid the hustle and bustle of the streets outside. The green walls, the swept and dusted order, and a lingering fragrance of incense all contribute to a sense of serenity. Swamiji himself speaks in a low voice. His body, relaxed and still, communicates ease to those who confront him. His humor dissolves the burdens that people bring with them, and his assertion of a cosmic order is reassuring. The visitors in turn are oriented toward him and bring with them currents of emotion that pervade the room. Swamiji speaks to people, and people speak to him, but there is little interaction between visitors in his presence. This is a focused gathering—a group of people engrossed in a common focus of cognitive and visual attention[7]—and the atmosphere of arrested attention carries its own powerful calm.

Colonel Khanna evoked the healing aspect of this atmosphere when he told me how meeting Swamiji had brought him tranquillity after the depression following his retirement. "Although he has not told me in any particular way, 'Do this, do that,' but you FEEL," Colonel Khanna said as we sat after lunch in his house. "I go to ask him something but when I meet him I forget to ask him that. I mean, that's the least important thing: speaking. I mean his presence itself inspires you for a better living. Isn't it?"

The emotional climate of *darshan* sessions is also what keeps many Westerners seated for hours as Swamiji meets with visitors and the conversation rolls on in a language they cannot understand. "Aren't you bored?" I asked English "Saraswati." She shrugged, "If I can't understand his words, I can only go on the feelings that I have when I'm with him, right? The peace and tranquillity. But every now and then, someone will be translating." Later I posed the same question to French "Kumari" who not only had no knowledge of Hindi but also had problems with English. She sat motionless day after day, her face brimming with emotion as she looked toward Swamiji. "You feel his *shakti*," she simply stated when I got my question through. Sometimes, she said, Isabel the nurse would also explain to her what had happened. Otherwise, Swamiji's mere presence was enough.

Commentaries

Once I had gathered what different people had to say, I realized that my plan to share my authority was not quite as simple as it would seem. I would have to select and arrange other people's voices, become a conductor who would orchestrate their polyphony.[8] I started by looking for patterns that might match up with social differences: did Indians, for example, have insights different from those of the Westerners present? Did women and men stress different features? My search for socially based differences, though, was stymied. I found that people who shared backgrounds often expressed divergent views: all Jewish American men did not think exactly alike; nor did Catholic French women, Maharashtrian farmers, or south Indian housewives. There was instead a good deal of intersection in the views expressed by different groups of listeners. Despite their far-flung backgrounds, to some extent they formed a bounded analytical set—an interpretive community[9]—in that they all saw Swamiji as a Guru. I ended up arranging my material according to themes I discerned in people's testimonies, regardless of who these people were. While it might seem anthropologically insensitive to juxtapose what an impoverished Nasik barber and a sari-wearing French nurse have to say, this is what has emerged from my materials and, in fact, this intersection of views vividly evokes the mix of cultures around Swamiji.

SWAMIJI AS TRADITIONAL STORYTELLER

I start with Swami R., another *sannyāsī,* sitting in a hut in central Maharastra. Swami R. was in his forties, but with his shaved head, round proportions, and ochre robes tied like a bib, he could look like a large baby. He had been an engineer before he took *sannyās,* and so he spoke Bengali-accented English with verve. Swami R. had known Swamiji for almost twenty years and, in fact, Swamiji was instrumental in his taking *sannyās.* They both shared a devotion to the Mother Goddess. His large eyes bright, Swami R. told me that Swamiji was a "very good person, with clean behavior, simplicity, sincerity, and complete devotion to Devi. He is trying to do his best in guiding all the persons who come to him." He went on to marvel at Swamiji's prodigious memory—"once he hears something, he remembers it"—and his independence. He commented on how Swamiji was "spiritually, a person of superb faith, with a thorough religious background, and knowledge of rituals, of scriptures. He has a very good communion with Devi." I recorded these views before I was interested in Swamiji's storytelling. Writing to Swami R. of my prospective plans, I received endorsement with his reply, "Yes, Swamiji's stories are the best part of him." I took this as an acknowledgment from a fellow *sannyāsī* that storytelling was a primary medium for many of the fine qualities he had already listed.

English "Dattatreya" had also hoped to become a *sannyāsī* (when last heard of, he was contemplating a Christian monastery instead). The son of a diplomat, he had been raised in many countries, and since childhood had borne a mystical streak. In 1983, he had already stayed near Swamiji for several years and looked very much like a white *sādhu* with his wispy blond beard and saffron cloth wrapped around the waist. I met with him one morning in 1983 at the house where Swamiji had lived previously. An altar remained in worship there, visiting ascetics and male disciples often stayed over for varying lengths of time, and this was where lunches were communally prepared. "Dattatreya" was chopping vegetables as he spoke. Though I had not brought up storytelling, "Dattatreya" observed that *sādhus* used many different means for spiritual edification, and Swamiji's medium was words. "He once told me," said "Dattatreya," "that *mahātmās* have a duty to elevate people. They do it in various ways. Some through silence, some through actions, some through speech. When he said this it seemed obvious to me that he uses sound to give *shakti* to people. That's how he gives grace to people, you know, through his words." Delicate features crumpling in a bemused smile, "Dattatreya" said, "He can go on all day. It's really extraordinary, the way he can go on talking!"

Chinmaya Baba, who now looks after Swamiji's old ashram, also saw storytelling as a *sādhu's* means of edification. A middle-aged *sannyāsī* with black-rimmed glasses, matted chest, and enormous belly, Chinmaya Baba said, "Yes, Swamiji tells so many stories. This is to have an effect on people's minds. The ancient seers and sages [*rishi-muni*] told these stories to set an ideal standard [*ādarsh*]. These are to show people a way to move ahead, the correct paths to tread. The seers and sages didn't make up these stories. They understood truths and gave them to us in the form of stories. These stories have all come down to us from those ancient times."

Madan (who was dubious about my understanding) spoke less of origins than of an enduring split between the ascetics who told stories and those who did not. Madan was a squat young man with deep set eyes and a moustache. He was a Brahman from a nearby town and had been working as a clerk. In 1985, he informed his parents that he did not want to marry and would become a *sādhu* instead. He came to Swamiji in the company of his uncle, who with an indulgent, amused air, acted as spokesman. Swamiji spoke at length about what it meant to be a *sādhu,* and the hardships involved: "You should help others, not earn. You should be willing to eat anything and sleep anywhere. . . ." Madan was adamant, though, and it was arranged that he would come live with Swamiji and try out the ascetic life before he was formally initiated into any order. Madan had already moved in when Swamiji had a severe bout of high blood pressure and remained inside his bedroom through afternoon *darshan* hours one day. As those of us gathered outside waited, wondering whether he would emerge, I began to chat with my companions. Without rising from his cross-legged position, Madan acrobatically scooted across the room to explain in Hindi:

> The *sādhu*'s temperament [*svabhāv*] is very different. In my thinking, there are two kinds of *sādhus.* Those who have matted locks [*jhaṭṭā*] and beards are full of anger. They can't live in society. They go off to jungles and caves. They live alone. They keep on doing austerities and austerities [*tapas*]. They gain such power they can create something if they wish. Vashishta, Durvasa, Bhishmacharya, are all like that.
>
> Then there are also *sādhus* who don't keep matted locks. They stay in society. They have a peaceful temperament. If a person makes a mistake they gently try to show him the right path. They tell stories. Only these ones without the matted locks and beards tell stories with love to instruct people. Swamiji is such a *sādhu.*

Champa also linked stories with loving teaching. She was a Maharashtrian Brahman who never married and, now, entering her forties, remained fiercely independent. She ran a cold drink stand in a village several hours away from Nasik, and occasionally stopped in to see Swamiji. In the past she had scandalized village society with her jeans and sunglasses, but now she compromised with the pants traditional to north India. When I spoke to her, she was wearing a lavender Punjabi outfit so brilliant it seemed to match her disdain of what others might see. Her gaunt face was animated as she echoed Madan's point. She had just remarked that Swamiji spoke with happiness on his face; the stories therefore had more of an effect on people than if he sternly told them what to do. "Other *sādhus* also bring out stories in the middle of talking," she said, "but there are only a few *sādhus* who can explain things with love."

Nathu Maharaj, the local barber, met with me in his garrett swirling with wood smoke and packed tightly with extended family. He must have been in his fifties, with a shock of gray hair and betel-stained buck teeth.

He said, "Many *sādhus* tell stories. But to understand a *sādhu* properly is what's difficult. And to recognize the worth of a true *sādhu* is very difficult, too. You might meet many *sādhus* but which one you pin your faith on is the matter of past lives." He had just told me that the fact that I had access to a car, many clothes, and practically a Ph.D. while he would never have any of these was also a matter of past lives. I felt oddly ashamed when this intelligent, articulate man qualified his observations with, "This is my un-educated [*anāṛī*] point of view."

Apart from Swamiji's being a *sādhu,* many people commented on the enormity of his folk narrative repertoire in an age when radio, films, and television appeared to be edging traditional storytelling out of use. Jagadish Seth's wife, Lakshmi Amma, marveled at Swamiji's prodigious memory as we chatted after lunch in her crowded home. She had just asked for a tape of Swamiji's rendition of the popular legend of Shakun-tala. "His stories give us peace of mind," she said in her Kannada-accented Hindi. "He doesn't gossip, he tells stories. These days who else tells stories like him? And so well?" I had to agree that I didn't know anyone who did.

Chandrakala was a single Punjabi woman who worked as an advertising executive in Bombay. She visited Swamiji on most weekends and often served as a translator. When I brought up the issue of his storytelling, she observed, "He tells stories you haven't heard of before. Even when it's the *Rāmāyaṇa* or the *Mahābhārata,* you think, 'Oh, I know it,' but he catches you. He'll tell you stories you don't find in any of the books. I've looked through translations and I just haven't found them. Then I asked him and he explained that there were many different versions." Chandrakala pulled her sari tighter around her shoulders and widened her eyes, "He'll tell ver-sions you *just* never heard of before!" Chandrakala's surprise, I think, de-rives from the orientation to a literate tradition she shares with many Indian elites. Though Swamiji's stories have moved through the oral tradi-tion, they have often eluded mainstream publication.

Mr. Karnad was originally from Swamiji's region but had worked as a journalist for a prestigious newspaper in Maharashtra for many years. He had remained a bachelor, and now that he was retired he lived with "Dattatreya" in Swamiji's old apartments. I approached Mr. Karnad after a group of us had gathered for our habitual lunch, and found that he linked Swamiji's carrying forward of ancient traditions with the patriotism of his youth. "He is very fond of his country," Mr. Karnad said, sitting on a metal chair wearing a white kurta and baggy pajamas, his eyes with a faraway look. "Very, very, fond of his motherland. Very fond. He wants us to be like that: that that was, the old tradition. He nurtures that old tradition. . . . The politicians, they only blah-blah about our heritage, great Indian heritage. Swamiji doesn't say anything about our heritage, he *lives* our heritage. In his conversations, in a practical way." Mr Karnad concluded with a nod, "Very practical."

NARRATIVE AS A VEHICLE FOR INSTRUCTION

Most of Swamiji's listeners had theories about the use of stories, and I found these views as insightful as anything I have come across in the scholarly literature on narrative. The very day I returned to Nasik I met Krishna Chaitanya, a *brahmachārī* who wore the ochre cloth of a *sādhu*. He must have been about forty, for there were flecks of gray in his hair. He was originally from Karnataka and spoke several languages with an alert intelligence. The morning I arrived, I sat on the floor telling Swamiji of my plans to tape stories. Krishna Chaitanya looked on, and when Swamiji left the room to spit tobacco, he turned to me. "The stories are nothing but the morals on which our society is based," he announced in vehement English. I nodded, startled that within my first few hours of fieldwork someone had so neatly encapsulated a theoretical approach I thought I had brought with me from graduate school: that folklore is an expression of deep-rooted cultural themes.

Most of Swamiji's listeners were aware that the stories contained teachings. Dr. Mukund, who looked after Swamiji, said, "He is telling these stories for our instruction." "Gulelal," the lumbering Jewish American who was visiting for a few months, asserted, "His stories are all lesson stories." Madan explained, "All *sādhus* tell stories for a target.*" Bird-like British "Saraswati" commented that the stories were often aimed at someone in particular. "He might be talking to you," she observed, "but what he says could be cutting someone else in the room to the quick; every story he tells." Lakshmi Amma simply said, "He tells us stories so we can change our lives."

As we waited for Swamiji to open his doors one morning, Champa explained, "There's always some kind of doctrine [*siddhānt*] in a story. A story is used to make people understand these doctrines. Then people remember them properly. The form [*rūp*] of a story makes people remember. There's always some reason for telling a story, but instead of saying it directly, he tells it by the long* route,* moving around the issue in the form of a story. As he wanders in a story, people listen. If he said something directly, it wouldn't have the same effect. When he reaches the meaning, it's accepted."

Pannalal, a local farmer in his fifties who has known Swamiji since 1960, spoke along very similar lines. He was a tall man with an elongated face and courteous bearing. Sitting on the floor in Swamiji's outer room, his head inclined and voice thoughtful, Pannalal said, "He teaches us through his stories. He tells us what's good. If he gave us a direct message we wouldn't understand. But if he tells it in the story form it sticks in our minds."

Dr. Khanna agreed. She was the Colonel's wife, a middle-aged professional wearing a flowered nylon sari and lipstick. I had asked if she thought Swamiji's stories were a form of teaching. "Yes," she said after a moment's reflection, "the story helps the morals sink in, because what happens with any human being is that it's very difficult to grasp any philosophical or moral point. But if it's illustrated by a story, the story is more engrossing because it doesn't involve you in philosophy or anything. It is *about* somebody else. And like a good entertainment, you listen to it and then you retain it. When you retain it, you know, at times you recall it. And when you recall it, slowly it gets kind of fixed in your mind. And the more the repetition of these parables, I suppose, the more it helps."

Swamiji did indeed repeat stories a good deal of the time; even with his variations, they were recognizable. Yet like Dr. Khanna, no one seemed to mind. Mr. Karnad said, "You never tire of hearing the same story again and again from him." A smile came over Mr. Karnad's face as he thought of Swamiji. "Even if he tells it one hundred times, the meaning will always be deeper in your mind."

All these listeners hit on key points in narrative theory. A story is a "cognitive instrument," a means of making sense of the world.[10] While straightforward analysis dissects principles within a timeless frame, stories dramatize these principles through characters in an unfolding plot.[11] Rather than leaping straight to the detachable conclusions—doctrines, morals, or commentaries on particular events—a story wanders through sequences, capturing listeners' imaginations as it proceeds. The point where a narrative arrives beams meaning backwards over what came before.[12] As Champa said, using the English words amid her brisk Hindi, a story takes the "long route" to meaning; it is precisely this leisurely progress through the dilemmas involving other characters that lends a story its entertainment value, luring attention in a way that straightforward moralizing cannot.[13]

Swamiji's stories are often called forth by particular dilemmas of his listeners. A story becomes "an implement for argument, a tool for persuasion."[14] It can be used to "shoot" morals at people[15] and to ease tensions by displacing the problem to another, structurally parallel level.[16] That many of Swamiji's listeners are aware of the didactic intent of storytelling adds a serious note to the entertainment value of his stories. People strain forward not just to be amused, but to find answers that may apply to their own lives.

STORIES AS PERSONAL COMMENTARY

Pannalal saw Swamiji's stories as a benevolent means of diagnosing the present, predicting the future, and commenting on the past. "He understands what's in someone's mind and tells a story to show them the right path," Pannalal said. "This is his teaching, to show us the right path [*mārg*] for living. If we follow this path we have good fortune. . . . I have known him for twenty-five years. He has never told us directly if there's going to be some trouble ahead, but he warns us through a story. We're careful then, and our path is cleared. Sometimes we might think, why is he saying something? But we should listen with a peaceful mind. We should try to understand what he's telling us. If you don't listen to what he's saying you can forget your path. You fall into difficulties. Then if you go back to him and say, 'I had troubles,' he doesn't say, 'I told you so.' Rather, he tells another story."

I asked why people listened with care, and Pannalal said, "This is because of the power of his worship. Anything becomes Bhagavan through worship. In this way he attracts people's minds." He looked at me across the floor and politely pointed out, "If *you* were to tell the same story it wouldn't stick in anyone's mind." I was thinking over the source of this dismissal—because I was a young woman?—when a housewife who had been vigorously nodding her head, added, "He has full faith in Devi. That's how everything happens." Swamiji's capacity to tell the appropriate story seemed, in the minds of listeners, to be vitally linked to his spiritual power.

Manjuben was a childless woman who came for a few days from her home in coastal Gujarat. Diminutive, and with heavy spectacles, she wore a bright orange sari in honor of her spiritual concerns. "He's telling the future in his stories," she said as we walked to lunch. "They are grand and full of morals [*tattvabharī*]. He comes and visits us and tells us stories. Sometimes only after he goes I understand what the story meant." Manjuben Amma confidentially whispered, "It *all* comes to pass."

Sahadev, on the other hand, was sure that the stories were commentaries on what he had just done. He was a round-faced man with a cherubic smile who ran a dairy farm in Khandesh, an inner region of Maharashtra

Swamiji is present at a disciple's altar, along with Ganesh, Saptashring Nivasini Devi (top) and Durga (below).

known for its thick milk. He commuted back and forth to Bombay several times a week, and he often broke journey to see Swamiji, arriving laden down with fruit and heavy garlands for the altar. I caught him outside the door one day as he was slipping on his shoes to leave. "Through stories he tells us about our own feelings," Sahadev said. "If you've made a mistake on the road he'll tell a story about it." The image of the road (*rāstā*, *mārg*), which Chinmaya Baba and Pannalal had also mentioned, could refer to Sahadev's moral path; it might also be linked to his perpetual travels—he was, literally, always on the road. "If you've done good deeds and said good things, his story will repeat what you did. You feel he was with you. He tells you how to behave and what not to do. His stories are completely advice.*"

STORIES WITHOUT COMMENTARY

There were, however, a few disciples who did not internalize the stories as comments on their own lives. "Narahari," a hypnotherapist I met in both Nasik and Albuquerque, assured me, wire-rimmed glasses glinting, "These stories are archetypes. They are energy patterns coming out of the void." The Jungian framework of archetypes allowed "Narahari" to strip the stories of Swamiji's personal imprint and the situational context alike. "He tells a story—it has nothing to do with him. It just comes out of his mind. . . . I don't think he sits there premeditatively saying, 'So-and-so needs to learn to change this.' He just has an archetypal world view." I had actually been present when "Narahari" appeared as a gullible disciple in one of Swamiji's stories and so was surprised that even this characterization did not carry personal meaning. When I asked "Narahari" about this he shrugged, adding, "I'm not a good metaphor person. I like things raw and direct." If Swamiji wanted to teach him something, "Narahari" said, he had to say it bluntly.

"Amrita," a nurse with whom I met in Albuquerque, saw storytelling as a strategy for interacting with many people at the same time. She had visited Swamiji for several weeks the previous year and had observed the stream of visitors from the neighborhood and further afield. "I felt that all these people came," she recalled, "especially from Bombay. He wanted to be with them all. It was just his love for them that made him tell stories. It's nothing more than that. The stories were giving him an opportunity to be with them together."

Chandrakala also underplayed any didactic intent. "He likes telling stories and I like listening," she said, speaking English in a clear, musical voice. "I haven't really thought about it much . . . sometimes there's a moral, I suppose, but not always. Basically I think he enjoys telling stories. He enjoys it and makes you enjoy it, too."

THE PLEASURE OF A STORY

The issue of Swamiji's and his listener's enjoyment that Chandrakala spoke of does indeed seem to be central to storytelling. Swamiji has a broad grin and a shine of enthusiasm as he launches into a story; his listeners, hearing that a story will be told, are often smiling in anticipation. Champa had pointed out that it was Swamiji's "laughter and happiness" that arrested people's attention. When I spoke with "Prabhu" in Albuquerque, he reminisced, "The thing about Swamiji was the way he used to delight in his own stories. He would tell these stories again and again."

Isabel, the frail French nurse, elaborated at the greatest length, speaking in gently accented English: "Swamiji is so much inside the story," she said, sitting on the floor by the altar, her brown eyes sincere. "He is *inside* it. His body, his words, everything. He is so happy to tell us a story. He could tell the same story every day, but change it a little every time. And if it's funny, each time he laughs and laughs and laughs. He never tells a story as though he *has* to tell it; he tells it with enjoyment. I really think it's the *shakti* that makes him speak this way. He is really giving himself when he tells a story.

"Then, he is not just one character," Isabel continued, smiling as she recalled Swamiji's delight in his stories. "He is everyone in the story. When he says a man is sleeping, he becomes that man. Or a bullock. Or a king. He *becomes* each character in a story."

Isabel evokes many facets of the riveting rendition of a narrative. The narrator's own pleasure is contagious; his smile lights a smile on other faces. The narrator participates in the situations and characters so completely that listeners are drawn in as well. Entering the imaginative space of a story with complete absorption, a skillful storyteller takes listeners by the hand, drawing them within this enchanted circle. Yet for each listener, the experience of the inner landscape may be different.

INTERPRETIVE VARIATION

Having observed that there was variation in the ways people made sense of Swamiji's stories, I began to ask my fellow listeners about their own views on this issue. "Do you think different people might hear the same story in different ways?" I would enquire. While some people gave me a dismissive "yes" (as though the point was so obvious there was no need to comment further), others elaborated. Isabel, for example, said, "I think we take what we need. We are open to what we need. He might tell a story to a special person, but everyone listens. People have different feelings inside and take something else." I was reminded, as Isabel spoke, of Swamiji's own attitude toward what any person remembers: "What is needed by the heart will settle in the mind." I also thought of Bruno Bettelheim's *The Uses of Enchantment,* in which he argues that beloved fairy tales metaphorically express the psychic conflicts of Western children growing up within a nuclear family. He writes: "The fairy tale is therapeutic because the patient finds his *own* solutions, through contemplating what the story seems to imply about him and his inner conflicts at this moment in his life." [17]

"Yes, different people see different meanings in his stories," agreed Peter, a dark-haired Swiss disciple who worked as a waiter in Berkeley. "Some people see a pretty story, some see a wise story, some just see a story. He who has ears to hear will hear; he who can't hear won't hear. That's from the Bible."

Peter was relating Swamiji's stories back to his own scheme of reference in the Christian tradition. In the Gospel according to Mark (4:1–20) as well as Matthew (13:1–24), Jesus is reported to have preached from a boat to a crowd at the beach. He tells the crowd a parable about a sower who throws out seeds: some fall on the path and are devoured by birds, some fall on the ground and are scorched, some fall among thorns and are choked, and some fall on good soil to bear a bountiful crop. He concludes with the cryptic statement, "He who has ears to hear, let him hear." Later, when a select group of disciples asks Jesus why he speaks in parables, he explains in Mark's report that these are a means of excluding uncomprehending outsiders, while in Matthew's version he suggests that parables serve as a means of clarifying teachings to common people. [18] Jesus goes on to explain that the seeds are the "word of the kingdom" which will wither or take root in people's lives depending on how receptive they are. As with Swamiji, the effect of a story would seem to depend on the active imaginative participation of the listener.

While Peter referred multiple interpretations back to the New Testament, Nathu Maharaj explained the same phenomenon in a Hindu idiom. "What these people say—these saints and *mahātmās,* is at a very high* level.* Each person extracts meanings from these stories according to their *samskār*." He paused to suck at a hand-rolled cigarette, and I reflected that although the first translation that came to mind for *samskār* was "effects of a previous life" it could also mean "a stage in life" or "inner refinement measured by rites of passage." "They see meaning according to this. I might say, 'This is the meaning!' but another person will say 'No, that's the meaning.' We have different levels of understanding. This is the issue [*yah bāt hai*]." Nathu Maharaj rolled his head.

After a digression on genuine and fake *sādhus,* Nathu Maharaj returned to differences in understanding. "You might have a pot and take away that much," he drew his hands about a foot apart. "I have a glass and can take that much," he indicated the distance between thumb and outstretched forefinger. "And a child will take just a tiny pot." The span between thumb and forefinger narrowed to an inch or two. "Each person fills water according to their vessel's capacity. And the Ganga flows on. . . ."

Swamiji's speech has been likened here to the Ganges river; a source of purity, a center of sacredness. The analogy illustrates the respect with which Swamiji's words are viewed. In contrast to the active Christian image of a preacher who scatters seeds, Nathu Maharaj's metaphor illustrates a more relaxed Hindu religious attitude. The detached *sannyāsī* moves along his own path, and the people who choose to visit him may take away what they please.

Though Swamiji did not bring up the issue of multiple meanings in conversations with me, my mother recalled an occasion on which he expressed his views. Several years before she had been translating the *Mahābhārata* for Swamiji (he periodically retells this epic in varying lengths). Someone asked him what it meant. "He said, 'You should never assign a meaning to a myth because if you assign a meaning, the mind clamps onto just that one meaning. Then it's no longer active, because when a story is active it allows for new beginnings all the time. Don't give meanings to anything,' he said, 'it doesn't ever mean just one thing.'"

Yet as the folk narratives I reproduce here show, Swamiji does sometimes follow a story with comments on the moral that can be drawn. His exegesis, though, is never detailed. It is not presented as a sole or authoritative opinion. Swamiji does not say, "I told this story because x here needs to learn y." Reflective listeners are free to discern multiple resonances in the story as they ponder over why it was told: For them specifically? As general teaching? For someone else? Carl Fellner, who advocates the use of religious parables in family therapy, describes the therapist in a way that encompasses Swamiji: [19]

He has not expressed an opinion, he has just told a story. However, in so doing, he has commented indirectly on several levels of meaning about an ongoing situation, and he has seeded a number of ideas, set in motion a number of forces. It is now up to the individuals themselves to make their own discoveries, their own interpretation, and thus move towards perceiving relationships in new ways, towards "tasting" new realities.

Stories as Therapy

"Gee, why he tells stories?" Bringing together his long fingers, "Prabhu" reflected on my question in Albuquerque. "Prabhu" was fair-skinned and dark-haired and had lived with his wife in India for several years in the ashram of Swamiji's Guru. Now he lived in Albuquerque where he studied hypnotherapy, a form of therapy developed by Milton Erickson which emphasized storytelling. Unlike Bettelheim or Fellner, though, Erickson did not recommend traditional stories so much as anecdotes improvised from a therapist's experience which in some way mirrored the patient's situation.[20] "Well, they use stories in hypnotherapy a lot. It's an easy way to relate to principles: to lessons, to learning. It's not confrontative, it isn't direct, it doesn't hurt you or put you off. It touches a place inside you where personally you can relate." "Prabhu" went on to describe how the "nice, light trance" provoked by a hypnotherapist was similar to the concentrated attention people brought Swamiji. This state of mind allowed messages to penetrate the subconscious, hastening a solution "according to their need." "Prabhu" observed, "It shows a great respect for a person not to try and teach them something directly, or moralize. . . . People have their own model of the world. Part of being a good therapist is to recognize the other person's model. A *sādhu* is like a therapist because he doesn't change anything, but tells stories so people can recognize their own outlook and make their own choices. This involves respecting the integrity and divinity of a person."

The therapeutic aspect of storytelling, then, seemed to hinge on the possibility of interpretive variation allowing listeners to extract meanings differently. Yet as a *sādhu*, Swamiji served as a therapist in a wider sense, and his storytelling was one aspect of this interaction. Other visitors whose worlds of reference spanned Gurus and psychotherapists also established a connection between these two roles. Dr. Khanna, for example, marveled over how Swamiji remembered all the different people who visited and their particular concerns. "He really sympathizes," she reflected, "so you unburden yourself. In Western words it's as though you're talking to a psychiatrist. It's just like that. He acts as your sounding board, then gives you correct advice. He tells you to accept what you get."

My mother made a similar observation. "Everyone comes with their secrets," she said, describing the time she had spent observing Swamiji. I agreed, saying that people needed someone to confide in. "A *sannyāsī* acts also as a psychiatrist," my mother went on to assert. "People tell them things they can't tell anyone. And very often, *sannyāsīs* are surrounded by some really weird people. Swamiji has great compassion for them—even a black marketer, a racketeer—because they have told him their innermost fears. Own fears, own innermost reactions; and he has compassion for that person. The person has opened up to him the dark areas of his soul that he will not have opened up to others."

Swamiji himself once compared a *sādhu* to a "psychologishta." He had been explaining the different ways that doctors drew blood to a man about to set off for a blood test. Then he began to talk about cricket with Krishna Chaitanya, who was an avid fan. My mind began to wander as wickets and runs were discussed. Jolted back to attention, I was surprised to find Swamiji holding forth on the principles of psychotherapy. There were a handful of nodding Indian listeners present. The Westerners sitting among them were following with difficulty since Swamiji's words were not being translated.

"A person is off balance," Swamiji said, "and what a psychologist does is lead them back. The psychologist sits listening sympathetically [*hamdard se*] and the person tells the story [*kahānī*] of their life. Through telling this, they recollect the moment when they went off balance. They understand the mind and the consequences of their life on the mind. Then they are freed. They are cured.

"A *sādhu* also cures," Swamiji went on to say, "but not by making people tell of their life. A *sādhu* cures with love [*prem*], faith in Bhagavan [*shraddhā*], and trust in other people [*vishvās*]. People's minds are taken off their troubles and they are freed. All a *sādhu* says is 'Worship Bhagavan.' The worship of Bhagavan gives you a peace greater than anything else. You eat, but you have a bad stomach. You give money, but then when you don't, people bear a grudge. Children love you if you speak kindly, but when you get mad at them they hate you. The only thing that is constant is the worship of Bhagavan. It has no ill effects. If you become addicted to worshipping Bhagavan, all other problems or addictions a psychologist cures fall away by themselves."

I was listening intently, though a little crestfallen that while Swamiji mentioned storytelling by patients, he did not see this as a form of therapy by a *sādhu*. The relationship with a Guru, I knew, had been recognized by psychoanalysts themselves as deeply therapeutic in the Indian context.[21] Surely, I reasoned, stories served as a medium through which a Guru could express affection, faith, and trust, and also educate listeners about worshipping Bhagavan—not just through rituals, but through an attentive responsibility toward other people. Stories point to a reality that transcends the troublesome flux of life in the world, the inner Self which remains free of illusion (*māyā*).

As I sat on the linoleum, my mind turned to an article by Claude Lévi-Strauss which compares shamanistic and psychoanalytic cures.[22] Lévi-Strauss describes how a Cuna shaman in Panama sings over a woman undergoing a difficult childbirth. He argues that the action of the shaman within the song text constitutes a psychological manipulation of the sick organ and in this way effects a cure. He goes on to compare the shaman to a psychoanalyst. Both, he asserts, bring a patient's unconscious conflicts and resistances (with their bodily corollaries) to the conscious level, allowing for a healing resolution. Through transference, both the psychoanalyst and shaman become protaganists in the narrative that will facilitate healing, and they create a relationship in which the patient can restore and clarify an unexpressed or confused situation. Yet there are differences between these roles. A psychoanalyst *listens* to a personal "myth," and when he speaks he has been supplied with words by the patient. A shaman, on the other hand, *tells* a collective "myth," speaking for the patient. Lévi-Strauss concludes by arguing that the structural parallels between a narrative and a situation of conflict give form and meaning to inchoate individual experience. Through symbolic analogies, healing occurs.

Like the Cuna shaman (and most traditional healers), Swamiji's strategy is also to place individual experience within collective symbolic structures, endowing it with meaning. The stories metaphorically express human dilemmas and, by reaching a resolution within the story, Swamiji supplies listeners with a moral that can be applied in their lives. Yet unlike Lévi-Strauss's rigid separation, it seems that a traditional healer may both listen and orate: visitors have confided their problems, often in a narrative form, and it is in response to these personal stories about what is wrong that a *sādhu* tells the appropriate folk narrative, reframing these troubles in the illuminated arena of cosmic principles.

Drawn from shared cultural traditions, these stories link personal experience with collective experience and weld the present to the past. Yet the meanings stemming from each story, as my conversations with those around Swamiji showed, lie ultimately in the engagement of the listeners. A *sādhu* can only offer traditional wisdom; it is the listeners' responsibility to extract morals and apply them to their ongoing lives. As Walter Benjamin writes, "The storyteller is the figure in which the righteous man encounters himself."[23] One can say the same for the righteous woman in search of counsel that will throw light on her path.

II

Storytelling Occasions

5. Loincloths and Celibacy

"Did I tell you the story of how a loincloth [*langoṭī*] created a whole worldly play [*saṃsār*]? Did Swami R. tell you this?" Swamiji asked on a September morning in 1980.

"No," I said, looking up from the notebook in which I had been frantically scribbling all he said. It was before 10 A.M. and Swamiji had already been talking for a few hours. He sat cross-legged on the floor beside the altar in this small Nasik house. The couple who had built the house for his use were now both dead, but their presence was established in two gargantuan plaster-of-paris busts that flanked the altar. The woman had a printed sari wrapped around her and pulled over her head. The room was filled with pictures they had collected through the years of Swamiji, other revered *sādhus,* and deities; now that he was living here he had added a few pictures of the couple, too. "Who are these people?" mystified visitors would ask, "Are they saints?"

In those days, Swamiji still had his teeth: crooked and tobacco-stained, they lent a lopsided charm to his smile. The last time I had visited him his vision was so bad that he could only discern outlines against the light, but in the intervening years he had had cataract operations and could see through heavy glasses. The red *kumkum* on his forehead had become smeared as he spoke, the round spot now lunging down toward his nose. Oblivious of how he might look, Swamiji sat unfolding his views on the nature of the universe and human life. I listened and wrote, stunned by the breadth and coherence of the vision that Swamiji presented. After four distancing years away at college, I found that India had become rich with material I wanted to record. Now that I was visiting Swamiji, I could not bear to let his words slide past without transcription. A few other people came in and listened, but I was the only one who wrote.

Swamiji had started at the very beginning, when there was only empty space (*ākāsh*) in the universe; then came wind, fire, water, earth. He spoke of the Self which pervades this creation and all the individual creatures in it. The sense of separateness in individual beings, he said, could be likened to glasses lined up beside an ocean: when a wave swept over them they were filled with the same salt water, yet the illusory sense of difference remained. Switching metaphors, Swamiji said we were all filled with divine energy (*shakti*), just as bulbs of various wattage, fans, refrigerators, and hot-water heaters were different but worked on the same electricity. Amid this unity, opposites such as "I and you" or "pleasure and pain" had to be recognized as illusory. For in the great cycles of time nothing was destroyed, only changed. Water rose to the skies and fell as rain; corpses rejoined the earth and brought forth food and life. Within all these outer differences, oppositions and cycles, Swamiji said, enduring happiness was inside. External happiness was always transient. To be rich or famous just made for further trouble. Even Indira Gandhi couldn't go anywhere without bodyguards. If she had wanted to bathe in the sacred pool at Tryambakeshwar like we had done yesterday, she wouldn't have had the freedom to do so alone: everywhere police and crowds would be monitoring her movements.

The views which Swamiji expressed were familiar to me, but I had mostly been exposed to them in fragments from other holy people or books. Swamiji was building these fragments into an elegant edifice decorated with everyday metaphor. I listened enrapt. Years later, when I read Marcel Griaule's conversations with the blind Dogon elder Ogotemmêli, and Carlo Ginzburg's reconstruction of the Italian miller Mennochio's views, I had the same sense of being presented with a vision of the universe that was coherent in its own terms. If one could believe in this framework, the arbitrary, changeable world just might make sense.[1]

Swamiji brought up this story to illustrate his point that happiness could not be found outside the individual. Pen alternating between fragments of Hindi and quickly translated English, I wrote down the tale. Later that morning I went home and, borrowing my father's rusted old Olivetti, I transmuted the scribbled words into an account. What I reproduce here is what I typed a few hours after I heard it, reconstructed from a series of disjointed words. I tried to be faithful to what Swamiji had said and can only hope that this is not too far from what would be presented had I taped it.

*   *   *

Once there was a Sadhu with just a loincloth. But the rats kept on eating at his loincloth. "This is bad," he said, "What can I do?"

The local people told him to get a cat. But after a few days he was again distressed. "What happened, Maharaj?" the people asked.

"The cat won't stay at home," he said.

"But Maharaj, to make a cat sit in one place you must give it milk."

"And where will I get milk?"

"Maharaj, you must get a cow."

So he brought a cow to live with him. But then he was so busy with his devotions [*bhajan*] that he had no time to graze it. "The cow isn't giving milk," he complained.

"Maharaj," the people said, "food makes milk. You must take your cow to graze." So he found a servant to take care of the cow.

Now the servant stayed with him for six days and on the seventh he wanted to go home. "Why do you want to go?" the Sadhu asked.

"Maharaj, I have a wife and children whom I love very much, and I want to visit them."

"This won't do if you keep running off, you must bring them here. There's some space in the garden here, and you can stay here with your family." So the family arrived.

One day the Maharaj was watching his servant and he asked, "Why are you so happy?"

The servant said, "I have a wife and children whom I love, and so I'm happy."

"I have no happiness," said the Sadhu, "so I'll marry, too."

This is how one loincloth created an entire world [*saṃsār*]. This is what the smallest desire [*kāmanā*] can do.

*   *   *

Swamiji chuckled as he finished this story. He went on to say, "Live in *saṃsār*, but don't let it live in you. See everything as Bhagavan. That way, there's no problem." He underlined his previous points about Bhagavan being a presence inside all people and the need to treat everyone with respect. Then he told another story about the legendary King Janaka who was detached from the world even as he presided over matters of state from his throne. This story was long and convoluted, and though I listened carefully, my note-taking soon flagged. Swamiji has not subsequently told anyone about King Janaka when I had a tape recorder in hand; arising from the oral tradition into the spoken word, for me the words of this other story have vanished into silence, leaving only the faintest smudge of memory.

Allusions and Versions

If an entire world grew from the Sadhu's attachment to his loincloth, an entire project was built around my enjoyment of this tale. It is the very first one of Swamiji's stories that I wrote down, leading to sheafs of typed papers, stacks of tapes, and this very book. I often collected several versions of particular stories on tape, but Swamiji never repeated this one. It is a folk narrative that he often tells, though, for others around him refer to it.

Setting up a kitchen with my three Western roommates in 1983, we found ourselves in ever greater complexity: a stove was procured, then pots and pans, then spices, jars, pickles, spoons. . . . When "Gayatri" was about to set off on yet another shopping trip to outfit the kitchen, she suddenly grinned: "This reminds me of that story Swamiji tells," she said. "You know, about the Sadhu who had just a loincloth." Since everybody knew the story, there was no need for explanation. We all laughed together: like the apocryphal prison inmates who knew each other's jokes so intimately that they could be referred to by number rather than retold in performance, we were familiar enough with Swamiji's stories that an allusion invoked an entire tale.

"Gayatri"'s analogy emphasized the accumulation of actual possessions, but two years later Dr. Khanna mentioned the story in reference to inner attachments. I had asked if there were any stories she particularly remembered, and she mentioned this one, "about that Sadhu with the loincloth. You see that was about attachment to the material world." I asked if she would repeat it. "*Swamiji* is the best person to tell you," she smiled. Obviously she did not consider herself to be in the same league of storytellers. However, she set down her mug of tea, wrapped her hands around her knee, and tried to retell it. "You start with one *langoṭī*, then keep a rat, keep a cat. . . ." She paused, then corrected, "Or the rat takes it away so you keep a cat, keep a cow, and a man. So attachment leaves you in such a labyrinth of further attachments that it's difficult to extricate yourself." Dr. Khanna's reluctance—or inability—to retell the entire story in anything but the most sketchy form is an example of how many of Swamiji's listeners remember his stories but are "passive" bearers rather than "active" performers of folk narratives in their full complexity.[2]

My mother said she had heard Swamiji tell this story to a young *brahmachārī* (celibate novice). This young man had visited Swamiji to ruefully announce that he was giving up his white robes and would allow his family to find him a wife instead. Swamiji had laughed heartily, and then told the story. "Why do you think he told it?" I asked. "Why do you think?" my mother asked, shooting me a glance that showed she did not appreciate my playing dumb. "It's a pretty obvious comment, isn't it? It was an analogous situation. The boy was trying to become a *sādhu* but he went on to rejoin the world."

As an excursion into tale-type and motif-indexes reveals, this is an Indic folktale.[3] Among the recorded variants is that of P. V. Ramaswami Raju. A lecturer in Tamil and Telugu in England during the late nineteenth century, Raju brought together a collection of short tales entitled *Indian Fables*. This collection was aimed at a European audience, and so it contains numerous explanatory asides on the customs of "the East." Raju does not state his sources and so it is not altogether clear where he dived for these "pearls from the deep" in the ocean of Indian oral traditions. Were these stories Raju had heard in his childhood? That he had collected as an adult with a book in mind? That he had gleaned from Tamil or Telugu collections? That he had heard from a Guru? These questions cannot be answered by looking through the book, but here, nonetheless, is Raju's version:[4]

The Man and His Piece of Cloth

A man in the East, where they do not require as much clothing as in colder climates, gave up all worldly concerns and retired to a wood, where he built a hut and lived in it.

His only clothing was a piece of cloth which he wore round his waist. But, as ill-luck would have it, rats were plentiful in the wood, so he had to keep a cat. The cat required milk to keep it, so a cow had to be kept. The cow required tending, so a cowboy was employed. The boy required a house to live in, so a house was built for him. To look after the house, a maid had to be engaged. To provide company for the maid, a few more houses had to be built, and people invited to live in them. In this manner a little township sprang up.

The man said, "The farther we seek to go from the world and its cares, the more they multiply!"

Like Raju, Swamiji is from south India, and though Kannada is his mother tongue, he also speaks Tamil and some Telugu. This is a Kannada story, too, though, as I found when I read U. R. AnanthaMurthy's moving novel, *Samskara*, and discovered a short retelling in the musings of Praneshacharya. This central character is a man revered for his piety and learning. Caring for his invalid wife, he seems to be living the life of a detached *sannyāsī* within the world. Yet when plague strikes the village, his deepest values are called into question. His wife dies, he finds himself in the arms of a beautiful Untouchable, and he leaves the disease-ridden Brahman settlement in turmoil. He wants to be alone to think things through but:[5]

> Whatever his decision, his feet still walked him close to the habitations of men. This is the limit of his world, his freedom. Can't seem to live outside the contacts of men. Like the folktale hermit's g-string: lest mice should gnaw at the g-string, he reared a cat; for the cat's milk he kept a cow; to look after the cow, he found a woman; and married her and ceased to be a hermit.

So this is a folktale in Swamiji's region and it is possible that he encountered it as a child. Or perhaps he heard it from other *sādhus* during his wanderings, for his question, "Did Swami R. tell you this?" seemed to indicate that other *sādhus* would be likely to use the story. Another possible source could be the *Gospel of Sri Ramakrishna,* a book he refers to in other contexts. This book consists of evocative accounts of visits made to the saint Ramakrishna by a disciple, "M." Though originally recorded in Bengali between 1882–1886, this has been subsequently translated into English and many other Indian languages including Kannada. In the English translation, one finds that on Saturday, May 24, 1884, "M." visited Ramakrishna (whom he calls "Master") at Dakshineshwar, outside of Calcutta. Among the other visitors was one Narendra Banerji. Because of friction within the joint family, Banerji had taken to living separately with his wife and children. Addressing himself to Banerji, Ramakrishna said:[6]

> You see, all these sufferings are "because of a piece of loincloth." A man takes a wife and begets children; therefore he must secure a job. The *sadhu* is worried about his loincloth and the householder about his wife. Further, the householder may not live on good terms with his relations; so he must live separately with his wife (with a laugh). Chaitanya once said to Nityananda; "Listen to me, brother. A man entangled in worldliness can never be free."

A footnote at the bottom of this page explains that the allusion to loincloths derives from a story that Ramakrishna often told his devotees. The story, paraphrased here, reads:

> There was a *sannyasi* whose only possession was a pair of loincloths. One day a mouse nibbled at one piece. So the holy man kept a cat to protect his

loincloths from the mouse. Then he had to keep a cow to supply milk for the cat. Later he had to engage a servant to look after the cow. Gradually the number of his cows multiplied. He acquired pastures and farm land. He had to engage a number of servants. Thus he became, in the course of time, a sort of landlord. And last of all, he had to take a wife to look after his big household. One day, one of his friends, another monk happened to visit him and was surprised to see his altered circumstances. When asked the reason, the holy man said, "It is all for the sake of a piece of loincloth!"

Despite minor variations, all these versions are nearly identical. They all mark the passage from a simple, solitary life to the accumulation of possessions and a settlement of people nearby. The story plays on the difference between the sphere of ascetics and of householders; between those who stand outside and within *saṃsār*. Though I have translated *saṃsār* as "the world," it is actually a term with no exact English equivalent since it includes meanings such as social enterprise, domestic life, and the cycle of birth, death, and rebirth. *Saṃsār*, the social and phenomenal world, is what a *sannyāsī* renounces; not the material world (*jagat*).[7] By describing the passage into *saṃsār*, this story encapsulates the ascetics' insecurity that they may yet be sucked back into the world they have left behind. The magnetic force drawing the solitary renouncer back into the world is attachment or desire: it can manifest in sexuality or the accumulation of possessions. Here in an entertaining folk narrative, then, is the corollary of Robert Gross's generalized ethnographic statement: "the sadhus stress that desire—*kāmanā*—continually creates desire which in turn is the basis for the formation of the entire phenomenal world."[8]

Sādhus and Loincloths

This story falls into the genre of cumulative tale in which one action leads to a chain sequence of other actions; its very structure emphasizes accumulation. The loincloth here is the source of complexity, the root of growing entanglements. The loincloth (*laṅgoṭī, kaupina*) is actually a central symbol of ascetic identity. A hymn popular among Dashanami ascetics describes the detached life of a *sannyāsī* with the refrain, "Only the loincloth wearer is truly fortunate" (*kaupīna vantam khalu bhāgya vantā*).[9] This hymn is attributed to Shankaracharya, and I have heard Swami R. sing it with great feeling on several occasions. Dashanami *sannyāsīs* are not alone in their good fortune, though: male ascetics of most orders are unified by the loincloths that they wear day and night. While householders may also wear loincloths, the *sādhus'* is shorter and narrower. Robert Gross, who lived among *sādhus* as an initiate, describes their loincloths as "often just covering the penis and leaving the testicles exposed." [10] As minimal clothing, the loincloth restates the commitment to a simple life of renunciation.

There are various kinds of loincloths that express sectarian differences or different degrees of ascetic practice. [11] The *Laws of Manu* (VI:44) advises the brahmanical *sannyāsī* to wear a loincloth of cast-off clothing, indicating the ascetic's indifference to the householder's world. Homespun cotton loincloths are most commonly worn among Dashanami *sannyāsīs*. Members of the Aghori sect, however, are required to wear a strip torn from a shroud picked up at the cremation grounds; this signifies that they are dead to the world. Ramanandi renouncers use a loincloth made of banana bark, which stands for their alliance with a ritually pure, natural world and a jungle environment. Another kind of loincloth made from plants is the coarse, scratchy *munjiā langoṭī* made of the reed-like *munjā* grass. It takes a dedicated ascetic to wear a loincloth of this sort, for as Gross observes, it is "comparable to the hair shirt worn by certain Christian penitents." [12] For this reason, the ascetics who wear such loincloths sport the title *munjiā* or *munjiā-bābā*. There are also ascetics who wear a wooden belt several inches thick and locked with brass hinges (*kaṭhiyā bābās*), and ascetics who live encased in metal loincloths of iron, steel, or brass.

The naked Naga ascetics claim to have internalized their loincloths. Part of the Naga initiation involves a violent jerk at the penis which, severing nerves and blood vessels, prohibits the initiate from all future erections. Since the tightly bound loincloth is believed to maintain celibacy, Nagas have no need for such external aids. They are well known, though, for other tricks they may perform with their limp penises. Robert Gross describes Nagas who pierce their penises with rings from which chains dangle, or who attach rocks to their penises to stretch and lengthen them. He goes on to mention a memorable "old and respected Naga Baba living near Ujjain [who] was reputedly able to wrap his elongated, flaccid penis around a bamboo pole and lift small children holding on the ends." [13] I have not witnessed such feats myself, but once when I was visiting Swami R., a Naga Baba came to the area who flashed pictures of himself pulling motorcycles and trucks by a rope attached to his penis. "You're all donkeys," he superciliously informed the men crowded around him in the tea shop. "All *you* can do with your penis [*lingam*] is make children!"

The association of loincloths and sexual control is evident in the north Indian colloquial usage of *langoṭ band,* "tight (closed) loincloth," for someone who is celibate and incorruptible, and *langoṭ kā kacchā,* "uncooked loincloth," for a lewd, promiscuous man.[14] The story of the *sādhu* so concerned with losing his loincloth can be viewed as a passage from celibacy, represented by the loincloth, to active sexuality, represented by the wife. The rats nibbling at the loincloth are like the sexual desires the *sādhu* cannot keep in check.

While Raju's version mentions a maid that is employed to look after the "cowboy," there is no indication that the holy man enters into sexual relations with her. Swamiji's, AnanthaMurthy's, and Ramakrishna's versions, on the other hand, mention marriage. Raju was an academic, but the others are *sādhus* or, as with Praneshacharya, *sādhu*-like. Since the maintenance of celibacy is a central ascetic concern, it is not surprising that these retellings emphasize the passage to active sexuality. Ramakrishna's amused statement, "the *sādhu* is worried about his loincloth and the householder about his wife," implies that the ascetics' sphere of loincloths and celibacy is a direct inversion of the householders' sphere of wives and sexuality. Yet the boundary between the spheres is more sharply delineated at the conceptual level than in practice.

Brahmacharya is the term used for celibacy; the related term, *brahmachārī,* refers to the student stage of life in the classical Hindu life cycle and also to novice ascetics like the young man to whom Swamiji once told the story of "The Sadhu and His Loincloth." Both the classical student stage and the novice apprenticeship are periods of training to become something else: the student prepares to become a householder involved in the reproduction of society, the novice ascetic rehearses to become a monk, well established in his celibacy. But if even fully fledged *sādhus* may fall back into the world, the danger is more pronounced with young men who are only trying out the *sādhu* life. Swamiji frequently gave refuge to earnest young men who wished to become *sādhus;* among them was my brother Rahoul. While some did go on to become *sādhus,* others eventually returned to the worldly life, much to their parents' relief. Rahoul, for example, went on to college and a career as a color printer and photographer; within a few years, his life in the United States was anything but *sādhu*-like. Let us turn then, to a story about a *brahmachārī* tottering on the edge of a return to the entanglements of a householder's life.

"Falling In"

Five Septembers after I had heard this first story, I was once again back in
Nasik during Swamiji's *darshan* hours as a steady stream of people came
and went. A white-haired man wearing a crumpled cotton *dhotī* arrived
from a distant village. He carved sandalwood *pādukās*—wooden clogs
worn by ascetics and often worshipped to represent the presence of the
Guru—and Swamiji chatted with him about his business. A smiling hotel
owner arrived to announce a fire ceremony (*havan*) at his house. He wanted
Swamiji to bless the occasion and all the regular visitors to stop in for
lunch. A neat, bespectacled clerk came in with his son. They sat together
on the floor until it was time for the chanting to start in the next room.
"Gulelal" sat listening, as well as Isabel and "Kumari." Between speaking
personally with people, Swamiji mused over current events. He discussed
the recent earthquake in Mexico City; the numbers dead, the buildings
that had toppled. Everyone present who had read the newspapers, listened
to the radio, or watched television news had comments to contribute. We
then chatted about the forthcoming appearance of Halley's comet. A young
man from Saptashring came in, hot and dusty off a bus. He was wearing
pants and had a Gandhi cap tilted at a jaunty angle on his head. I did not
know this man, and I leaned against the wall, day-dreaming as the conversation bounced back and forth between him and Swamiji. News was being
exchanged about people, crops, the chances of rain, and my mind slid further away. I zipped my tape recorder away, certain that there would be no
more stories told that day.

When the Saptashring man left, and others present had adjourned to
the next room to receive children for the evening chanting, Swamiji turned
to me and French "Kumari." We were alone in the room, and from outside
strains of children's voices floated in. He glanced up at the clock with
pot-bellied Ganesh. It was half-past five. "There's still half an hour left,"
Swamiji said. "I'll tell you a story." I scrambled to extract my tape recorder.
Isabel returned as Swamiji started speaking. He leaned back against an
orange-dyed Australian sheepskin covering a pillow, legs stretched out on
the bed that had replaced his chair. We three women sat against the wall to
his left. Since neither of my French companions was fluent in Hindi, I
translated each sentence into English as Swamiji spoke.

*   *   *

There was a Swamiji. There was an ashram. He had some Brahmacharis staying with him. They all lived on a mountain; that ashram was on a mountain. Yes? And there was a small city*—a town—some distance away. There were devotees there. If they wanted to get supplies for the ashram, someone had to go to town.

One day a disciple [*chelā*] was sent to town to fetch supplies. The Swamiji sent this one Brahmachari. "You go. Go to such-and-such Seth's house. Bring the supplies from there."

[A Seth is a wealthy man, a merchant, or proprietor. Swamiji often addressed prosperous male devotees as "Seth"; knowing that Isabel and "Kumari" would recognize this word, Kirin left it untranslated.]

"All right," he said. He set out. He went and met the Seth. Evening came. Night came. The Sethji said, "Now it's night, where will you go? Stay overnight. Go tomorrow morning."

"All right," he said. He had dinner and so on. Then they gave him a space to sleep on the verandah. He bound up all the supplies, and went to sleep on the verandah.

That day a marriage procession* was passing by. There was a boy. And there was a girl. They were both nicely decorated. The boy was made up as Ram; the girl was made up as Sita. They were sitting in a car. A band* played loudly as they went along. Many people were going with them. Everyone was watching, and many people were going along with them.

The Brahmachari also watched from afar. His heart was filled with love. He thought, "My taking birth has now become meaningful [*sārthak*]. [Kirin pauses in translation, and Swamiji repeats the sentence for her benefit, then goes on.] I've seen Ram and Sita."

There was a betel leaf [*pān*] shop nearby. He went and stood there. He kept staring, eyes wide. He said to the betel leaf vendor [*pān wālā*], "Look brother, my taking birth is now meaningful. My Guruji did a wonderful thing. He sighted this day and sent me here to bring the goods. I have seen Sita-Ram."

"Where?" the betel leaf vendor asked.

"Look, they're going in the car."

The betel leaf vendor said, "You fool! Do you think these are Sita-Ram? These are people who just got married and are going home. They're in a marriage procession.*"

"When you say 'marriage,' what do you mean?" the Brahmachari asked.

"A girl gets together with a boy. Then after the marriage, there's a procession.* Now they're decorated and taken out in a procession.* In about an hour's time this will all be over, and the makeup will be removed. You don't know anything," he said. "You haven't seen anything yet. This is neither Ram nor Sita."

"I didn't know any of this," the Brahmachari said [in a low, awed voice]. "What will they do next?"

"What else will they do but lead a worldly life? They'll lead a worldly life, they'll have a home!" [loud and exasperated].

"What will he do with this girl when he takes her with him?"

"He'll make a home, then they'll get ahead in their worldly life [*saṃsār chalāigā*]. They'll live in joy. They're hardly celibate like you!" the betel vendor said. "Just sitting on a mountain you haven't seen anything. When someone says 'marriage' [*shādī*] you don't even know what this is. You have no idea about the pleasures it bears. Look, this is the kind of thing that happens in the world. Just see how joyful everyone is, how happily they're celebrating. Your Guruji is just making you work for him and nothing more. What pleasure do you have in your life?"

The Brahmachari thought this over [one hand rubbing his chin, voice lowered]. "You're right, sir. Now what do I do?"

"Go take your burden [*bhoj*] and give it to the Guruji. Become a worldly person too."

"All right," the Brahmachari said. "I'll take all these things and give them to the Guruji. Then I'll get married too."

This is what came into this mind. Now who was going to wait until morning? It was still night, but he set out anyway. "I'll go straight to Guruji," he thought as he was walking. It was very far. As he went he got sleepy. It was very dark. He had to climb a mountain. There was a well on his way. Around the well was a platform. He lay down on it.

As soon as he lay down he fell asleep. In his sleep he had a dream. He was married, he was experiencing great joy. In the midst of his delight, he fell down. He fell into the well. Once he had fallen in, he couldn't climb out.

In the morning some women came to fetch water. They looked in. "Look, Babaji's Brahmachari has fallen into the well!" So they brought him out and sent him to the ashram.

The Babaji said, "What, brother, what happened to you? How did you fall in?"

He said, "Guruji, this is what happened. I had gone yesterday, and saw this and that. I was returning to ask you about this immediately. As I was coming back, I fell like this into the well."

The Babaji said, "Just thinking about marriage, remembering this and that, you had a dream and fell into the well. Now if you'd actually fallen into the world, think of what a huge pit you'd be in! Now you've been saved from that: don't fall in!" [Laughter is reverberating through Swamiji's words. Isabel, "Kumari," and Kirin all smile.]

This is what he says, this is one story. The Brahmachari said, "I don't want marriage."

*   *   *

Still laughing, Swamiji repeated, "This is one story."

"It sounds like a story about Saptashring and Nasik," I observed, wondering whether this was about the young man who had just come and gone. It seemed plausible that Swamiji had lifted a slice of his own experience and transformed it into a story. He too had been a Guruji on top of a mountain; he too had possibly sent young *brahmachārīs* to fetch supplies from the town nearby. The scene of newlyweds decked out with fine garments, tinsel crowns, and garlands riding along in a car was familiar to me from the Nasik streets. Swamiji's description of the car inching along amid a crowd of relatives and a band blasting music paralleled actual weddings. As he had spoken, I could hear the strains of the Nasik band favorite from my childhood, "Come September," in my head. Also, there were betel leaf vendors on many street corners, perched cross-legged in small shacks and ready to chat with loiterers. Up on the mountain, I knew there were wells and that women most certainly drew water in the morning. This could so easily be a true story, I thought, that Swamiji had transmuted into the style of a folktale.

"No, it's not about Saptashring and Nasik," Swamiji erased my hypothesis with a shake of his head. He went on to say it was a traditional story, but he retold it in his own way. He never did identify though, the source from which he learned this tale.[15]

The Two Stories Compared

I immediately thought of the "Sadhu and His Loincloth" when I heard "Falling In." These two stories are almost inversions of each other, and share many common themes. While the Sadhu renounces the world to live a solitary life with just one loincloth, he ends up rejoining it. The Brahmachari, on the other hand, leaves his ashram, considers entering the world, but ends up returning to the celibate life. In both stories, ascetics live apart from householders, and association with householders leads them off their path.

"Falling In," like "That's Good, Very Good," has a tripartite structure similar to a rite of passage. The story begins and ends with the ashram on the mountain, with a transformative threshold period in the city. As a settlement of householders, the city represents economic enterprise and active sexuality. Unlike the ascetic Swamiji on the mountain, the betel leaf vendor in the city is a Guru of worldliness. The association of betel leaf and eroticism is a cultural undercurrent to the story, an undercurrent that extends from ancient texts to contemporary films. The *Dharma Shastras* or Hindu law books, for example, forbid celibate novices to eat betel, for it is heating.[16] In Hindi films today, betel leaf being slipped into another's mouth often carries erotic connotations. So while the young Brahmachari is so naive that he mistakes newlyweds for deities—confusing representation and reality—it is appropriately enough a betel leaf vendor who informs the young celibate man about marriage and its pleasures.

The betel leaf vendor advises that the Brahmachari return to the Guru and give up his "burden." This burden seems to be the maintenance of celibacy in the midst of a sexual world. Returning to inform his Guru that he too would like to get married, the Brahmachari falls asleep. His dream is obviously an erotic one, and the "falling in" might be a metaphor for ejaculation. The well that he tumbles into can also be interpreted as a vagina and pit of worldly attachment. For the illusion (*māyā*) which maintains *saṃsār* is feminine; it is from the womb of illusion that the phenomenal world springs into being. That the Brahmachari is pulled out of the well by women the next morning indicates a rebirth, or a movement into another plane of understanding. The Guru receives his wiser, chastened disciple with the advice that he should not fall into the pit of the world. The Brahmachari agrees. He has gone through three phases—separation, margin, and aggregation—and now he returns to his ascetic pursuits with a more mature understanding of what he has renounced.

In both "The Sadhu and His Loincloth" and "Falling In" the ascetics come across as simpletons who have no inkling about the ways of the world. The local people patiently advise the Sadhu that rats can be routed by cats, that cats need milk, that cows need to eat to give milk. The servant explains that he is happy because he has a wife and children whom he loves. The Sadhu listens, earnest and troubled. Similarly, the young Brahmachari stares wide-eyed at a marriage procession, without the faintest idea of what it all means, and the garrulous betel leaf vendor must enlighten him. By heeding the advice of householders, the Sadhu reenters the world and the Brahmachari considers the renunciation of his celibacy. Householders, these stories state, are dangerous to the ascetic enterprise. They embrace two things that *sādhus* must reject: sexuality and possessions.

Sexuality

Though these stories acknowledge that marriage and sexual fulfillment hold an alluring happiness, by linking this happiness with *saṃsār,* they also argue that it is fleeting and contingent. Sexuality is a key force in sustaining the illusions of *saṃsār.* With its strong outward-oriented drives, sexuality deflects the preoccupations of the ascetic from within to without; ideals fall away in the face of passions; altruism is replaced by individual gratification.[17]

I have never heard Swamiji discuss sexuality in depth, probably because I am unmarried and so it would be inappropriate to mention such matters in my presence. There have been occasions that couples have come asking the boon of a child, and Swamiji has consulted horoscopes, told stories, and dispensed folk remedies (including small seeds that resemble the phallic *lingam,* which, if swallowed by a woman, are supposed to help her conceive). "It seems to me," Swamiji mused one day, "that just sex doesn't make children, Bhagavan makes children. Otherwise why is it that some people keep trying and never have a child, and others don't want children and they keep having children? Think about it: children come from Bhagavan."

This comment indicates that Swamiji accepts sexuality as appropriate for householders. For ascetics, on the other hand, he views sexuality as a transgression of ideals. He seemed deeply disturbed in 1983 when he learned that a well-known Guru openly had affairs with women disciples. These days, Swamiji observed, there were hardly any true *sādhus* around, and the entire enterprise had been reduced to a "business." His troubled musings extended for several weeks. One afternoon during this time, English "Dattatreya" came in and asked, face puckered with earnest concern: "Swamiji, these days, how does one become a good *sādhu?*" Without hesi-

tation Swamiji rejoined, "These days, you go find a girlfriend*!" "Dattatreya"'s face fell and those listening laughed. Swamiji went on to enumerate the various Gurus who were known to use their gatherings of female
disciples as extended harems.

The ascetic ideal of celibacy is deeply rooted in the Hindu world view,
affecting the ideology of householders, too. Sex—like any other act that
involves the spilling or exchange of body fluids—is seen as impure. Purity
is central to the conceptual ordering of the caste hierarchy, with the most
pure ranked uppermost, and the most impure relegated to untouchability.[18] The preoccupation with purity and celibacy is most pronounced at
the upper rungs of the caste system, particularly among Brahmans. An orthodox Brahman must abstain as far as possible from sex, using it only to
procreate. Also, the conservation of semen is linked to the powers of men-
tal concentration. In Hindu folk theories, forty days and forty drops of
blood are believed to make one drop of semen; stored semen makes for
strength and radiance. G. Morris Carstairs summarizes the views of upper-
caste Rajasthani men:[19]

> Semen of good quality is rich and viscous, like the cream of unadulterated
> milk. A man who possesses a store of such good semen becomes a super-
> man. "He glows with radiant health," said Shankar Lal. He excels all normal
> men in strength and stamina, both moral and physical. As an example, I was
> always told of idealised holy men, unlike those imperfect exemplars we had
> actually seen, whose life of celibacy and piety had brought them to this peak
> of condition. . . . The "arrived" worshipper of God acquires . . . super-
> natural powers by virtue of the increase of god-like qualities in him, and
> their physical counterpart is the intact store of rich, uncurdled semen in
> the head.

To conserve semen is to increase vitality, and to sublimate sexuality upwards, into "the head," is to bring about a gain in power.[20] In traditions of
yoga, the man who has lifted semen into his head, and who is ever thereafter unperturbed by sexuality, is called an *ūrdhvaretas* ("uplifted seed").
Even in the tantric practices which prescribe intercourse with a woman,
semen is never supposed to fall; to emit semen, in this view, is to waste
vitality and succumb to the phenomenal world of death and decay.[21]

As Wendy O'Flaherty has shown with verve and brilliance, asceticism
and eroticism are two complementary but opposing Hindu ideals.[22] Using
the corpus of myths surrounding Shiva, "the erotic ascetic," as the base for
her analysis, O'Flaherty demonstrates how the abstention from sexuality

generates heat with tremendous creative power that can be used for pro-
creation or for liberation. So the ascetic, by virtue of celibacy, if filled with
erotic power. This power leaves the chaste ascetic vulnerable to seduction,
even as it allows his counterpart, the unabashedly lustful ascetic, to seduce.

Indian folklore and ancient literature are indeed replete with lecherous
ascetics.[23] Perceived by the pious as wise and celibate, ascetics have no
problem winning over trust and then exploiting their disciples. This entrenched theme carries over into modern mass media. In Hindi films, for
example, holy men are often presented as lewd characters who have put on
their robes to gather female disciples around them. Even as they meditate,
they occasionally unscrew their eyes to leer at women nearby. Indian scan-
dal sheets revel in the sexual exploits of various Gurus. Rumors fly that a
particular Guru gives initiations in his inner rooms, that another "in-
spects" the *chakras,* or centers of spiritual energy, two of which are in the
genital region. Occasionally, a Guru who prefers boys is reported. It would
seem, as B. D. Tripathi dolefully states in his *Sadhus of India,* that "sex urge
may entrap even the biggest spiritualist."[24]

Possessions

As these two stories show, *sādhus* are dependent on householders for their
material subsistence. Who provides the cat, the cow, and the servant but
the village people? Who sends goods to the ashram but a wealthy Seth? If a
sādhu is not careful, zealous devotees may engulf him with possessions,
making him more like themselves. Swamiji himself struggles with the paradox that faces *sādhus* not just in folklore but in real life. Though he has
renounced material possessions he is bombarded by disciples with offerings. Swamiji has no box inviting donations, but people bowing before his
altar often fumble in their pockets for a rupee or two; if Swamiji notices,
he waves a hand saying "No money!" The money that comes in, particularly on festival days, is redistributed to poor people or *sādhus* who come
by. Most offerings are in the form of goods instead, ranging from perish-
ables like fruit and sweets which are immediately redistributed, to larger
objects such as shawls, chairs, clocks, thermoses, and so on. Swamiji gives
away most of these objects but there is also always a backlog in his room.
He lives amid these objects but does not see them as his. As he says, "For a
sādhu, the stomach [*peṭ*] should be the only trunk for storage [*peṭī*]."

In keeping his environment relatively simple Swamiji has had to actively circumvent his disciples. To honor a Guru, disciples all over India will surround him or her with luxurious items, especially symbolic tokens of royalty and divinity like thrones, crowns, yak-whisks, silk. When an ashram is established, large donations and land grants can turn the Guru into an extremely wealthy personage. Monasteries too often own expanses of lands which are leased to tenants. The *mahant*, or head of a monastery, is in the folk imagination an indolent person lolling in riches: to call someone a *mahant* is to insinuate that he is lazy, willful, and enjoys a life of ease. This is a far cry from the ascetic ideal, yet ironically, it is an outgrowth of veneration of this ideal. As Max Weber puts it: [25]

> The paradox of all rational asceticism, which in an identical manner has made monks of all ages stumble, is that rational asceticism itself has created the very wealth it rejected. Temples and monasteries have everywhere become the very *loci* of rational economies.

Swamiji would surely agree to this. He often spoke of the contradictions present in ashrams when wealth accumulated and shifted the focus from religious concerns. Earlier the same day that he had told "Falling In," he told us a parable. It was morning, and a group that included many regular visitors had gathered. "Gulelal" had established his bulky presence on the wall facing Swamiji, and the two French women, earnest in saris, were beside me on the women's side of the room. Swamiji had been talking about Reagan's policies of cutting federal assistance to welfare programs, and "Gulelal" leaned forward, eyes brightening as heard his president's name. "There's a difference," Swamiji observed, "between getting rid of poverty and getting rid of the poor!" I translated this for "Gulelal"'s benefit. While on the theme of wealth and poverty, Swamiji turned to ashrams.

"A rat makes a hole," Swamiji said, "to store food, to bring up its children, to take refuge. The snake watches. It sees the rat coming and going. It observes the place the rat lives. Then the snake enters the hole. When the rat next comes, it eats it up. What was meant to be for living becomes a place to die."

He laughed to himself while we stared at him, wondering what he meant. Swamiji then clarified, "In the same way, the poor are eaten up. They take refuge with a Swamiji; he's like a hole. Then people see all this coming and going. They think that this gathering can be of use to them. It will help promote their business and make connections. So they enter the place and become devotees of the Swamiji. Once the big people take over, there's no place for the poor. They're thrown out."

Many contemporary Gurus do indeed start out with a following of pious peasants, but as word of their greatness spreads, film stars, industrialists, and foreign exchange—laden foreigners flock around them. A board of international trustees is likely to be established; a Swiss bank account or two is opened as well. Fees may be charged for staying or eating in the ashram. Fees may also be levied for initiations. Swamiji worried about these trends, particularly in the case of the Gurus who had gone abroad. He speculated that there must be something in the "air and water" of America which made Gurus who had been there money-hungry. "It's a sin for a *sādhu* to sell three things" he often repeated in a rhythmic formula: "To sell food, to sell women, to sell religious teaching [*anna vikraya, strī vikraya, dharma vikraya*]."

So while both these stories suggest a polarity between ascetics and householders, they also show how fragile the boundary between these lifestyles can be. Though an ascetic has renounced the worldly life it encloses him on all sides. Swamiji's comment, "Live in *saṃsār* but don't let it live in you," suggests that while there is no escape from living in the world it is possible to eradicate the world as a state of mind. By this he means attachments, desires, and egoistic divisiveness.

When Swamiji speaks more generally about the necessity of freeing oneself from attachment, he tends to refer to the *Bhagavad Gītā* (II:62–63). In this view, desire born of attachment leads to anger, confusion, loss of memory, and the destruction of intelligence. It is necessary to act in the world, yet action should be performed out of selfless duty rather than desire; additionally, one should have no attachment to the results of actions. What is meant to happen will happen. These principles, Swamiji felt, held for *sannyāsīs* as well as for householders. Speaking to local people who were not *sādhus*, Swamiji used a parable about dealing with desire: "As you walk along the path of life," Swamiji said, "look down. If you look up, to people who have more, you might stumble and fall. Desires are boundless, like the sky. There is always something you don't have. You have some money, but you want more. You live in a flat but you want a house. You have a car, but you want two. That's why even rich people are dissatisfied. But if you look down, you will feel compassion for those who have less. You will be grateful for what you have. You can keep walking and you won't fall. That's why, when you walk, look down."

6. False Gurus and Gullible Disciples

One July morning in 1983 conversation had drifted to a contemporary Guru and his ashram. Swamiji noncommittally noted that the ashram had grown very wealthy through the last few years. Someone described workshops at which, for a fee, one could sign up for a mystical experience. One of the men present, Mr. Advani, had helped to organize such a workshop locally. He boasted of the numbers that attended, and extolled the spiritual awakenings that occurred.

Swamiji listened with interest, left elbow resting on the arm of his deck chair with his hand under his chin. There was a break in the conversation when a few visitors stood up to leave. "Hail to the Mother of the Universe, Hail!" muttered Swamiji as they saluted him. He presented them with bananas. As the screen door creaked behind them, he asked us, "Haven't you heard of the Narayandarsimat?"

"The what?" we asked.

"The Nose-Cutters [*nāk kāṭne vāle*]."

"The *what?*"

"The Nose-Cutters," he repeated, looking around the room. He scanned all our faces. "She's heard it!" he pointed to "Gayatri" of New Jersey who sat at his feet, wearing a sari of light blue silk. She looked to me for clarification, but this allusion left me nonplussed as well. Gupta Saheb who was visiting from Kanpur in the North rolled his head: "The—Nose—Cutters" he slowly repeated in Hindi, then added in English for the benefit of the three Western women present: "A group."

Apart from "Gayatri," the others sitting beside me on the women's side of the room were "Saraswati" from London and "Bhavani" from New York. All three women were under thirty-five and had been associated with ashrams elsewhere. That summer I shared an apartment with them. As Swamiji started in on the following story, I jumped into action, reproducing each sentence in English for my Western companions. Joining Mr. Gupta and Mr. Advani there were several local men present whose names I did not know. A young couple had brought in their baby to be blessed. The teenager mother had two oiled braids, and as Swamiji spoke she rhythmically patted the tiny baby at her side.

Beside the altar, the tape recorder played the *Durga Saptashati,* "700 verses to the Goddess Durga," and a man's mellifluous voice intoned Sanskrit.[1] This modern rendition was set to music reminiscent of Hindi films, and flutes, sitars, xylophones, and bells rippled through each verse. That year, the tape was a great favorite of Swamiji's and the entire cycle of verses was played every day. As Swamiji launched into the legend of the Nose-Cutters, the music composed a backdrop against which the story was told.

*   *   *

There was a Guru, like me. He had many devotees. He wasn't really like me . . . he was greater than I. Consider him to be a little like me. He would tell his disciples, "I'll give you *darshan* of Bhagavan." And the disciples spread the word: "Our Guruji reveals Bhagavan." This was the kind of propaganda [*prachār*] they did. This world exists through propaganda. The more advertising you do, the greater a thing becomes. That's why companies* all advertise: on the radio* on the television.* The products themselves are nothing much, that's why they must spend so much money advertising them.

[Swamiji is chuckling, and we all laugh.]

The Guru advertised himself in the same way. Say the disciples meet someone like you—especially the important officials ["officer* *log*"]— they would say, "Our Maharaj gives people *darshan* of Bhagavan." Now everyone wishes to see Bhagavan. You'll say, "Yes, I would very much like to see Bhagavan."

"If that's so," the disciples would say, "then you must donate 10,000 rupees."

"All right, I'll give you 10,000 rupees" [Swamiji agreeably rocks his head]. What's it to you if you have a lot of money? Certainly, seeing God is worth the expense. So you would be taken there by the disciples.

The Maharaj was quite handsome. He'd put on a jeweled crown. In his own hands he'd hold a conch and a discus. A disciple hiding behind him would hold a lotus and mace. He'd sit on a throne wearing golden yellow garments and a shawl. He'd sit there, just as Bhagavan Narayan sits, with all the attributes of Narayan.

[Narayan is another name for Vishnu, Preserver of the Universe; nobody looked toward Kirin.]

This was in a dark room.* A person would be led in through one door. A small light would be lit.

"Look, you can see Bhagavan for just one second.* If you look at him any longer than that, you'll be blinded."

So the person would be led through. The Guruji would do this—

[Swamiji straightens up in his chair, sententiously fluttering his eyelids, flexing his arms bent at the elbow first upwards, then down: Narayan has four arms.]

And then the person would be led through the other door. "I have seen Bhagavan," the person would say [in a voice muffled with awe].

In this way, the Guru earned a great deal of money. You've had *darshan,* so you tell someone else. The second person tells a third. And so, there's a lot of advertisement.

[Swamiji pauses. We wait. Over the tape recorder, the narrative of the Goddess vanquishing demons has ended; a man's and woman's voice interweave to the throb of drums.]

One day, the Guru died. He died, leaving a lot of disciples. None of them was quite like him. There was one disciple—like me—yes? Wherever he went, he stole.

[We laugh uncertainly. Just what could Swamiji mean?]

The king of that place gave the order* that his nose should be cut* off. The police* cut off his nose. As soon as this was done he began to dance. He danced,* then fell at the feet of the man who'd cut off his nose. "You've done me a great service!" he said, and he began to dance once more, to dance away.

[Swamiji bobs from side to side, clicking fingers to palm.]

The police* looked at him, wondering, "Why is this man dancing?" [in a baffled voice].

The man danced his way out. Everyone asked [brows weighted with concern] "Why do you dance?" And he said, "I see Bhagavan everywhere."

"Is that so? You see Bhagavan?"

"Yes, I can see Bhagavan."

Then he met someone—like our Gayatri—"Oh Baba, why don't I see Bhagavan?" she asked.

[Swamiji is grinning at "Gayatri," whose eyes widen. She seems disarmed by this appearance in the story.]

"You can see Bhagavan, too. I'll show you Bhagavan. Come with me."

Gayatri came. He said to her, "Cut off your nose and you'll see Bhagavan." ["Gayatri" adjusts her sari, smiling with an uncomfortable air.] She came. He cut off her nose. "Now you too should dance like me," he said.

[Swamiji's white, stubbly chin is raised and he exudes droll enjoyment in the tale. "Gayatri's" face folds in theatrical horror, but then she smiles broadly at those who have turned to her with grins on their faces. Kirin, for one, is convulsed and has trouble suppressing her laughter as she translates.]

So Gayatri began to dance. "I see Bhagavan, too!" she said. By then Saraswati appeared.

[Now "Saraswati," face pale beneath her curly red hair, looks alarmed.]

"Why can't I see Bhagavan?" she demanded. They told her: "You cut off your nose, too, then you'll see Him." Her nose was sliced off. She began to dance, too. In this way, the group grew. There were a hundred, there were two hundred, there were a thousand. All people without noses. They danced all the time, cymbals in their hands. They didn't rest for a minute* they danced so much. "We're all seeing Bhagavan!" they cried.

Doing this, they traveled to another kingdom. By then the group had grown to four or five thousand people. They would just camp in a park. They never had to worry about money; the disciples would take care of all that.

Then once there are so many followers, a religion should be given a name. They gave themselves the name "Narayandarsimat," the group that gives you *darshan* of Narayan. This was the name. After they gave themselves this title, they began to travel. They went to another kingdom and stayed in a park. They ate rich sweets and fried bread [*halvāh aur pūrī*]. And they danced.

Some people came up and asked, "What, *jī*, who are you?"

"We're the people who can show you Bhagavan."

"Is that so? How come we don't see Bhagavan?"

"It's because you have a nose, blocking your vision of Bhagavan."

Those people said, "Who knows, maybe this so. . . . " They sent this news on to their King. The King was the same. He immediately came to the gardens where the visitors had camped.

"Who are you all?" the King asked. "None of you have noses. What does this mean?"

They said, "We are the people who reveal Bhagavan. Our religion is called Narayandarsimat."

"Is that so? How come I don't see Bhagavan?"

"Your nose blocks your vision, that's why you can't see Bhagavan."

"If I cut off my nose, will I see Bhagavan?" the King asked.

"Yes, certainly you'll see Bhagavan. We'll show you."

"Fine!" said the King. So he called his Pandit. Every state has a royal Pandit. "Tell me an auspicious time to see Bhagavan."

The Pandit said, "Tomorrow at ten is an auspicious time."

The King said, "You're such a great Pandit, you're the Pandit for the royal family. And you only tell me now that such an auspicious time is coming up tomorrow! Those people had to come here to bring this to your attention. How fortunate we are!"

The King sent his drummers out to announce,* "Tomorrow at ten o'clock everyone in this kingdom will see Bhagavan. Whether they are men or women, everyone can see Bhagavan. This is the King's order. The auspicious time is tomorrow at ten."

[Swamiji pauses again. Now the singing in the background is slow and reverential. We sit tensed and silent.]

Now a King's Prime Minister is smarter than a King. He thought—like our Gupta Saheb—

[Gupta Saheb, a dark man with a narrow, alert face, sits impassively though all eyes now turn to him.]

"No matter how much I reason with the King, he won't listen," he thought. He went home. That evening he met his grandfather. The grandfather asked, "What's new in our kingdom? What's going on?"

The Prime Minister said, "It's like this. Some people called the Narayandarsimats have come to our kingdom. The King has issued the order that everyone's nose is to be cut off tomorrow. No matter how much I reason with him, he refuses to listen."

Then the old man said, "Look here, where's the nose and where are the eyes? How can a nose block your vision? There's something fishy going on [lit. "something black in the lentils"]. There's some mistake.* The King is ruining everyone. They'll all be trapped, deceived. We can't let this happen."

"What can I do?"

"Take me to the King."

So the Prime Minister took his grandfather to the King. The old man said, "King, don't do this, something's wrong here. It's not right."

"What do you know?" asked the King [impatiently]. "You're just an old man. This is a new age. These kinds of things go on these days. These people who've come are great scientists. Your nose blocks your vision. You haven't seen Bhagavan, you don't know anything. These people have come to show us Bhagavan. Why do you block their way?"

The grandfather said, "But who in our kingdom has seen the Bhagavan they show? You're just assuming this is true."

"No, in our kingdom, no one has seen Bhagavan," the King agreed.

"I won't lie," said the old man. "If you want to do it, do it, but let my nose be cut off first. I'll tell the truth. Don't wantonly cut off your nose and spoil yourself. You're my King and these are all your subjects. Don't ruin them all. Let my nose be cut off first."

"All right," said the King.

The next day, the army ["mili-tree*"] surrounded the park, on all sides. The Nose-Cutters had all their knives ready. Then all the subjects arrived, along with the King. The Guru came in and sat down.

The King said, "Look, Maharaj, this is the most venerable minister in my kingdom. The old must always be respected. That's why he should be shown Bhagavan first. You can give us *darshan* of Bhagavan after him."

The Guru thought, "Thousands have had their noses cut off, does one more matter?" He said, "All right, send him in." So the old man was sent to the Guru. The Guru took his nose in one hand. In the other hand he held a knife.

[Swamiji tilts back his head pinching his nose with the left hand and straightening the right hand above it as though ready to slice. Murmurs of apprehension rise around the room.]

He cut the old man's nose off.

At the time of initiation, a *mantra* should be whispered in a person's ear, shouldn't it? At that moment, the Guru said, "Look brother, your nose has now been cut off. The nose that's gone will never come back. The whole world will make fun of you. The whole world will laugh on seeing you. That's why you should do as we do: say you've seen Bhagavan. The entire world will raise you up; you'll get a lot of reverence and respect."

[Swamiji notices that the young mother with oiled black braids has set her baby down on the orange carpet folded against the wall. "Pick up your baby," he advises. "He might pee. This is where everyone sits, and if he pees there's no one to clean it up." The woman hurriedly lifts the baby, patting the carpet with her handkerchief. "Has he peed?" Swamiji asks. "No," says the woman. "No," echoes Prakash Seth examining the carpet. "Babies don't know anything," Swamiji gently observes. Then he resumes the story.]

So the old man's nose was cut off. He came out and he said, "I didn't see Bhagavan, I didn't see anything. I'm in terrible pain. In one ear I was told, 'Say what we say, else you'll be mocked by the world.' These people are just rogues. Round them up."

The army was already there, surrounding the place. They caught hold of the Nose-Cutters and began to thrash them. Then each one began to cry out. "I don't see anything, I don't see anything! I said I did because so-and-so said so. So-and-so said so because he was told by someone else."

[Swamiji's voice has speeded up, he is grinning broadly. We laugh: the mounting tension we felt has been released.]

This was the Narayandarsimat sect. One King was able to cut them short. There is a book called *Satyarth Prakash* and the story is written there. I read this as a child. This isn't a lie, this story actually happened in our India. Finished.

*   *   *

The story was done, the *Durga Saptashati* had also run to completion. We sat silent for a minute, attention still fixed on Swamiji. He adjusted his spectacles and looked around the room. When he spoke again, his voice was low and earnest. "The Lord [Ishwar] has no form," he said. "You can't see Him with these eyes, but you can perceive Him through wisdom. Wisdom is the Lord. Then, if you look into the matter, your own form is the Lord's form. Everyone's true identity is divine. Why don't you understand that everyone is Bhagavan? People need to stop hating each other, to abandon jealousy, malice, backbiting. For who is it that you attack? No one other than the Lord."

By this time, the hour of *darshan* was well over. The doctor's little boy had come and gone, having dropped off a tiffin box with Swamiji's lunch inside. The visitors started to surge forward and bow before they left. A man asking for holy water to heal his daughter deflected the conversation. As usual, Swamiji put a banana into each person's cupped hands. Then we emerged into the bright sunshine on the terrace.

Interpretations

At the time, interested as I was in a life history, I did not think to elicit "oral literary criticism" from everyone who was slipping on their shoes lined up by the door. What had they made of the story? Mr. Advani seemed unruffled. Maybe he had not caught on that there might be an analogy between the workshops he was so fervently organizing and the Nose-Cutters' initiation. Gupta Saheb, who had been portrayed as the

Prime Minister, nodded goodbye with a grin. But that was no indication that he was pleased by this characterization or that he agreed with the story, for he always courteously smiled.

Upstairs, the group of us living together spread newspapers on the floor in preparation for lunch. "Gayatri" and "Saraswati" made passing reference to the tale. Both seemed amused about having had their noses sliced off. "As though I'd do a thing like that!" "Gayatri" said, grinning and shaking her head. "Am I as gullible as all that?" "Saraswati" mused in her clear British tones. "He always has a *message*, you know, I wonder why he said *that*." I silently remembered that they had both previously been involved with large religious institutions.

"Bhavani"'s comment came a few days later. New to India, she had quite literally absorbed the story as one more insight into the complex civilization. "Far out," she said. "This country is too much! Do you know when this happened? Do you know who the King was who stopped the Nose-Cutters?" I burst into laughter but had to agree when she pointed out that Swamiji had stressed that the story was true.

My mother, when I interviewed in Berkeley, recalled Swamiji offhandedly telling this legend when a small group gathered around him when he visited a large ashram in the late 1970s. She remembered Swamiji telling the story in reference to a particular instant enlightenment experience offered at this ashram. "The story was like dynamite," she reported. "It's explosive to tell an anti-cult story within a cult!" Despite her uneasiness, no violent explosions followed the retelling. On that occasion, she said, Swamiji had compared himself to the old Prime Minister in the story. "He was an old man like me and he had nothing to fear," Swamiji said as he introduced the character; like the character he was taking a risk in unveiling what he perceived to be the group's illusion. "It's interesting to see which characters he identifies with and how," my mother reflected.

"Gulelal" also referred to this story one afternoon in Nasik. It was two years since I had recorded it, and meanwhile I had written a paper in which it had been used.[2] I mentioned this to "Gulelal" and he said, "When I went to America last time, Swamiji told me not to cut off any noses." I grinned, understanding that "Gulelal" had been advised not to set himself up as a bogus Guru. But then "Gulelal" offered a very different explanation: "What he meant was: don't destroy anyone's faith. When you cut a nose, it's the central part of their face and their faith." As "Gulelal" saw it, Swamiji was referring to "Gulelal"'s disillusionment with another Guru; to reveal a loss of faith to disciples who were still involved was to "Gulelal" equivalent to cutting off their noses. He had spent twelve years involved in an ashram that he had eventually lost faith in, and so losing the central belief in one's life remained a crucial and worrying concern.

Though I acknowledged that different interpretations could be offered for a story, I also openly disagreed with "Gulelal"'s account of what Swamiji meant. "I think he was telling you not to masquerade as a Guru," I suggested. "Gulelal" repeated that, no, he was sure this was advice on how he should approach other disciples from his previous ashram. Having spent weeks mulling over the meaning of the story as I wrote my paper, I felt certain that I was right, and so I offered "Gulelal" a copy of this paper. No sooner had I done this though, than I became uneasy myself. It was awkward to have my two worlds collide; would someone who knew Swamiji agree with my representations in a more academic voice? I thought of a moment two years before when "Saraswati" had taken a picture of Swamiji and me, both grinning broadly. As she clicked the camera, she had said in an undertone, "Ethnographer and Subject." This caption for what was essentially Swamiji and me sharing a joke had seemed wonderfully absurd at the time. Giving "Gulelal" a paper in which the Ethnographer proved her mettle in describing the Subject, I felt extremely tense.

The next afternoon, "Gulelal" broached the issue with Swamiji himself. He announced that he had read something I wrote about the Nose-Cutter story. As I translated, I squirmed, wondering what "Gulelal" might report about my academic productions. But he just reminded Swamiji that he had been told not to cut off noses. "What did you mean?" "Gulelal" asked. Pushed into defining a meaning, Swamiji said, "Don't cut noses means don't deceive others!"

Other Versions of Nose-Cutters

In order to write the paper that I gave "Gulelal" I had looked in the university library for the book Swamiji cited as his source for the story. I found it in Hindi as *Satyarth Prakash* by Swami Dayananda Saraswati and in English translation as *The Light of Truth*. Swami Dayananda (1824–1883) was the founder of the Arya Samaj, a Hindu religious and social reform movement. Swami Dayananda—like Swamiji—left his Brahman background to wander through India in search of spiritual wisdom, eventually taking the vows of a Dashanami *sannyāsī*. On the orders of his blind Guru, Swami Dayananda campaigned for a return to a pristine Hinduism based on the

Vedas. He condemned idolatry, emphasized humanitarianism, and bitterly critiqued other religions, Gurus, and sects. In the *Satyarth Prakash,* first issued in 1875, Dayananda synthesized the views that he had delivered orally in lectures through north India.

Sure enough, in this book I found the story that Swamiji had told, though in a very different form.[3] The story appears in chapter 11, "A Refutation and Advocation of Indian Religions," which presents an unabashedly biased history of various sects within Hinduism. There are spirited exposes of the supposed logical absurdity in the mythology surrounding various deities; there are tirades against Gurus and sarcastic descriptions of the average ascetic's conduct. Many parts of the book are in dialogue form. When Swami Dayananda is asked about the Swami Narayan sect, he launches into a description of the founder's wiles.

The Swami Narayan sect was founded in Gujarat during the early nineteenth century by Swami Sahajananda, also known on account of his devotion to Vishnu (Narayan) as "Swami Narayan." As Raymond Williams has shown in a historical overview of the sect, this was a period of extreme political instability in the northwest region of India; Sahajananda's appearance was seen as consonant with the traditional view that during times of stress Vishnu himself will come to earth. One of Sahajananda's major patrons was a wealthy landlord, Dada Kachar, who provided a residential base from which Sahajananda proceeded on tours. As more devotees gathered, a growing phenomenon was the state of mystical union (*samādhi*) that followers claimed to experience.[4]

> What made this unusual was that it did not result from long practice of the yogic path of ascent to higher consciousness—thought by many to be the only path of its attainment; it came immediately through contact with or meditation on Sahajanand Swami. There are hundreds of stories of persons in the trance state, especially from the early part of his ministry. A constant theme in the stories is that the men and women who had such visions saw Sahajanand Swami as the Supreme Being served by other divine figures, e.g., Rama or Krishna.

Swami Dayananda, preaching several decades later, did not approve. He distrusted these visions and did not hesitate to say so. According to his account, Swami Sahajananda dressed up as the four-armed deity Narayan to win over the powerful landlord of Kathiawar, Dada Kachar. His disciples led Dada Kachar through a room with a one small lamp, and allowed the landlord to glimpse the Guru/deity for a brief minute. Swami Dayananda then writes: "a parable is apposite here" and starts on the story of the criminal whose nose is cut off and claims to see God.

The story of the noseless man who dupes others is an Indic tale type[5] with other recorded variants. For example, the following rendition of this story appears in a collection of Tamil folktales recorded by the missionary E. J. Robinson.[6]

The Nose a Sacrifice

In a certain country a man without a nose, who could not bear being laughed at by many that saw him, devised within himself a method of relief, and put it into execution. Every time the offence happened, he lifted up his eyes to heaven and said, "Lord of the world, I meditate on thee, salute thee, worship thee. Give thy sacred hand to a wretch lying down pained in this sinful world. With what shall I compare the splendour of thy holy body?" While he thus spoke, his eyes filled with tears, and his frame trembled. Afterwards, looking on the people standing round, and affecting to pity them, he said, "O people behold! See the god standing! Alas! Why do you loiter vainly?" Some, believing him, fell at his feet and said, "Sir, you must make the god known to our eyes also." The noseless man answered, "Would you see the god distinctly? You would see if, like me, you were without your noses." So they cut off their noses and discovered that he had cheated them. There was no god visible. Fearing that people with noses would laugh at them also, they said, "the god is well manifest to our eyes. At a small loss, what great profit we have gained! What bliss is ours! Believing this, all the people in that country cut off their noses in a few days. It is thus that one of a false religion tries to draw others into it.

In this version, there is no reprieve; everyone's nose is lopped off. Similarly, the *North Indian Notes and Queries* for the year 1894 bears an entry entitled "The Man Without a Nose." Here, a man without a nose assures those who mock him that his noseless state enables him to see the "Lord Almighty." Others follow him to cut off their noses, and though they find themselves duped they continue to uphold the collective fiction that God is revealed. Eventually, everyone cuts off his nose, and no one is left to mock the original man who had no nose. The editor, William Crooke, does not state the source of the story. He does, however, link it to the Hindi proverb "*ānkh ke āge nāk, sujhe kyā khāk,*" or "How can a man see with his nose in front of his eyes?"[7]

The story is linked to another north Indian proverb in a book published the same year: Pandit Ganga Dutt Upreti's *Proverbs and Folklore of Kumaun and Garhwal.* The proverb is "*ho paṛhosina mai jasi,*" or "O neighbor be like me." Here, the outline of the story is essentially the same. A man without a nose pretends to entertain the gods, and assures astonished onlookers that to see the celestial gathering each must cut off his nose, as it is "the root of haughtiness and vanity." The first person to do this is told, "My dear son, do you not know that the leper wishes to have the whole world become like himself, and so also a sinner?" The group grows until it is driven out by a King.[8]

In all these variants, the interpretive thrust built into the tale is slightly different. Swami Dayananda concludes his retelling with the summary statement, "In this same manner, all the opponents of the Vedas are clever in stripping others of their wealth. Such is the imposition of sects. The followers of the Swami Narayan religion illegally make money, practice frauds and tricks."[9] He turns this story into a critique of sects that oppose his own emphasis on the *Vedas* and gain wealth and followers through means that he considers fraudulent. This exegesis resembles Robinson's less specific statement, "It is thus that one of a false religion tries to draw others into it." Upreti's summarizing proverb "O neighbor be like me" does not address religion but rather generalized human nature, in which people wish others to share their defects. The proverb "How can a man see with his nose in front of his eyes?" is a quip at people so gullible that they might actually think a nose blocked their vision. The same story, then, can be slanted in different directions to address different, albeit related, issues. When Swamiji finished up his own rendition, modeled loosely on Dayananda's, with the comment, "This isn't a lie, the story actually happened in our India," I heard this assertion of the story's veracity as implying that deception by false Gurus was well established in Hindu practice, and that Westerners should know "our India" harbored charlatans as well as saints.

Swami Dayananda drew on this traditional tale to comment on what he perceived to be the actual practice of a fellow Guru. In his view, it was a historical fact that Sahajananda decked himself out as Narayan to gain disciples. Swamiji, in turn, adapted both the "factual" description and the accompanying folk narrative to comment on Gurus in his own time. In his retelling, reference to the sect under attack was omitted, and both sequences were linked into a single legend set in a past unmoored by identity or place. By making the thief whose nose is cut off a disciple of the Guru who decks himself out as a deity, Swamiji linked the two sequences through a Guru-disciple relationship. As the Guru, so the disciple, the link suggests. Fakes breed further fakes.

A detailed comparison between Swami Dayananda's written account and Swamiji's orally performed one is a potentially endless undertaking. There are differences in the use of language, the names of characters, details about when and where events occurred, and even in the style of the two English translators. Yet the basic outlines of the story remain the same. Both Dayananda and Swamiji address the enduring cultural theme of the false ascetic and the power he can wield as Guru; both question instant experiences of God and comment on the plight of devotees who cannot admit themselves duped; both, as ascetics, are making a reflexive statement on their own role.

Gurus and Nose-Cutting

The various versions assembled here reveal several connotations of the nose. Noses are cut off of criminals; for the gullible, the nose blocks spiritual vision; the nose is the seat of vanity; lepers may lose noses; to cut a nose is equivalent to deceiving others. And as "Gulelal" points out, a nose is "a central part of . . . face and . . . faith." Still, how does all this relate to false Gurus and sects?

As psychoanalytic theory tells us, the unconscious device of upward displacement links the genitals with the nose. To cut a nose is symbolic castration for men and women alike. Ironically, Nasik marks a famous nose-cutting incident from the *Rāmāyaṇa*. Here, Ram's younger brother Lakshman is believed to have cut off the nose of Ravana's sister, Surpanakha. The reason he did this was that she was lusting after Ram and had tried to kill his wife, Sita. Cutting her nose, Sudhir Kakar writes, is "a fantasied clitoridectomy, designed to root out the cause and symbol of Surpanakha's lust."[10] The implications of this act were enormous, for Ravana sought revenge, abducted Sita, and a great war ensued.

In the *Kathāsaritsāgara,* "Ocean of the Streams of Story," dating from the eleventh century A.D., I came across an odd story featuring nose-cutting and Gurus. This story emerges in the course of numbskull tales related by a minister called Gomukha in order to bring solace to a pining prince.[11]

Story of the Man Who Tried to Improve His Wife's Nose

There lived in some place or the other a foolish man of bewildered intellect. He, seeing that his wife was flat-nosed, and that his spiritual instructor was high-nosed, cut off the nose of the latter when he was asleep: and then he went and cut off his wife's nose, and stuck the nose of this spiritual instructor on her face, but it would not grow there. Thus he deprived both his wife and his spiritual guide of their noses.

If one pursues the psychoanalytic track, the wife's flat nose would seem to indicate a clitoris; the high nose of the spiritual instructor or Guru, a penis. The folk belief that storing of semen makes for great powers perhaps explains why the man should find his Guru's penis so attractive. On the other hand, why should he want his *wife* to have it? Here we are in the realm of the "narcissistic personality" which Philip Spratt has attributed to Hindu men.[12] The Guru often stands in the relation of a father to a man,[13] and Spratt's assertion that there is a passive homosexual attitude toward the father by the narcissistic son helps explain why the man in this story might want his sexual partner to be endowed with the Guru's penis. Indeed, I have often heard it asserted by other Gurus (though not Swamiji, who emphasizes the relationship between child and mother) that men must stand in the relation of a woman to God. There are actually sects where men dress up as women to worship a form of Bhagavan.[14]

Returning to the Nose-Cutter sect, why should a man whose nose was cut off declare himself a Guru and cut off others' noses? That his nose was cut in the first place indicates that he had transgressed certain social rules. Though posing as an ascetic, he is already marked a scoundrel; any pretended celibacy, then, is not a source of power (for he lacks spirituality) but is equivalent to a self-castration. In drawing others into his sect and advocating that they be celibate like him, he is also castrating them. As with many sects, the front is one of purity and spiritual revelation; backstage, there is a welter of human foibles. A Guru may be preaching celibacy, but in his inner rooms he may be sleeping with female (or male) disciples.

This story expresses a cultural paranoia over the duplicity of sects and plays on this paranoia at several levels. To cut noses is equivalent to deceiving others about the nature of spirituality and the sect; to cut noses is to jeopardize people's ties with ongoing social life (as in the case of devout couples who have abstained from sex, even though their ostensibly celibate Guru is himself sexually active); to cut noses is to mar a central feature of people's faith in the integrity of their Guru. And now for another story about a false Guru.

The Greatness of Lies

In August 1985, Swamiji was leaning back in his deck chair and chatting with the assembled people. Swami Turiyanand, who is a disciple of Swamiji's, had come to visit, and Swamiji teased him about his newly acquired false teeth. A dark man with a shining shaved scalp, Turiyanand sat with his lips tightly closed as Swamiji coaxed him to flash a white smile. Krishna Chaitanya sat beside Turiyanand and also wore ochre robes. Behind them were Purshottam Seth, an old man with a hooked nose who wheezed up the stairs with a walking stick every day. Nathu Maharaj had breezed in after finishing a few morning shaves. Mr. Karnad stood near the door, his arms crossed. "Gulelal" sat at the back of the room, a cotton T-shirt and ochre drawstring pants covering his large frame. (A few days later, he was to forget to secure the drawstring and so perform the Chaplinesque stunt of dropping his pants when he stood. Swamiji commiserated, saying that once at his Guru's ashram he had been presented with silk robes which almost slithered off him during a ceremonial procession.) Beside "Gulelal" was "Narahari" in an outfit that made me grin: a plaid cowboy shirt and white *lungī* wrapped around his waist. In addition there was a local rick-shaw driver with a ceremonial red streak on his forehead who had come in to ask Swamiji for a *mantra*. Swamiji had asked him to come back another time, explaining that *mantras* should be imparted privately, falling on no more than four ears—the Guru's and the disciple's—but the man had stayed.

On the women's side of the room there were also several Westerners, all wearing saris that showed varying degrees of expertise with the folds and pleats. Isabel and "Kumari" sat side by side. Australian "Ahalya Amma," an august, white-haired woman in her sixties sat beside "Gayatri," who was back for another visit, two years after she had appeared in the Nose-Cutter story. Two local women had also come in leading squirming children by the hand. But they only stayed for a short time before setting off to resume their domestic duties. Amid this coming and going, the room redolent with offerings of ripe bananas, I sat with my tape recorder awaiting the quarry of a story or two.

There was a nip in the morning air and so Swamiji was wearing a red vest over his ochre robe. He sometimes wore this vest back-to-front, with the "V" dipping down his back, but today it was at his chest. He was reminiscing over a recent visit to the hermitage of Swami R. There had been a magnificent feast, and all the foreigners, not knowing how rich feast food could be, had gorged themselves and now had upset stomachs. While on the theme of understanding customs across cultures, Swamiji went on to air one of his pet hypotheses, that Hindus and Jews were closely related. "We say Brahma, they Ibrahim. It's the same thing, isn't it? When one person says 'strong' and another person says 'istrong' they're saying the same thing even if they say it differently. And then, Jews worship the Ganesh Yantra." Swamiji grinned at the array of Jews present, and explained that the symbol for elephant-headed Ganesh who removes obstacles was just like the star of David. "Gulelal," "Narahari," "Gayatri," and "Ahalya Amma" were Jewish, and they all listened intently as Swamiji spoke. Sometimes Krishna Chaitanya translated, and sometimes I did. It was not clear to me what the connecting link to the story was, but suddenly Swamiji announced, "There was a King." Looking distant as he recollected the tale he was about to tell, he amended, "No, not a King." He started again with a Guru instead.

*   *   *

There was a Guru. He had three or four devotees. They were sitting together and the Guru started to chat with them. He said to them, "What are your thoughts? What are they, tell me. What do you think is good? What's important in the world? What's true? What kind of man can earn well? What brings good earnings? What's good?"

One disciple said, "Where does happiness lie?"

Another said, "Guruji, in my thinking, eating good mutton* brings a lot of happiness."

[Kirin, who is translating, is thrown off track by the mention of mutton. "What did you say in the beginning?" she asks. Nathu Maharaj and Swamiji chime together, "Where does happiness lie?"]

He said, "Eating mutton brings great happiness. This makes everyone glad."

Yet another said, "How can there be happiness in doing that? When you eat too much your stomach hurts. So that's no good." So there was a fight* between them.

Another said, "Guruji, it's like this: in bad* character.*"

Another said, "What's the happiness in that? There's no happiness there because when a woman has a child she has so much pain. The woman thinks, "I don't want a child again." She can't eat or anything. But in a few days people return to their old ways. Once more they find themselves in the previous condition. There's no happiness there."

The third disciple said, "There's happiness in doing big business.*"

The second one said, "What's the happiness in business? The Government* comes and casts a net. There is income* tax.* Your employees go on strike.* There's no happiness in that."

The fourth one said, "Guruji, there's great happiness in telling lies [*jhūṭ*]. It's deceiving others that makes us all happy."

[Nathu Maharaj goes into a hiccuping paroxysm of laughter. He sways forward and backward as he laughs, hunched over on the floor. Others smile, but aren't so amused. Swamiji grins down at Nathu Maharaj.]

By then a King had arrived there. He heard the first three, but when he heard the fourth, he got angry. He said, "There was some truth in what the first three said. But what this man is telling us, to lie and deceive, is wrong." He asked him, "Tell me, what happiness can you get by telling lies and deceiving others? Which man would come near you? Tell me this."

"Maharaj, just give the opportunity and in six months I'll show you. Else allow me a year and you'll see everything."

"All right," said the King. He gave him that much time.

Fine, so the King had given him this time. This man left. The fellow left. He let his beard grow like mine [Swamiji strokes the white growth on his chin]. He was a young man. He decked himself out in ash and other things [*bhasma-bhisma*]. He wore nice clothes. There was a city: small, like Nasik. He met a man like our Seth here.

[Swamiji indicates the Purshottam Seth, sitting in starched white clothes with a Gandhi cap on his white head. Purshottam Seth nods majestically, looking out toward other listeners with the faintest shadow of a smile.]

The Seth had a bungalow. He had two or three rooms. This man rented a room here; he rented an entire block* of the house. Yes? He got himself a hall* like this.

[Swamiji is looking around the room, his own "hall" with amusement. The women with children, and a few others who have just arrived stand to leave. There is an interruption as Swamiji blesses them and hands out bananas. Kirin switches off her recorder until Swamiji has once again settled back in his chair to resume the story.]

So this Babaji rented a block* of the house and sat down in a hall* like this. And . . . he kept aside an inner room. He put an image of Vishnu in there; a very beautiful image he'd had made. He lit an oil lamp in front of the image. He made a throne and put it in there. He decorated the image and sat it down. Then he surrounded himself with a few people from there. They did the usual disciple's thing [*chelā-bāji*]. They spread the word that he was a very fine Babaji.

Then someone would say, some disciple of the Babaji like our Nathu Maharaj, some disciple: "Our Babaji shows people God."

[Nathu Maharaj grins, buck teeth splayed out and downward-slanting crinkles fanning out from his eyes.]

Then someone came, like our Gayatri. "Babaji, I want to have *darshan* of Bhagavan."

["Gayatri" leans forward, beaming from ear to ear.]

"Fine, you'll certainly see Bhagavan [Swamiji rolls his head with assurance]. You're the kind of person who sees Bhagavan. Bhagavan is sitting in there. Go, meditate there. Bhagavan will reveal himself to you, he'll give you *prasād*. Go see him in there."

"All right," she said.

"There's just one thing and that is, Bhagavan won't show himself to people who lie. Only people who tell the truth can see him. Go, now mediate."

She sat, she sat for a little while. Then "ha ha ha!" she came out laughing aloud.

"What, did you see Bhagavan?"

"Yes, I saw Bhagavan and he waved his hand" [Swamiji lifts a palm towards us in a gesture of blessing].

Then Narahari appeared. "Gayatri saw Bhagavan, why didn't I?" he said [in a petulant voice], "I want this, too."

["Narahari" stares intently through his wire-rimmed glasses. His eyes are fixed on Swamiji but he does not smile.]

"Yes, look, you'll see Bhagavan, too. Go, do some meditation.* But this won't be possible for a person who tells lies. Go sit."

So he went and sat inside. He sat for a while, then he too came out laughing. "Bhagavan gave me some holy water from his conch!" he said.

Next "Gulelal" said, "I'll go in, too."

["Gulelal" smiles forebearingly from his position slumped against the wall.]

And he, too, reported, "Bhagavan gave me some *prasād*."

So one after another people began to flock in. They stood in lines [number* *lagāyā*], line upon line. The lines grew till they spanned the distance between Bhadrakali and Ram Kund. People kept coming. Everyone said, "I saw him, I saw him [*darshan ho gayā*]! How wonderful Bhagavan is! What lovely golden-yellow garments he wears! How he is revealing himself!"

The Queen came here, too. After hearing about it from her, the King came as well. He went in. As he left, the Babaji said, "Look, King, you asked what the greatness of a lie was. Everything I said was a lie. All the people who came here told lies. [Swamiji's laughter bubbles between his words.] There was nothing, no one saw anything. I had said that lies were very great. Yes? I had said that lies brought happiness. All this is a lie. That's why I said lies are very great."

*   *   *

We were all laughing as the story ended. "What do you think, Nathu Maharaj?" Swamiji asked.

"Yes, there's a greatness to lies," Nathu Maharaj said, head vigorously rolling in agreement. "But. . . . "

Swamiji added, "A person who tells lies is quickly ensnared [*jaldi phans jātā*]." He went on to cite a Kannada proverb "are customs ridiculous or people [who follow them] ridiculous?" (*jātra marulā, jana marulā*). Then he launched into another story about a false *sādhu* who distributed miraculous lockets with hair from his own beard (or perhaps it was even his pubic hair, Swamiji mischievously said at the end). Since this was a very sketchy rendition of an extended traditional story [15] I do not reproduce it here. "This is the kind of thing some Gurus distribute," Swamiji grinned. "And then they laugh about it later." This information set Nathu Maharaj laughing so hard that he had to pull out a handkerchief to wipe his eyes.

A Variant of "The Greatness of Lies"

In Charles Swynnerton's *Indian Night's Entertainment,* among the many Punjabi stories he gathered in the upper Indus region is a folktale very similar to the "The Greatness of Lies." Though Swynnerton is lavish in his romanticized descriptions of the area, he provides little information on the identity of the narrators he rounded up, apart from their being "villagers." I am tempted to speculate that the narrator may have been a woman and a householder, for this recasting of the story involves a smart girl who ends up marrying a King. [16]

To summarize, four girls chatting among themselves extoll meat, wine, love-making, and lies as the most pleasant of tastes. They are overheard by a King, who calls each one in separately for interrogation. The first three girls defend their assertions, and the King agrees that, indeed, meat, wine, and love-making are very pleasant. But he will not accept the fourth girl's statement that lies are the most pleasurable of pursuits. She assures the King that he, too, will tell a lie. She requests a large sum of money and six months. Then she builds a fine palace and announces that God dwells here, but that He is only visible to those who are born in lawful wedlock. All the King's ministers, afraid to be dubbed bastards, claim to have seen God. The King claims the same. The girl then chides him for lacking a conscience and insight. "How could you possibly see God, seeing that God is a spirit?" she asks. The King is so impressed by the lesson the girl has taught him that he ends up marrying her. She becomes his advisor in all matters, and her fame spreads through many lands.

A comparison of Swamiji's and Swynnerton's versions once again re-veals the manner in which the stories Swamiji tells pivot around ascetic concerns. In Swamiji's retelling there are not four girls but four disciples of a Guru. The pleasures of eating meat, of sex, and of business are all cri-tiqued by the disciples as fleeting: indeed, this view that pleasures of the flesh are only temporary is central to world-renunciation. To prove his point about the power of lies, the fourth disciple sets himself up as a Guru in his own right. He promises a vision of Bhagavan to those who are com-pletely truthful, dramatizing an emphasis on moral fiber; the threat of being revealed as base-born, on the other hand, reveals a concern with so-cial esteem. In describing the hordes that flock to the room where Bhagavan supposedly presides and the various things they all claim to have seen, Swamiji mocks the faddish aspects of a sect. The story is transformed into a commentary on Gurus and disciples, and the ease with which a collective illusion can be built from deceit.

The Two Stories Compared

The similarities between "The Nose-Cutters" and "The Greatness of Lies" struck me even as the second story was being told. Both deal with false Gurus and the visions of Bhagavan they promise. In both cases, Gurus offer *darshan,* or a glimpse of Bhagavan, and people are eager to see him. The first Guru in the Nose-Cutter story sets up a viewing room very like the room in "The Greatness of Lies": there is a throne, a representation of Bhagavan, a small light burning. The ecstatic behavior of those who have supposedly seen Bhagavan is also very similar. They start to laugh or dance in what seems like a parody of ecstatic devotional sects. According to the *Bhāgavata Purāṇa,* an ardent devotee "loses all sense of decorum . . . and like one possessed he now bursts into peals of laughter, now weeps, now cries, now sings aloud and begins to dance in a singular way."[17]

The Gurus in both stories are uniformly fake (except for the one who starts off "The Greatness of Lies" with his question). The stories differ, though, in the responses of disciples. In "The Nose-Cutters" the first group of disciples who flock to the Guru masquerading as Narayan are mixed: while some help the Guru with his fancy dress and lead visitors through the room, there are other innocent disciples who truly believe they are seeing Narayan. The second group of disciples who gather around the noseless Guru are gullible to start with, but by going on to tell others they see Bhagavan they become fellow conspirators in the hoax. The four disciples debating in "The Greatness of Lies" are intelligent young men dealing with the nature of the world rather than with delusions. But the disciples who come for *darshan* of Bhagavan are all independently liars. The stories, then, differ in the amount of collaboration between false Gurus and disciples. While deceit is collective among those without noses, it is individually constructed among those who do not wish to be branded liars. Even as these stories criticize false Gurus, they mock the disciples who were misguided enough to choose these Gurus and to spin contributions to the grand webs of deceit.

Characterizations as Social Commentary

When Swamiji placed himself and his listeners within narrative frames, he seemed to be making certain points. Though I cannot presume to spell out Swamiji's intentions in making particular characterizations, it is worthwhile to reflect on who was drawn into a story to play which role. Exploring the junctures at which narrative and outer reality intersect, both spheres are given sharper outlines.

In the Nose-Cutter legend, Swamiji likened himself to both the masquerading Guru and the thieving disciple-turned-Guru. The foreign women, "Gayatri" and "Saraswati," became noseless initiates. Gupta Saheb was compared to the Prime Minister. When these analogies were made, there was a stir among those of us listening. (The baby slept on and Mr. Advani remained benign and impassive.) We smiled, exchanged glances, and listened with the added intent of following the fates of those present who now found themselves buffetted along by the story's flow.

Telling "The Greatness of Lies," Swamiji compared himself to the disciple who was about to perpetrate the hoax. Swamiji stated that the man grew a beard like his own; that he enthroned an image of Bhagavan in a "hall" like the one in which we sat. He came to a city like Nasik, and rented out a block of rooms from a wealthy man like Purshottam Seth. The disciple who helped spread the word that this freshly established Guru would reveal Bhagavan was like Nathu Maharaj. "Gayatri," "Narahari," and "Gulelal" were three visitors who entered the room where the image was installed, and all three claimed to have direct experiences of Bhagavan. Also the lines that extended through the city were as long as the distance between "Bhadrakali and Ram Kund"; two sacred spots in Nasik which are at least several miles apart. Since this story was never as violent as "The Nose-Cutters," we listened to these comparisons to the world of daily life with greater hilarity and less tension than when the people involved were having their noses sliced off.

Swamiji's comparison of himself with various characters reveals various planes of self-identification. As my mother reported, on another occasion Swamiji compared himself to the old Prime Minister; so old that he had nothing to lose. In these stories then, Swamiji asserted his identification with the categories of disciples, Gurus, and wise old men. Drawing a parallel between himself and the two scoundrels in "The Nose-Cutters," as well as between himself and the masquerading "Babaji" in "The Greatness of Lies," Swamiji made reflexive statements on his role as ascetic. This role, he seemed to emphasize, is potentially subject to abuses, and disciples would do well to keep this in mind.

"A Prime Minister is always smarter than a King," Swamiji said when he likened Gupta Saheb to the Prime Minister. Like the Prime Minister, Gupta Saheb was a reflective and cautious man. A few weeks later, he offered some interesting comments which linked the Nose-Cutter legend with Swamiji. Wearing a bush shirt and trousers, he spoke eloquent Hindi interspersed with English words. "I have met with many *sādhus* and saints," he said, "because we are from U.P., but this one [Swamiji] is totally different from the others." U.P. is short for Upper Pradesh, a state in the North liberally dotted with pilgrimage sites where *sādhus* flock. Eyeing my tape recorder, Mr. Sharma reiterated, "We are from U.P., the very sphere of *sādhus,* and have met with numerous *sādhus,* but this *sādhu* is very different. The reason* is that most *sādhus* are obsessed with money. But for him, there is no question of wealth. There is no motive* to* extract* money.* The second thing is that an individual* can only find Bhagavan through his own efforts. *Sādhus* and saints cannot show you Bhagavan. It is not possible* that you come into contact* with them for a day or two and then see God. You must perform your own duties." Wealth and instant spiritual experiences were of course two aspects of self-serving ascetics critiqued in the Nose-Cutter legend. While echoing the story, Gupta Saheb turned these themes to a positive commentary on Swamiji's own behavior. Ending in a spurt of English, Gupta Saheb asserted, "Swamiji's philosophy is that you are human and you treat others as human. This is the main philosophy which I like."

I never found a chance to interview the venerable, white cap–wearing Purshottam Seth, but I understood that he had a large house nearby. In drawing him into the story as the owner of a house, Swamiji could have simply been indicating his status in the community as a man of means. Yet lacking knowledge of his biography I could be deaf to imbedded allusions. For example, I do not know if Purshottam Seth or someone in his family had at some time patonized a false *sādhu.*

As for the barber, Nathu Maharaj, there was a lively joking relationship between him and Swamiji. Often when Nathu Maharaj swaggered in, the pockets of his once-white cotton drawstring pants bulging like holsters, Swamiji would tease. If a story was being told, Nathu Maharaj was often drawn into it. Nathu Maharaj had a forebearing, amused attitude toward the various roles he played in Swamiji's stories. He did not take offense. When I asked him about his characterizations he just laughed, and said these were all "jokes.*"

I later asked "Gayatri" what she had made of the story "The Greatness of Lies" and her role in it, and she too assured me, "It was just a joke." "Ahalya Amma," who had also been present, declined interpretation, saying that she had been tired and unable to pay proper attention. "Gulelal," though, was certain that it referred to the Guru whose sect he had been involved with. "There's no doubt about it, we were all made fools of," he sighed. "That was a facetious story." On the other hand, "Narahari," whom I spoke to later in Albuquerque, interpreted this story as "archetypes coming out of the collective unconscious" and denied that his role in this story carried any kind of personal comment.

I found it significant that when both these stories about deceitful Gurus were told, there were several Westerners present. They were portrayed as the gullible disciples, loathe to admit having been duped. How did these stories, I began to wonder, comment not only on scoundrel *sādhus* but also on the attitudes of disciples gathered from abroad?

False *Sādhus*

As I have already mentioned, since *sādhus* are often itinerant it is easy for pretenders to present themselves as holy men. Fugitives, criminals, and even inquisitive anthropologists[18] all have adopted ascetic disguise. The use of ascetic costume as a front for other activities dates back many centuries. For example, Kautilya's *Arthashastra,* a manual for government dating from the fourth century B.C., suggests that spies should pose as ascetics. The various kinds of ascetics and their life-styles are described in meticulous detail: recluses whose ashrams are actually enormous syping corporations; ascetics supposedly engaged in austerities in the suburbs of a city with merchant spies as disciples; female ascetics who worm their way into honor at court; ascetics who nonchalantly park themselves in the vicinity of forts.[19] Even among *sādhus* themselves, there is a clear dichotomy established between the genuine ones and the fakes. As Robert Gross reports:[20]

> Some of my informants mentioned that there are two basic types of sadhus: *pakkā, virakta* sadhus, i.e. those who have taken initiation from a guru, follow a sadhana [spiritual path] and are controlled and dispassionate, and the *nakali* (false) sadhus or *mowāli-bābās* ("riff-raff") who have disguised themselves to look like sadhus.

While genuine *sādhus* are sincere about their spiritual practices, false *sādhus* use the role to exploit others and gain material comfort. When Swamiji described *sādhus* to Madan, who aspired to become one himself, he explained, "There are two kinds of *sādhus:* those who show you the way to find peace of mind, and then those who show you the way to collect money. I'm telling the truth!" Genuine religious teachers, in Swamiji's view, would never be concerned with amassing money. "One doesn't become a *sādhu* to earn," Swamiji went on to say, eyes solemn behind his spectacles, "but to help others." Swamiji's comments relating authenticity with a lack of interest in money are similar to the observations made by Mrs. Sinclair Stevenson:[21]

> The quicksure test . . . that Brahmans tell you to apply when you are not
> sure whether a man is a true ascetic or not, is to give him money. The real
> *sanyasi* refuses it, the false ascetic accepts it gladly and even begs for it.

When elevated to the role of Guru, a false *sādhu* comes to wield great
power over disciples' lives. Because of the sacred nature of the relationship
with a Guru, a disciple will often unquestioningly obey the Guru. As a
superhuman, almost divine character, the Guru stands beyond established
codes for behavior in society. There are stories about Gurus who rolled
about in their own shit, of Gurus who threw stones at disciples, Gurus
who demanded the sacrifice of life or property as a test of devotion. In
most of these cases, the Guru turns out to have been a saint detached from
his body and social categories, but ultimately benevolent to disciples. Yet
given this latitude in acceptable behavior, false Gurus out to dupe disciples
can go to great imaginative lengths in their scams. In an article on Gurus,
K. A. Padhye presents some hilarious reminiscences: [22]

> According to the test laid down by the Upanishads and by the Deccan saints,
> the Sad-Guru ought not to be engrossed in worldly affairs and should not
> attach any value to money. I know of one bogus Guru, who had been to
> Bombay some years ago. He represented to his audience that his age was
> 9900 years and that he had the rare fortune of dining with Shri Rama, the
> hero of Ramayana and his consort Sitabai. He further made his audience
> believe that he had seen Bhagwan Shree Krishna, Buddha, and Shree Shivaji
> Maharaj. Some of the intellectuals in Bombay whom I accompanied to his
> place believed in his representations. He was thoroughly exposed when he
> was confronted with a copy of his deposition in a Court of Law wherein he
> had stated his age as 80 years; but until he was exposed by this convincing
> evidence, he made a lot of money from the Bombay citizens. Instances can
> be multiplied. In 1907, a young man appeared at my native place (Thana)
> and represented that he was dropped down by Shree Datta Maharaj from
> Heaven for the purpose of the spiritual uplift of the people and for leading
> them to Heaven along with him. Thousands of people flocked to him with-
> out enquiring as regards the truth or otherwise of his representations. He
> went on exploiting his followers especially females for about three or four
> years. He was thoroughly exposed when a gentleman from a sacred place
> near Kolhapur proved by documentary evidence that he was the resident of
> that place and was driven out from that place . . . for his bad character.

Padhye is a Maharashtrian, and the Deccan saints he cites are from the
region near Nasik. Padhye's account once again exposes the two key viola-
tions attributed to false *sādhus:* the acquisition of money and sexual exploi-

tation ("bad character," as Swamiji also put it). Far from being free of attachments and desires, the false Guru turns out to be like any other self-serving human being, but more dangerous since he bears the power to tamper with other lives.

Initiation (*dīkshā*) can take a variety of forms as people are introduced to the specialized esoteric knowledge held by a sect: nose-cutting is an absurd and extreme example. Though initiation transmits *shakti*, the offer that this will be accompanied by instant mystical experience may lure the curious but arouse the suspicion of outsiders. For mystical experiences are generally thought to be the result of many years of spiritual practice, something more to be attained by lengthy personal endeavor than to be bought for money or secured by an exercise swift as cutting off a nose.

If these stories mock offers of initiation that include instant mystical experience, they equally play upon the anxiety of disciples that they have indeed experienced whatever the Guru offers and are not spiritual dullards. A friend who was once involved in an ashram which mass-produced spiritual elevation confided her extreme sense of insecurity and depression when her meditations were uneventful but everyone else seemed to have spectacular experiences. It was tempting, she admitted, to say that she was having an experience just so she would not feel so excluded. But a false claim of this sort is considered reprehensible. As David Miller and Dorothy Wertz write in regard to how greatly *sādhus* value a vision of the deity: "To be deceitful in such a serious matter is considered an unforgivable sin that would cause a major setback on the road to release."[23] Furthermore, to broadcast spiritual accomplishments, whether true or false, also goes against the grain of asceticism. As Swamiji once enquired, when the issue of Gurus advertising their powers was raised, "Does a diamond need to declare it's a diamond? When you pass a sandalwood tree, can't you tell it by its scent?"

Swamiji's renditions of these two stories are thus shot through with the cultural bias against false Gurus, but the bias is recast to address the historical moment. Like many twentieth-century Gurus, the men in these stories charge exorbitant numbers of rupees for initiation; they advertise in a manner reminiscent of an industrial corporation (Advani's Guru could be found in full-page newspaper ads); they claim to have a "modern" message, presenting themselves as "scientists" who will usher in a "new age." Spirituality becomes a commodity that can be bought and sold. And at the forefront of the buyers are foreign disciples.

Gullible Foreigners

To reiterate a point made in earlier chapters, the "spiritual" East in contrast to the "materialistic" West is a historically embedded construct that derived from colonial perceptions of an Other. Though the source of this construct is with the West, the supposed bifurcation was appropriated by educated Indians who used it for their own ends: nationalism and Hindu reform. The foreign seekers of ultimate truth at the feet of Gurus are heirs to this construct, and by rejecting their own cultures in favor of a more "authentic" spirituality in the East, they only sustain the illusion of a polarization between East and West. Gurus can become the epitome of all that is good, wise, beautiful, and other-worldly. The sober fact that they may be fallible human beings—crafty, grasping, lusty—is all too often overlooked.

The first Guru to accept foreign disciples, as I have already noted, was Swami Vivekananda at the close of the last century. Through the twentieth century, interest in Gurus has waxed and waned in response to wider trends in Western culture. Despite the faddish aspect of some of this interest, a steady stream of Westerners has been finding its way into the ashrams of Gurus in the West as well as in India. Lacking a cultural context in which to place the roles of ascetic, Guru, or disciple, Western followers tend to be the shining-eyed purveyors of ideals. Gurus may be disapproved of in the wider culture, but within the pocket of a sect, the trope of the mysterious East comes into play. Even if in their own religious tradition there is folklore mocking monks, priests, rabbis, and other religious orders, the healthy cynicism maintained by anti-ascetic folklore in India is unknown to most Westerners who link up with a Guru. Through eyes colored by visions of the wholly spiritual land, the average *sādhu* is to be viewed more likely as a saint than the scoundrel he well may be.

In telling these stories about deceitful Gurus to audiences of Westerners, Swamiji appeared to be presenting them with the background of cultural knowledge about the potential pitfalls of sects. Characterizing "Gayatri," "Saraswati," "Narahari" and "Gulelal" as gullible disciples, Swamiji seemed to be exhorting them on the need to be discriminating. By comparing himself as the masquerading Guru and the nose-cutting disciple, Swamiji warned that discrimination should be applied in all cases, even to himself. Many of the foreigners who had been involved in other ashrams felt that Swamiji was different from the other Gurus they had known, in that he led them to question why they were in India at all, and why with him. "Go home to your country," Swamiji often said, "Bhagavan is there, too." He never levied fees for his teachings, and he encouraged them to visit other Gurus if they were interested. As "Gulelal" said, once again bringing up his disappointment in the ashram he had been lured to by the promise of instant enlightenment:

> Swamiji here encourages independence. He wants you to travel around, do *yātrā* [pilgrimage], be responsible for yourself. God visits people very rarely, and it's always terrifying when it happens. To create a world-wide spiritual movement on the basis of something that's not true is to dupe people. It can give you a few years of faith, but with a bitter aftermath.

Swamiji was often embroidering playful reasons for why the world was the way it was today, and one hot afternoon in 1983 he came up with a hypothesis for why foreigners were so involved in ashrams. After an afternoon nap, I had entered through the screen door to find Swamiji lying flat on the cool floor as Prakash Seth, a farmer from a nearby village, and "Pagaldas," an American from Oakland, sat nearby. Swamiji was musing over why it was that some contemporary Gurus kept foreigners "like slaves" in their ashrams. How could there be such injustice in the name of religion, he asked. He told us that according to his "upside-down thinking," Americans had previously taken slaves from Africa. Now the cycle of *karma*—consequences of past actions— brought retribution to the descendants of the slave-owners. Dark-skinned Gurus were hauling off these descendants to ashrams, rather than plantations, in India. The three of us present were all speechless with laughter. "Pagaldas," who had lived in other ashrams (where he learned Hindi and received this name), laughed loudest, nodding his frizzy, graying head of hair. Looking up at us from his position on the floor, Swamiji just grinned.

7. Death and Laughter

On the fourth of July in 1983, Swamiji's morning *darshan* was proceeding as usual. Prakash Seth, who had been helping Swamiji since his illness, opened the wooden door at 10 A.M. A group gradually grew around Swamiji's chair, assembling into the habitual divisions of space. On the women's side were "Gayatri," "Saraswati," and "Bhavani," as well as Meena Gupta and I. On the men's side, Swami Sadananda (who oversees the children's feeding program at the Saptashring ashram) sat closest to the altar, occupying the deerskin reserved for visiting ascetics. Gupta Saheb was beside him. Prakash Seth and Mr. Karnad stood, their arms crossed, near the back of the room. The *Durgā Saptashatī* tape was playing and incense smoke looped up from the altar. As Swamiji chatted with particular people the rest of us looked on, relaxed.

Half an hour into *darshan*, Vyas Dada, a dark, pot-bellied man who runs a restaurant in the vicinity, sailed in chewing betel leaf. With him was Bapu, the younger brother of the woman who had given Swamiji the house where he previously had lived. Bapu was a slight young man in his early twenties who worked with Vyas Dada. The appearance of garrulous Vyas Dada and retiring Bapu created a stir. As they settled down near Swami Sadananda, Swamiji's attention became focused on them.

"Bapu is my *bāp*," Swamiji teased, looking over the altar toward Bapu. "Maybe he's my father come back."

Bapu smiled and bashfully played with his fingers. The rest of us grinned.

Swamiji had been on a storytelling binge for the last few days. He had been privately telling me his life history, but also, in the public gatherings, he recounted a wide array of folk narratives. For the visiting Westerners, he ran through a condensed version of the *Mahābhārata,* starting with a jaunty English, "One day King, walking, going," and then lapsing, amid laughter, back into his usual Hindi which I translated. He told us humorous stories of *paṇḍits* who "fasted" by eating just rich sweets, of wandering storytellers, of cycles of wealth and worship. He launched into legends surrounding pilgrimage sites. He narrated fragments of the *Rāmāyaṇa,* asserting that there were always multiple versions, and that all over India the landscape was marked with stories of Ram, Sita, and Lakshman's wanderings. Just the day before, he had narrated the legend of "The Nose-Cutters." Today, when he began to grin broadly, the regular visitors who had been his audience through this spate of stories leaned forward. We sensed that another story might be at hand.

Sure enough, as melodies rippled from the tape recorder by the altar, Swamiji started into a legend, his voice strong and pleasure shining on his face. He looked at first toward Bapu but soon the story was addressed to all of us in the room. I switched on my own recorder and began to translate. Gupta Saheb, who sat nodding assent and punctuating Swamiji's sentences with "Humms," corrected me on occasion.

*   *   *

There was a Seth [wealthy proprietor; merchant]. The Seth's name was Nagpal.

[We laugh, for Nagpal is a wealthy industrialist known to most visitors. "Not your Bombay Nagpal," Swamiji assures. "Yes?"]

He lived in Ujjain. He was a very wealthy Seth. He built many houses.

["Did you hear this story?" Swamiji looks around through his glasses. Heads shake: No. Swamiji resumes, the smile broadening on his face.]

He built a house, a house that was very beautiful. He called in many skilled craftsmen. There was no other house like this in Ujjain. After building this house, there was still a little work left before it was completed. Just one or two days of work were left. Statues had been made all over the house: statues.* Many statues had been made. They all had to be painted. Then he was telling the craftsmen, "Look brothers, this house, my house, has turned out beautifully. No one here in Ujjain has a house like this. Even the government* doesn't have buildings* like this."

Those people said [respectfully], "This is true, Maharaj."

"As you paint these, give them the kind of color that will last for seven generations. It should appear very beautiful. For seven generations!"

[Kirin has been waiting for Swamiji to finish the last few lines before she translates, but he turns to her clarifying the Hindi pīṛhā with the English word "relation." "Generation*!" amends Kirin. Swamiji nods, his attention flicking from her back into the plot.]

"It should stay that beautiful.*" Just as he was finishing saying this, a Babaji like our Sadananda arrived there.

[Sandananda's eyebrows lift and he grins. He is a long-limbed, bearded man on the verge of middle age, with an ochre cloth wrapped around his waist.]

He arrived there and saw them just as the King was finishing what he said. Not the King, the Seth. [Swamiji hastily corrects, "The Seth, the Seth."] The Sadhu witnessed this. He laughed. He laughed inside his mind. Then he walked away.

The Seth saw him. "Why did this Maharaj laugh? What does this Babaji know? Babajis only know how to eat off other people! [We laugh.] What does he know about this house? He just laughed for no reason. He doesn't even know how to wear proper clothes!" ["Bhavani" lets out a chortle, possibly because Swamiji himself can be somewhat "tospy-turvy" in his appearance.] He kept quiet. But it stuck in his mind, "What did I do wrong? Why did he laugh?"

Then, he had a shop, a big shop. In the morning, he would give work to everyone and then go sit in the shop. He went there and sat down [Swamiji sneezes, then resumes], and as he sat . . . his business went on, tens of thousands of rupees of business. In front of him, all his employees packed things up; they filled trucks* of goods: all this went on. The Seth was sitting inside. There was a space for the Seth to sit and he was sitting there. He was keeping track of the cash.*

Just then a goat, you know, came running up to the Seth. He came and stood this close to him—[Swamiji's hands move to his right shoulder]. Behind him was a man who slaughters goats: a butcher. ["Slaughter*" echoes Gupta Seth, addressing himself to Kirin.] He came in, too. He said, "Seth, this is my goat, and I was taking him to be slaughtered. He slipped out of my hands and came up to you. Just push him out please. I want to take him to be slaughtered."

It came into the Seth's mind, "This goat has come to me. It's my job to save his life. Then, too, I am so rich." He asked the butcher, "How much does this goat cost? Let him go and I'll give you the money."

He said, "Maharaj, give me fifteen gold coins [*mohur*] for him."

[Kirin blithely mistranslates gold coin (*mohur*) as peacock (*mor*). "*Mohur, mohur*," corrects Meena Gupta grinning from beside Kirin. "Not peacock!" says Gupta Saheb in English. "What's a *mohur*, Swamiji?" Kirin asks in confusion. "Gold coin," Gupta Saheb explains. "Not just gold," Swamiji explains. "When you say one *mohur* you mean about four rupees. So fifteen *mohur* means sixty rupees. Yes?"]

"Give me that much money, and I'll leave the goat for you," he said.

It's a habit of Seths to think, "Why fifteen gold coins for a goat?"

[Amusement ripples from the Indians listening, for merchants are prover-bially stingy.] He said, "I'll give you fourteen gold coins for him." If you say ten rupees, it's their habit to say five!

["They want to negotiate," Gupta Saheb clarifies in English.]

The Seth said fourteen. The butcher said, "Maharaj you won't get him for fourteen. There's fifteen rupees worth of mutton* in this goat: fifteen gold coins. I brought him just after weighing him. If I slaughter him and sell the flesh, it's worth sixty rupees. That is rightfully mine. Now if you give me that much, I'll give him to you. Otherwise I can't give him to you." He said this once.

"Fourteen," said the Seth. Then he thought, "Whose goat is this any-way, and why pay money for him?" He didn't want to give even fourteen rupees. [We know Swamiji means *mohur,* but no one corrects him. We laugh again for the Seth is acting up to the tight-fisted stereotype.] "I don't want to slaughter this or anything else: what do I have to do with this goat? Why waste* money for no reason?" So he thought, "Somehow I should take back my words." He said, "If you want to give him to me for fourteen *mohur* then hand him over, otherwise take your goat away."

He said, "I won't give him up for fourteen *mohur.* If you won't pay fif-teen, give back the goat."

He said, "Fine. Take your goat away." He grabbed the goat by the ears and handed him over like this [Swamiji extends both hands].

As he was handing him over, just then the Babaji came up in front of him. The Babaji saw him doing this. The Babaji looked at him and laughed. As he was handing him over [Swamiji's hands are frozen in front of him and his head turns towards Sadananda], he saw the Babaji. The Babaji was laughing. He thought, "I've seen the Babaji again, what's going on? The Babaji is laughing." Then he remained silent. The Babaji went off.

Then after doing all his business,* the Seth went home around twelve or one o'clock. That day it was one year since his child was born. He had just one son. For a long time, he had had no children.

His wife was waiting for her husband to return. She had made nice food. It was a year since the child's birth. ["Burtha-day*" Swamiji ex-plains in English. "Bhavani" lets out a low, delighted chuckle.] As the hus-band was coming, she had set out a silver plate [*thālī*]. When he saw his father, the baby wiggled his head like this—[Swamiji bobs in his seat, shaking his shoulders, rolling his head]—the baby who was sitting in his mother's lap. She had made all kinds of preparations, was doing all kinds of things, had set out lots of fine sweets. She served sweets, she served fried bread [*pūrī*], she served all kinds of good things to eat. He was eating.

The baby was sitting in his mother's lap, wiggling his head, jumping around. [Swamiji demonstrates: an oversized infant wearing ochre. Watching him, it is impossible not to laugh.] He was jumping, the way babies do, pushing up straight [hunching his back, then suddenly flexing it; arms raised from the elbows and clenched at the fists]. When his mother saw this, she said, "Look how happy this child is when he sees you!"

He said [reaching out his hands], "Give him to me." He sat the baby down in his lap.

"Now you too feed him a bite or two since he's one year old," she said. So he also put a bit of those sweets into the baby's mouth. [Left elbow crooked as though supporting the baby, Swamiji thrusts the bunched fingers of his right hand toward it.] It was a baby. You have love* for a baby don't you? Just then—it's a baby's habit—he let out a stream of pee—*chulllll!* [Swamiji flings out his hand to show how far the pee went. Along with him, we are all helplessly laughing.] When he peed, it fell all over his father's clothes. "*Che-che,* he's peed!" he did this [distastefully flicking and wiping at his robes, then swiftly depositing the imaginary bundle over the edge of the chair]. When babies pee, you know, they pee quite a distance! Some fell on the plate, too. "What has this baby done peeing?" he said.

His wife said, "So what if he peed, he's your own child." She took the baby back.

Then he was sitting there eating from that very plate. The food that had been peed on was on one side, and he was eating from that very side. Not too much pee, just a little had fallen on the food.

Just then, once again the Babaji appeared. "Give me alms," [*bhavatī bhikshān dehī*][1] he called. Yes? The Seth heard this as he was eating. It was the same Babaji. The Babaji was laughing from over there.

Then he couldn't endure this in his mind. "I've seen him *three times* today, and all three times this Babaji has laughed! I must have made some kind of mistake, and that's why this Babaji is laughing. There seems to be some secret on his lips." So he immediately left his food. He went and prostrated at the Babaji's feet. "Babaji, what's going on? I've had *darshan* of you three times. I'm very fortunate to have done so. All three times you laughed; there seems to be some secret hidden in your lips. You're not saying anything. Why do you laugh, what is the reason? Tell me, what did I do wrong?"

He said, "It's nothing, *jī.* We *sādhus* are always laughing."

"No, no. There's something or the other in your laughter. You'll have to tell me."

He said, "If you want me to tell you why, you must come alone in the evening to the banks of the Sipra river. ["The Sipra river in Ujjain," Swamiji adds as an aside.] Come, and I'll tell you: at five o'clock."

"Fine," the Seth said.

He went there at exactly five o'clock. Talking away, the two of them walked some distance along the river bank. When they reached a deserted place, the Seth caught hold of the Babaji's feet. "Now tell me, why did you laugh?"

The Babaji said, "Forget about it, *ji*, why do you ask about everything? I just laughed for no particular reason."

"No, no, you must tell me something."

"What's this about? What should I tell you? Ask me."

He said, "This morning, as I was telling the employees to paint the statues. At that time, you looked at me, laughed, and went away. You didn't say anything, you just looked, laughed and left. What was the reason for this?"

["I'll give you a banana, Doctor Sahib," Swamiji motions to the doctor's youngest son who had come in with his lunch and is now slipping out the door. "I'll give you a nice banana." He breaks one from the bunch and hands it over as he continues speaking.]

The Babaji said, "Look, it's like this. What I specially saw was the great hopes a soul [*jiv*] has. You're going to die in seven days. You're thinking about seven generations. After you die, how does what becomes of the house matter to you? Why are you worrying about seven generations now? When I saw this, it made me laugh. He'll die in seven days and he's thinking about seven generations!"

"Will I die in seven days?!" [eyes widened with alarm].

"Oh*yes*!" [Swamiji's droll enunciation of English makes us all—especially the Westerners—laugh.]

"All right *ji*, let's forget that." [Swamiji's voice drops into a mumbling, worried, undertone, hand to his chin. We sit silent. There is a pause, and then his voice gathers strength for the next question.] "Then, when I was sitting in the shop and handing over the goat; at that time you laughed. Why was this?"

"Forget that *ji*, forget it," he said.

The Seth said, "You have to tell me that, too."

"Do you know who that goat is?" he asked.

"Who is he?"

"He's your father," the Babaji said.

"My father!" [Swamiji stares with alarm. Another wave of laughter breaks over the room.]

He said, "That butcher was a porter before. Your father told a lie about sixty rupees, he wrote this off and embezzled it from him; he wrote false accounts. Your father did a bad thing with this money when he embezzled it. Then your father died. When he died, according to his past actions [*karma*] he took birth as a goat. Then, the man who had been a porter couldn't earn enough and started working as a butcher instead. Now your father was a goat. He had to repay the money; the goat was caught. He had to repay the money, right? What does a goat have? His mutton would have to be sold. 'I gave my children great riches. My child will release me': he thought this and came to you.

[Here Kirin's tape snapped to the end, and, turning it over, she missed recording the next line: "The butcher asked for fifteen gold coins but you only want to give fourteen."]

"If you had only given the fifteenth gold coin your father would have been saved. You were miserly about four rupees, though you had eaten so much of his wealth—just because of four rupees you couldn't save your father. He had to give his mutton* to free himself of the debt. [Swamiji laughs low, amusement bubbling between his words.] By dying, he could return the debt. It was paid* off."

And the third thing the Seth asked was, "When I was at home, why did you laugh? The time I was eating my food."

He said, "Just forget about that, *jī*."

"No, you must tell me that, too."

"Do you know who your child is? Do you know why your child looked at you and laughed?"

He said, "What is it?"

"That child was your wife's lover in the past. He loved her. You had money in hand, you had him murdered. To get his revenge this man took birth as your child, in your house. You killed him then, and now he sits on your wife's lap! When he sees you, he wiggles his head, he laughs. [Laughter—especially from the women.] 'Now, what will you do to me? I sit here with such authority. Watch, I'll show you. You've talked about seven generations; in one generation I'll ruin your name. I'll make your name a bad name. I'll finish off all your wealth.' The child looks at you saying this. Then as you sit and feed him—you eat off a silver plate, right?—he says,

'Eat my piss' and he pees. [Laughter shakes the room.] You feed him with love. When I saw this, it made me laugh. You couldn't save your father because of four rupees; your enemy pees and you eat it! Thinking about the ways of the world, I laughed. No one knows what lies ahead. The Lord's play is strange and marvelous [*ajab*]. This is what made me laugh."

He said [brow laden with worry], "Will I really die in seven days?"

"You'll certainly die."

"How will I die?"

"You'll have a sharp pain in your head. [Kirin hesitates while translating and Swamiji proffers in English "headache!*"] You'll die because of this."

"If this is so, then what should I do?"

"Since this is so, you should divide your riches into four portions. One portion should be given to the poor. One portion should be kept for your wife and child. One portion should be given to a temple or a mosque. And one portion should be given to some friend or old person. Then this will all be of use to you. You'll definitely die."

That story is now finished.

*   *   *

"I said that Bapu is my father, that's why I told this story." Swamiji was smiling broadly as he emerged from the plot. He spoke in a low tone from the back of his throat. "He, too, is thinking over this."

Bapu, looking embarrassed, mustered a smile.

Swamiji laughed, turning from Bapu to the rest of us present. "I left home and came here; my father said, 'You left me, and now I won't leave you.' That's why I call him Bap; *bāp* means Father.* Finished."

It was now time to go. Though this had in many ways been a solemn story, Swamiji had told it with such verve and hilarity that we had been laughing through most of it. Smiles lingering on our faces, we stood up to receive bananas and move out the door for lunch.

Swamiji on Reincarnation

I returned later that afternoon to find Swamiji resting on the floor in the outer room. He leaned against one green wall with his legs outstretched and a tobacco box in his lap. Prakash Seth and "Pagaldas" were sitting beside him. Swamiji began to speak of Saptashring Nivasini Devi's shrine on the mountain. He described the symbolism of the image and how she was like Kundalini: the power coiled at the base of the spine which unfurls, through spiritual practices, to finally merge with the Supreme Divinity at the top of the head. After describing the Devi's form emerging from the rock face, he added that some people believed there was a cave behind the image. No one had ever seen the cave. And yet it was said that within this cave there was another, smaller image.

"Bhagavan only knows whether this is true or false," Swamiji laughed. "People, you know, start out with some small idea and make it big. It's possible, but no one has ever seen it. When no one has seen something, then I say, 'In your last life you were this and in the life before you were that. Who knows? You don't know, and I don't know either. But you can just accept what I say!'"

Swamiji went on to describe how a certain Guru he knew was believed to have been a king in a past life; someone had a dream about this, and the idea had grown to such proportions that it had actually become part of official biographies. I told Swamiji that in America I had heard of psychics who did "past life readings." "Why just America?" Swamiji asked, launching into a description of all the different Indian divinatory traditions that would tell a person of their past lives. "But there's no way to check," observed "Pagaldas," and Swamiji agreed.

So despite the comments linking Bapu with his father, Swamiji's discussion of reincarnation in other contexts indicates that he sees reincarnation as a possible hypothesis but not a foolproof explanation for the way lives turn out. A week later he told me about a girl in Lucknow who could remember her previous life in detail. Once again his attitude was that this was interesting material for a yarn, and yet there was so much to think about in this life that it was worthless to spend too much time worrying about past ones.[2] There were occasions, though, when Swamiji called on reincarnation as a possible way to comprehend suffering. One afternoon a few weeks later, as I chatted with him we could hear the screams of a burned girl who had been brought into the hospital next door. Swamiji had sent holy water and a packet of *kumkum* for her earlier. As the screams reverberated through the walls, Swamiji was visibly upset. "Why should this happen?" he asked. "She was cold from working in the rain in the fields, and warming herself, she came too close to the fire. Why should this happen? Maybe it was her destiny from a previous life [*prārabdh*]."

When Swamiji teased Bapu about having been his father, he was primarily punning on the nickname Bapu has carried from birth. *Bāp* means "father" in colloquial Hindi, but other people had called him this before Swamiji. Perhaps there were certain characteristics that Swamiji's father shared with Bapu; perhaps Swamiji saw a similarity between his own relationship with his father and his relationship with Bapu. Or perhaps this was a statement of guilt for having left home, and the sense that retribution would inevitably follow: "I left my father and came here, and now my father says, 'I won't leave you!'" There is no doubt a tangle of conscious and unconscious motives underlying the equation of Bapu and his own father, but I am wary of attributing intention to Swamiji's actions and prefer to go by what he has actually said. Laughing as he likened Bapu to his father, Swamiji seemed to be projecting more of a playful possibility than a solemn belief.

A Range of Occasions and Interpretations

Bapu also seemed to take Swamiji's words in jest. A few weeks later I asked him what he had thought when Swamiji called him his father. Bapu shrugged, smiling, "Yes, Swamiji sometimes says that. He teases me, but who actually knows?" Bapu was sitting cross-legged on the floor, his hair freshly oiled and his eyes earnest. He had just come in from his job in Vyas Dada's nearby hotel. Though more at home using Marathi, to me he spoke a rough, Marathi-strewn Hindi. He had been describing how he met Swamiji through his sister, and how gradually his affection for Swamiji grew. "When you talk to Swamiji," he said, "you feel that you are talking to Bhagavan. In every word of his you feel love flowing, just as though he's Bhagavan. When you talk to him, you feel peace in your mind. Sometimes Swamiji tells stories: short or long stories.* People listen to these attentively, and I, too, listen with care."

Of course, Swamiji tells this story on many different occasions when Bapu is not listening. "Narayani," a Jewish woman so dark she was regularly mistaken as an Indian, remembered this story as one Swamiji had told when a baby peed in her lap. A local woman had brought her baby along for *darshan*. "Narayani" had good-naturedly picked up the infant, overlooking the fact that plastic-lined Pampers are not generally used in India. Cooing and clucking, "Narayani" unexpectedly found her lap soaking wet, and the mother hastily retrieved her child. Swamiji was vastly amused and started off on the story of "The Seth and the Sadhu." He did not end by offering a hypothesis of who the baby could have been in a past life. But sitting on a sagging sofa in Albuquerque, "Narayani" grinned ruefully as she recalled the event. "He made me realize you just don't know what karma you have with anyone," she said.

Mr. Karnad, the retired journalist, used this story to comment on the way Swamiji retold stories on different occasions, to stress different themes. As he sat on a folding tin chair after lunch, Mr. Karnad opened the conversation by referring back to an exchange about storytelling that had occurred between Swamiji and me earlier that morning: I had observed to Swamiji that he told stories differently each time, and Swamiji had agreed. Mr. Karnad said, "At first I used to wonder why he was deviating from the original text. But now that you've told me, now, I've been realizing that there is a purpose in deviating from whatever he has said the previous time. Now, it occurs to my mind that on a particular occasion a particular theme must be stressed."

I asked Mr. Karnad if there was any story that he could think of to illustrate how Swamiji's retellings varied, and he began to narrate what he called the "Merchant and the Sannyasi." Given the nature of oral transmission, this version itself deviated from Swamiji's. Wrapping up the sequence along the river bank, Mr. Karnad said, "This story Swamiji tells in different forms, at different times, and stresses different points. . . . If I'm very greedy for money, I want fame or something; then he will stress on this point of building, and this and that and all, because I'm not going to take that thing away. . . . And if somebody is very jealous; say husband is jealous of the wife, or wife is jealous of the husband. They come and complain about it. 'Swamiji, see my husband is drinking, see my husband is not coming early at home.' Ah? All kinds of things Swamiji is told. See, for that he'll say, '*Abhī kyā karegā?* What can I do now? That is your husband, he's a grownup man now.' Then when he gets an opportunity, when they're there, husband and wife, then he'll just stress that point of being jealous: 'Don't murder like the paramour. This is a karma; bear a karma.'"

I reminded Mr. Karnard of the time, two years before, when Swamiji had told the story using reincarnation as a theme. "He said Bapu was like his *bāp*," Mr. Karnad clucked. "I would be very happy if Bapu could only understand the depth of meaning in this story." He went on to tell me that Bapu had subsequently married and moved away. From Mr. Karnad's point of view, this story was no jest, but had been used as an attempt to convey to Bapu that there was a strong tie between him and Swamiji. Mr. Karnad felt that Swamiji needed a young man like Bapu to help him with errands and other tasks. Bapu had not understood the story—understood that he was needed—and had departed to make his life elsewhere. (I should add that during my stay, Swamiji received several letters from Bapu and always spoke of him with warmth rather than as a deserter.)

"Narayani" and Mr. Karnad helped extend my sense of the multiple occasions that can spark a story and the multiple meanings toward which a single story can be slanted by Swamiji. A baby peeing like the child in the story; a pun like *bāpu*; the suspicion that someone is too possessive and unable to accept their mortality; the confessed jealousy of husband and wife: these constitute a sample range of occasions when this story about the Seth and Sadhu is evoked. Yet as long as Swamiji is still creatively applying stories to situations, the range remains open-ended.

Karma

Both Mr. Karnad and "Narayani" mentioned karma in their interpretations of why Swamiji told this story. The term "karma" is not only used by Indians today but has also seeped into the vocabulary of many young Westerners; I have heard it used almost as often in Berkeley as in Bombay or Nasik. It is often translated as "the fruits of past actions," and so would seem to be a simple enough notion. As a Hindu cultural concept, though, it is subject to historical variation in textual exegesis and to differing emphases in ethnographic regions of India.[3] In order to shed light on this story I began to read up on karma, to transform the implicitly known into a form that could be communicated.

Max Weber lauded the theory of karma as the "most consistent theodicy ever produced in history"[4]—by theodicy he meant an explanation for the existence of human suffering. Anthropologists who have done fieldwork in different parts of India point out, though, that karma is actually only one among the several explanations that may be offered when unfortunate events take place. One may have acted badly in the past; additionally, a deity might have been angered, a ghost may be hovering in the area, or some malicious person might have worked sorcery or cast the evil eye.[5]

Karma is what propels the individual soul forward on the roundabout of *saṃsār*, both in terms of "worldly" life and of rebirths. Good actions create good karma; one's next life is better than the last. Bad actions, such as swindling a porter, may cause one to fall from human birth to that of another animal like a goat. In another story that Swamiji tells, a dog whose head has been split open by a Brahman asks for justice; the punishment he requests is that the Brahman be put in charge of the biggest temple. This seems more like a reward than punishment until the dog explains that in his past life he had been the head of the very same temple, and it was because he embezzled the tempting temple funds that he now is condemned to life as a cur. Also, apart from folk narratives, classical medieval texts could go to great lengths in enumerating misdeeds and the kinds of animal birth that would ensue.[6] Of the life forms that one may be reborn in, the human body is considered the best. As Swamiji told the assembled group one afternoon:

> The human birth is the highest. Better than a tree, a fish, an animal, a bird, is birth in the human form. Why? Because human beings have the capacity for knowledge [*jnān*] and wisdom [*vijnān*]. With this power, people could even visit the world of the moon, and now we are going to Saturn. Any place that people have visited, and any disciplines they have practiced are because of knowledge and wisdom. If you want to earn knowledge and wisdom, you can do it through meditation [*dhyān*].
>
> How does one meditate? Meditation is within us, it is not something to be acquired from outside. Just sit resolved and tranquil. Don't worry about anything. Then the will-power* grows. The power of knowledge grows. If you worry—this thought, that thought, this thought—none of the thoughts add up to anything. Hold onto just one thought, putting your full trust into it.

Swamiji went on to describe the practice of listening to divine sound (*nād*), one of the many techniques he recommends for stilling the mind in meditation. Through meditation, Swamiji says, echoing many Gurus before him, people can come to know their inner divinity and eventually be freed from the weary cycle of births and rebirths. Through meditation and other spiritual practices, a *sannyāsī* can burn up past karma, change the karma of others, and triumph over death itself.

Karma is carried forward from past lives and created through actions in this one. Yet karma is not sealed in the destiny of one individual. It can in fact be exchanged between people who are closely connected: a wife may take on her husband's karma, a son may carry his father's karma, and so on. Karma can also be neutralized through the grace of a deity or holy person and by the performance of pious actions which include telling and listening to religious stories.[7] Disciples of a Guru often feel that he or she has the power to absolve their bad karma.[8] For example, I have heard it observed that a certain Guru often fell sick after festival days when too many people had touched his feet; it was believed that he had absorbed their illnesses and sins and then worked them out within his own body. Swamiji voiced a similar opinion one day when he had a severe bout of what he announced as "arithmetic . . . asthmatics . . . arthritix" (arthritis). He began to ponder over why so many *sādhus* were afflicted with bad health. He had already been playing with the analogy of a *sādhu* being like a washerman (*dhobī*) who washed other people's sins away. Now he extended the metaphor. "The dirt is washed out through worship. But dirt can stick to the person who is washing, too, can't it? Don't the washerman's clothes get dirty? So, the sins of others can stick to a *sādhu*'s body."

The average person is seen to be bound up in a tangle of relationships bred from past karma, generating new karma as he or she bumbles along. The enlightened *sādhu*, though, is freed from attachments and desires. This detachment allows him to act without manufacturing fresh karma—the world, to him, is a spectacle, a "play" (*līlā*).[9] He can discern the patterns of fate that entangle deluded others and even smile, like the Sadhu in this story, at their blindness. Although old karma propels the enlightened one's body forward, new karma is not created. So when a *sannyāsī* dies, there is no longer any impetus of karma remaining to throw the soul out into a new body. The enlightened holy person is said, at death, to achieve "union" (*samādhi*).

Commentary on the Story

The story of the Seth and Sadhu is one of the longest, most involved stories that I have heard Swamiji tell. In terms of genres, this story straddles the line between legend and folktale.[10] Taking place in a named locale, with a named person, Nagpal, it has the historical aroma characteristic of legends. However, the time frame is not pinned down, and events actually seem to occur in the suspended world of a folktale. The place where Swamiji locates this story is Ujjain, a pilgrimage site in central India, and one of the four places where all sects of *sādhus* assemble to bathe every twelve years. Like Nasik, other Kumbha Mela centers tend to draw *sādhus* even during the regular flow of daily life. Therefore Ujjain is a likely setting for an arrogant Seth to be confronted by a wandering *sādhu*. The holy river Sipra and the temple of Mahakala ("Great Time"), a form of Shiva, are the particularly sacred centers of Ujjain.[11] The divinization of time in the form of Mahakala lends a poignancy to a story set in Ujjain which plays on the mysteries of time and fate.

In Swamiji's retelling, contemporary time is fused with a lost past. Though gold coins are still in circulation, goods are transported in trucks. The Seth, boasting that his mansion filled with statues was even better than the government's buildings, brings images of colonial architecture to mind. Within the story, the time frame covering just one day unfurls back into the Seth's father's life, and forward seven generations. From the Seth's point of view, his conception of a life extending onward without a horizon is curtailed to just seven days. Interestingly enough, the number seven, which recurs in this story, can be linked to a *sannyāsī*'s divinatory powers. As the Abbé Dubois reports:[12]

> The sannyasi's staff with its seven knots is not merely intended to aid him in walking. It is, like Aaron's rod, an instrument of divination. The seven knots are also not without a mysterious significance. Who has not heard of the perfection of the number seven? The high esteem in which it is held by the Hindus is clearly proved by the numerous sacred places and objects which are always spoken of in groups of seven.

The Sadhu in this story is not described as having a staff, yet he bears the power to penetrate the mysteries underlying destiny and time expressed in terms of seven. The structure of the story is oriented around an unveiling of the Sadhu's power and a revelation of the mysteries which bring a laugh to his lips. The story moves forward in four sequences. Three times the Sadhu laughs. Implored by the Seth to tell why he laughed, in the fourth sequence the Sadhu explains. He laughed at the vanity of a man who worried about a mansion lasting seven generations when he had only seven days to live. He laughed at the miserliness of a man who neither recognized nor would rescue his father reborn as a goat. He laughed at the man eating food spattered with urine from his wife's ex-lover, whom he had arranged to be murdered yet who was now his son. Finally, the Sadhu assures the Seth that he will die but instructs him on a way to shed the bad karma clinging to him. By dividing his material goods, the Seth can absolve himself of the past.

From the Seth's point of view this is a tale of revelation. As the story proceeds, he grows increasingly respectful toward the Sadhu. This growing respect matches the movement from distrust to veneration that accompanies recognition of a particular *sādhu* as a man of power. "What does this Babaji know?" thinks the Seth in the beginning. "Babajis only know how to eat off other people! What does he know about this house? . . . He doesn't even know how to wear proper clothes!" These attributes that the

Seth criticizes are precisely those distinguishing the ideal ascetic committed to a life of poverty, simplicity, and wandering. The second time the Seth sees the Sadhu laugh, haughty derision is displaced by a growing disquiet. With the third laugh, the Seth is humble. He prostrates at the Sadhu's feet: an act signifying respect and submission. The Seth who had sneered is now a supplicant. He beseeches the Sadhu to explain the "secret on his lips" and ends up understanding this secret as his own, mysterious destiny. Though the Sadhu will not avert the Seth's death, he can advise the Seth on the actions that will expunge his sins before he dies. In terms of pro-ascetic cultural propaganda, this is the story of a man who jeered at an ascetic and then learned better.

From the Sadhu's point of view, on the other hand, the story emphasizes the irony of a householder's life. His perspective on the situation is that of a liminal outsider to the settled world of householders. The Sadhu appears momentarily on the outskirts of houses and shops, but comes into his own in the solitude of a sacred place. The wealth of the Seth, who builds grand buildings, amasses money, and eats off silver plates accentuates the contrast between the life-style of householders and ascetics. Yet, though the Sadhu wanders possessionless outside the lives of householders, he understands their lives better than they do. His detached, liminal perspective allows for a breadth of vision that moves beyond specific events to karma extending over lifetimes. The vision (*drishti*) of a realized Guru (who, in Swamiji's interpretation, is also a principle pervading all beings) is extolled in the *Guru Gītā* (59) chanted in the morning in many ashrams and also around Swamiji's altar in Nasik.[13]

> Creating all the worlds, nourishing all things,
> A vision that understands the scriptures in entirety,
>   a vision that discerns the emptiness of wealth.
> Obliterating all defects, a vision fixed on the ultimate state.
> Though giving rise to worldly qualities,
>   a vision set on the path of salvation.

Falling at the Sadhu's feet and beseeching his guidance, the Seth is acknowledging him as Guru. The Guru's penetrating vision becomes the source of his salvation. The Sadhu discerns that the Seth who has defined himself through wealth can only shed the accumulated bad karma by giving this all away. Only then will the material riches be "of use" to him in a spiritual sense that spans lifetimes.

All through the story, money is represented as a source of evil. The means to build a house even grander than the government's breeds pride in the Seth. As he sits in his shop doing tens of thousands of rupees of business, his attachment to money blocks him from spending the sixty rupees required to free the goat. The goat, in turn, is what his father has become to pay back the porter from whom he embezzled sixty rupees. To gain this money, the porter must slaughter the goat (and from the brahmanical point of view, slaughtering an animal is also a sin). Because of his money, the Seth could have his wife's lover executed; now the lover returns as a baby who pees on expensive sweets and plots to finish off the family funds. Just as karma is transferred through a lineage, it is also passed along with the money deviously amassed by the Seth's father.

While another one of Swamiji's stories illustrated the theme that "money earned through hard work buds, swings, and blossoms," this story dramatizes the principle that money earned by dishonest means will only bring ruin. This ruin can only be averted by division and distribution of his riches. By giving only one quarter to his wife and child, he will curtail the murdered lover's plan to squander all the accumulated wealth. The other three quarters will go to charitable causes: the poor, the old, and religious institutions. The Sadhu's nonchalance as to whether the religious institution to be endowed is a Hindu temple or Muslim mosque reflects Swamiji's own attitude that all religions are equal. (This view extends beyond Swamiji to his hero, Mahatma Gandhi, and to saints associated with the *bhakti* movement who synthesized Hindu and Islamic elements in their formulations of religion.) According to this story, then, tainted money can be laundered by being poured into worthy causes, regardless of the boundaries separating religions. Significantly, the Sadhu does not ask for any money himself. Unlike the greedy false Gurus encountered in the last chapter, the Sadhu demonstrates by his poverty, modesty, and readiness to help others that he is genuine.

Other Versions

In Swamiji's version and in Mr. Karnad's retelling, the Sadhu predicts death but will not alter it. In two other cognate north Indian variants I have manged to unearth, the ascetic who has laughed is also willing to dispense advice on how to forestall death.

The first variant is from Maive Stokes's *Indian Fairy Tales*.[14] Stokes was the daughter of a colonial administrator who filled her spare time on the hot subcontinent by coaxing her servants to tell stories. Her ayah, Muniya, told this story in Hindustani, and Stokes entitled it, "How the Fakir Nanaksa Saves the Merchant's Life." Here, the holy person who laughs three times at a grain merchant is the Fakir Nanaksa, identified in a footnote as the founder of the Sikh faith, Guru Nanak (1469–1538). The title *fakīr* is a Muslim equivalent of *sādhu,* and Guru Nanak is well known for his harmonious blending of Islamic and Hindu elements in the construction of Sikhism.

The Fakir laughs when a goat being led for slaughter escapes from the person leading him and hides behind the grain merchant, only to be sent off to meet his death. He laughs again when an old woman being escorted for execution hides behind the merchant and she is also evicted. The third time he laughs is when the merchant's baby daughter wakes up and begins to scream, pulling at her mother's clothes. In all three cases, it is the merchant's wife who observes the laughter, and it is she who confronts the Fakir, demanding to know why he laughed. Brandishing a knife, she even threatens to kill the Fakir if he does not disclose the reasons that he laughed. He explains that the goat was her husband's father, who, for just four rupees could have been saved. The old woman was the husband's grandmother, and with just twenty rupees he could have bought her a reprieve. The child was the husband's sister whom the wife had tormented while she was alive; now reborn, she tormented her mother. The Fakir then goes on to proffer the unsolicited information that the husband will die the next day at ten. He instructs the wife to make sweetmeats and go out to waylay the angels of death. The angels eat the sweets and return to God without the merchant. With all the authority of a cosmic administrator, God writes a letter assuring the merchant of a twenty-year lease on his life and dispatches it down with the angels. At a thanksgiving dinner, the Fakir instructs everyone to hide their hands in their faces and worship God. He disappears as they do so and is never seen again. The merchant and his wife, on the other hand, live on happily.

Another variant was recorded in Jaunpur, north India, by a schoolmaster called Raghunath Sahay fifteen years later, in 1895. He elicited this story from one Gokul Prasad and contributed it to the journal *North Indian Notes and Queries* founded by colonial administrators to understand the "native mind."[15] This is an example of an "educated native" eliciting folklore from his fellows and sending it to a British editor for European consumption. In this story, it is Narada Muni (who appears as "Narad" in

Chapter 10) who laughs three times. He laughs first when he sees a man hauling along a male goat; the goat asks the man in a language he does not understand why he is causing him so much trouble when in his past life he brought him comfort. The King of the land has ordered that whoever laughs must be brought in for an explanation. Narada Muni is arrested, and he haughtily informs the King that he laughed because it was his pleasure. He is fined a *lakh* (10,000 rupees) and as he has no money, a banker pays for him. As he goes home with the banker, the banker orders one of his employees to collect an outstanding payment, and Narada Muni laughs again. He is brought to court a second time and is fined a second *lakh* of rupees. Again the banker pays, and again Narada laughs. Once more, the banker produces the sum. The banker's son then enquires why he laughed. Narada explains that he laughed when he saw the father collecting money because the father was to die that night and did not know it. The boy asks how he will die and how to avert the death. Narada advises that a tank should be dug for a *lakh* and a quarter of rupees and that the father should be placed on it; when he dies, the snakebite should be ignored and the death should instead be blamed on Parameswar ("Great Lord," indicating Bhagavan Vishnu). Then Narada proceeds to Vaikuntha (Vishnu's Heaven) where he refuses to salute Parameswar. Parameswar asks why, and Narada accuses him of killing a man. Parameswar denies this, but Narada insists that he come and see. They descend to earth and witness the son beside his father's corpse bewailing that Parameswar killed him. Parameswar is suitably embarrassed, and brings the banker back to life. Then the two return to Vaikuntha. The editor, William Crooke, adds a note to the story—"A curious example of the manner in which these great saints bully and control the greater gods."

A saint and a rich man; three laughs; a goat being led away; an underlying reason for laughter connected with money, past lives, or forthcoming death—the continuities between these two stories and Swamiji's indicate that they are all related. Whether the Sadhu, the Fakir Nanaksha, or Narada Muni, all three holy men in these variants display a distance from affairs of the world and a capacity to penetrate the underlying workings of fate.

Although the Sadhu can predict death and issue instructions on how to alleviate bad karma, he has no interest in prolonging life. The difference between Swamiji's version, where fate cannot be transformed, and the two versions cited above, matches a deep-rooted paradox in Hindu thought that the Sanskritist W. Norman Brown has discussed in terms of folk literature.[16] As Brown points out, many stories illustrate the futility of overcoming human destiny, which is ruthlessly preordained. There are other stories, though, that show how destiny may be overcome: by human shrewdness or by divine aid. The two views identified by Brown in folklore appear to operate in ethnographic contexts as well. Sheryl Daniel, who conducted fieldwork in Tamil Nadu, labels these opposing views as Free Will versus Determinism and observes that people may call on either concept according to the situation that requires interpretation.[17] Lawrence Babb, building on Daniel's data, points out that the shifting between Free Will and Determinism produces differing emphases on human responsibility: people are either accountable for their actions or unwittingly play out the results of past actions.[18] Amid the fog of "psychological indeterminacy"[19] hovering about the theory of karma—can people ever know how the past and future are arrayed around the present?—an enlightened *sādhu*'s penetrating vision is like a shaft of sunshine throwing destiny into sharp relief. Swamiji, his disciples say, is a *sādhu* who can see the past and the future; to their ears, stories are among the ways he tosses out clues.

Oedipus and Reincarnation

All three versions of "The Seth and the Sadhu" dwell upon the relationships between children and parents. In the version featuring Narada, hostility between a parent and child of the same sex is not commented on (unless one argues that the son's hearing of the father's death represents a wish-fulfillment). In the versions of both Stokes and Swamiji, though, the Oedipus complex is clearly an issue. It is considered from the parent's rather than the child's point of view,[20] and is phrased in the idiom of reincarnation. A woman's lover, murdered by her husband, returns as her son to sit in her lap and suckle at her breast; he kicks his father, and shows ultimate disdain by polluting the father's food with urine. Stokes's version is told by a woman from a woman's perspective, and the rival from the past life is the husband's sister. Because the jealous wife mistreated her sister-in-law, after dying the sister-in-law is reborn as a daughter to punish her. The bond between brother and sister in the traditional Hindu family bears an emotional intimacy that is rarely shared with a wife.[21] The choice of a sister-in-law rather than lover as the rival for a husband's affections makes sense in terms of the logic of Hindu familial relations. In both Swamiji's and Stokes's versions a child has been intimate with the parent of the opposite sex in a past life and experiences strong emotions of dislike and revenge toward the parent of the same sex.

In the kinship systems of northern India, a daughter is "born to be given away"; her place is in her husband's family. A son, on the other hand, bears responsibility for the welfare of his father's soul and the future of the family name. It is the son who offers rice balls (*piṇḍ*) in rituals for the deceased, to nourish the soul on its journeys after death. This dependence on a son after death is expressed by the father, now a goat, running to the Seth or grain merchant to be saved. In Swamiji's version, the father's helpless dependence on a son for what transpires after death is also mocked by the baby boy. "Watch, I'll show you," says the child enthroned on his mother's lap. "You've talked about seven generations; in one generation I'll ruin your name."

In Swamiji's version, fathers and sons figure largely in terms of both actual blood relations and symbolic paternalism. There is the Seth and his father-turned-goat. There is the Seth and his plotting son. But also, the relationship between the Seth's father and his porter is equivalent to that between a father and son, and an employer's abuse of an employee leads to retribution. Furthermore, the Sadhu himself is a father figure. He is, in fact, addressed as "Babaji," which is an affectionate way of saying "respected father" and is a term widely used for holy men, including Swamiji himself.

Adopting a Guru is like adopting a father, with all the connotations of submission that the father-son relationship carries in traditional India. The Sanskritist Robert Goldman has argued that in the great Indian epics, Oedipal conflict is often presented in a disguised form, involving surrogate father figures such as a Guru or elder brother.[22] While Goldman's evidence of conflict with Gurus cannot be denied, it must also be balanced with the widespread idealization of the Guru-disciple relationship. For as G. Morris Carstairs points out, the Guru is viewed by many as a benevolent parent figure; the tension and sense of restraint present in relating to an actual father are absent with the Guru, who is perceived instead as compassionate and powerful, and generous in his blessings and promises of self-knowledge.[23] The Guru, in fact, seems to mix both masculine and feminine qualities: the authority of a father and the warm nurturing of a mother. As a perfected being, the Sadhu in this story, though father-like, meets the Seth without tension. Rather than being caught in the egoistical bonds of a relationship, the Sadhu stands aside, compassionate but amused.

Laughing at the World

As an isolated act, laughter can span a range of meanings from joy and delight to impishness, irony, sarcasm, and outright malice. The Sadhu's laughter in this story is presented as a characteristic he shares with other *sādhus*. When the Seth asks him why he laughed, he brushes off the question saying, "It's nothing, Sir. We *sādhus* are always laughing." Laughter has been identified as a recurrent "psychic motif" in Hindu fiction by Maurice Bloomfield, who summarizes Stokes's version of this story, then goes on to cite other stories in which *sādhus,* both genuine and false, laugh.[24] Swamiji himself was often laughing, his gums toothless and his shoulders shaking; around him, people broke into laughter, too. Why in all these instances are *sādhus* associated with laughter? What is it in their relationship toward the world that causes them to laugh?

As the Sadhu in the story explains, "Thinking about the ways of the world, I laughed. No one knows what lies ahead. The Lord's play is strange and marvelous. This is what made me laugh." In other words, he was laughing as someone outside the world viewing those entangled within it. His laughter is associated with his liminality. From the ascetic perspective, the world filled with attachments and plans is nothing but a fleeting illusion: a divine play (*līlā*). While householders scramble about, *sādhus* have the leisure to stand back and watch, deeply amused.

"Prabhu," the hypnotherapist, described Swamiji in a way that reminded me of the Sadhu in this tale. "People would come," he said, "whole families, with problems. They would be telling their problems so seriously but Swamiji would begin to joke and laugh and tell a story. Nothing is below his dignity; everything is valid in its own way. So people naturally feel welcomed. Whatever you may be experiencing, he would listen very sincerely. What amazed me was how he would turn it around and be amused. It wasn't at the expense of the people. It was just a deep amusement at the ways of the world."

On these occasions that "Prabhu" describes, people sometimes seemed a little startled. Here they were unburdening weighty concerns, and here was this old man leaning back in his chair, laughing as though these concerns were light and insubstantial. After a moment, the surprise would melt, and they often joined in the laughter. This was especially the case if Swamiji had told a comic story about a similar dilemma. (There were other times, however, that when a troubled person came in empathy would glaze over Swamiji's face, his brows would draw together, and his voice would fall into low, comforting tones.) When telling stories, Swamiji's delivery and droll characterization often bonded his audience in laughter. As laughter flooded through the room, hierarchy and differences were momentarily leveled. Men and women, Indians and Westerners, *sādhus* and householders, the old and the young: these differences were temporarily swept away by our waves of laughter.

While humor suspends hierarchy to generate the warm bonds of communitas—however temporarily—it can also challenge established patterns of thought.[25] In the case of the *sādhus,* these established patterns which laughter subverts are related to attachments in the world. The laughter derides excessive seriousness, a clinging to possessions, plans for the future in which death inevitably looms. The laughter calls attention to what endures, for while karma generates karma, the Inner Self remains undauntedly serene. As Swamiji said (and I have tried to remind myself on gloomy days), "You should go through life laughing. In times of happiness, laugh. In times of trouble, laugh too. The trouble doesn't touch the Inner Self. *That* is always joyful."

Death and Asceticism

"Everyone has to die someday," Swamiji informed a young couple who visited one morning from Poona. They were solicitously asking after his health and looked very taken aback when the conversation bounced directly to death. "You might as well die laughing," Swamiji continued. "This is what I think. You can go crying or laughing. You *have* to go, but you can choose how to do it." The couple smiled at this statement, rolling their heads in agreement.

This comment is typical of Swamiji, who speaks without embarrassment about dying. Like the Sadhu in the story, he has a matter-of-fact acceptance of death. He sees it is an inevitability, something to be confronted and laughed about rather than glossed over. My notes are full of his quips about his own forthcoming death. During my 1983 visit, he was still recovering from a severe heart attack. "My ticket up was canceled," he grinned. "Because I'm ready for death any moment it seems that death is avoiding me." He made repeated references to the body, which would go, in contrast to the soul (*ātman*), which is eternal, everlasting, and divine. "Everybody's body will go," he earnestly tapped his arm. "No one's will stop over. Don't meditate on this but what's inside. *That* is imperishable." He refused to make engagements even a few weeks ahead, because he said it was a good thing to keep one's word, and who knew whether he'd still be alive? "When I go to sleep at night," he observed, "I think I might not be here in the morning. The Mother gives life and She takes it away."

Throughout my 1985 stay, my brother Rahoul was seriously ill in the United States. There was little hope that he would recover, and in fact, he died soon after my return. My daily interactions with Swamiji were shadowed by the loss my family was facing and by an acute sense of being split, even in sorrow, across continents. Swamiji's attitude was of gentle concern. He asked me every day whether I had received any news. He enquired about the illness and all possible modes of treatment. He placed the entire issue in the hands of the Divine Mother. "If She wants to do something, She'll do it. He will recover. It's all up to Her." When I left India, Swamiji sent blessings to my brother, along with packets of *kumkum* from his worship of a silver Shri Yantra, symbolizing the Goddess. We placed this *kumkum* daily on my brother's forehead until we were placing it on a corpse in a hushed hospital room. Swamiji's calm acceptance, his location of the terminal illness within a framework of divine will, and his contribution of ritual materials that gave us something to do when we were helpless showed me just how a *sādhu's* detached perspective can soothe those confronting the crisis of death.

On the afternoon of Dashara, a festival day in October, Swamiji sat sampling and distributing sweets from all the boxes people had brought. Isabel remonstrated, reminding him of his diabetes. Swamiji looked up from the box of luscious milk sweets in his lap and declared, "Lots of sugar! If you don't eat sugar on Dashara, then when will you? I have mathematics, no arithmetics. Arthritis. It will be with me till my death. Like your brother. . . ." Swamiji pointed his chin in my direction and said, "There's nothing now for me to do but wait and see when I die. I'm eating to hurry it up." Isabel was shaking her head, vehemently repeating, "*No* Swamiji, *no* Swamiji!" But Swamiji continued, unperturbed. "What's it to you?" he asked Isabel. "Do *you* get a stomach ache if I eat sweets?" "It's bad for your health," Isabel said. "I want to die," countered Swamiji. As I wrote that night, "Makes death seem a game; something to be met with a shrug of the shoulders and a laugh."

Swamiji's flippant attitude makes sense in terms of the classical model of *sannyās* as the fourth stage of life in which a person prepares for death. The *Laws of Manu* enjoins the *sannyāsī* to behave much as Swamiji does:

> Let him not desire to die, let him not desire to live; let him wait for (his appointed) time as a servant (waits) for the payment of his wages [VI:45]. . . . Let him quit this dwelling, composed of the five elements, where the bones are the beams, which is held together by tendons (instead of cords) where the flesh and the blood are the mortar, which is thatched with the skin, which is foul-smelling, filled with urine and ordure, infested by old age and sorrow, the seat of disease, harassed by pain, gloomy with passion, and perishable [VI:76–77]. . . . He who leaves this body, (be it by necessity) as a tree (that is torn from) the river bank, or (freely) like a bird (that) quits a tree, is freed from the misery (of this world, dreadful like) a shark. [VI:78]

The initiation ritual for *sannyās,* in fact, involves the performance of one's own death rites, and so a *sannyāsī* symbolically dies to the world even before the body is ready to go. This is a social death preceding a biological one,[26] and since it can be controlled through human actions, it represents a triumph over death. Yogic practices like the retention of semen, the suspension of breath, the stilling of the mind, are also involutions of life-processes and so put death within the province of human control.[27] With *samādhi,* union, the ultimate state of mystical practice, all dualities collapse and the bounded individual self merges with the divine Self. Outer activity ceases as concentration becomes focused within. In this state, it is said, a *sādhu* can choose whether to become dissolved in a cosmic union or to return to action in a body. This is why it is widely believed that enlightened ascetics can predict and decide the hour of their death. As Shri Shankar Lal, interviewed by Carstairs, explained:[28]

> Such a man, who is coming near to perfection, he is able to see his death before it comes, and tell his family that on such a day, at such a time, he will die; and so it happens. There are others who leave the world of their own will, at a given moment they tell their followers to bury them alive, at such a time, and then they sit in meditation and so they are buried, without having died: this is *samādhi.*

When life leaves an ascetic's body, the linguistic convention is not to say that he or she "died" (*mar gayā, guzar gayā, dehānt huā*) but rather that he or she "left the body" (*sharīr choṛā*) or "took *samādhi*" (*samādhi liyā*). The shrine where the body is interred becomes known as a *samādhi* where the spiritual presence of the ascetic remains alive. In fact, if the ascetic slipped away during meditation, there is some question as to whether death even occurred. At Alandi, a several hours' trip from Nasik, the *samādhi* of the young poet-saint Jnaneshwar has drawn pilgrims since the thirteenth century, and it is widely believed that he sits within, peacefully oblivious to the flow of time.

Other saints who take *samādhi* do not even leave a body behind. This is the case with Tukaram, another poet-saint, who is believed to have ascended into the sky as he sang praises of Vithoba, the form of Vishnu who has sparked such rich Marathi devotionalism.[29] Swamiji himself had an ancestor who floated up into the sky, leaving his clothes behind. He told me about this man in the course of relating events from his childhood. Swamiji was sitting on his bed, legs resting on a stool and shoulders slumped against a cushion. The light was soft in this room, and the scent of incense strong as he told me how he had gone to live with his maternal uncles near Mysore after his mother died.[30] Beside this house was a temple and also a *samādhi* shrine.

> There was a man; my mother's, mother's father's father. [Swamiji counted these off on his fingers, then raised his hand.] Four generations. At the time of leaving his body he became invisible. I didn't *see* this, I just heard it. What happened is that he sat to perform worship [*pūjā*]. He was wearing ochre. It was the month of Dhanu—November, December—on a full moon day. And in the middle of doing his worship, he began to ascend. He rose up into the sky as the people were sitting and watching. Then the ochre clothes he was wearing fell down, but not his body. They made a *samādhi* with these clothes. There, in my mother's grandfather's house. The *samādhi* still stands today.

This ancestor was not a *sannyāsī*, Swamiji said, but wore ochre when he worshipped. If *karma* is passed along through the blood, the piety of this man can be seen as carrying on in Swamiji himself. It was significant, I thought, that on the winter full moon of this *samādhi* Swamiji recognized Saptashring Nivasini Devi as the large-eyed face that had appeared to him in his childhood. Though Swamiji does not directly connect his *sannyās* to the saintly ancestor, this man is probably among the models that orient Swamiji's view of his role and life.

When an enlightened being does not outright ascend into the clouds but leaves a lifeless body behind, this is treated differently from a lay corpse. Cremation, the norm for lay adults, is virtually never performed for a *sannyāsī*. This is because with cremation, the body is presented as a sacrificial offering to the fire.[31] Since a *sannyāsī* has already sacrificed himself on initiation, he is no longer a worthy offering. Instead, the *sannyāsī* is thrown into water or interred in salt. When Swamiji spoke of his own inevitable death with almost chilling ease, he reminded us that he wanted his corpse to be thrown into the Narmada river so crocodiles and fish could be helped out with a meal. Swami R. urged that he should have a *samādhi* shrine, perhaps on the Saptashring mountain, but when I left nothing had been decided.

I have never seen a *sannyāsī's* funeral rites, but once again, scholarship provides a window into unknown experience. The most lively account I found is by J. C. Oman and dates from the turn of the century. Oman's eye for comic detail sometimes carries the danger of parodying "the natives" but he has quite a talent for evoking the chaos, color, and startling juxtapositions of collective events in India.[32]

> One morning about ten o'clock I overtook a strange procession—strange even for India—wending its way slowly through the Lahore Mall between the Chief Court and the Cathedral. A loud brass band led the way, discoursing music—European music, too; for it was not difficult to make out the tune of the once-popular song—
>
> > Just before the battle, mother,
> > I was thinking of you.
>
> Behind the musicians came some three or four men carrying smoking censers of sweet incense. They were marching in front of a litter borne on the shoulders of a few men . . . the occupant was a dead *sādhu*, sitting in vacant contemplation with his legs crossed in the approved manner. He was tied to the upright back of the litter and was covered with strings of flowers, which formed a sort of floral veil over his face but could not conceal the hideousness of death, as the unconscious head rolled helplessly from side to side, keeping time, in a sort of grotesque mockery, to the measured step of the bearers as they marched slowly along the wide road. . . .
>
> I ascertained that the party was on its way to a selected spot where the *sādhu*, a Sanyasi [*sic*] would be buried in a circular grave, sitting upright and covered over with salt. This funeral procession brought to my recollection a similar one I had seen many years previously at Rajamundry, in the Madras Presidency. On that occasion, the dead *sādhu* was placed in a sitting position in his grave, a quantity of salt was piled up above him, and earth thrown in till the body was nearly covered up. Then upon the top of the shaven head, still exposed to view, a large number of cocoanuts [*sic*] were broken in order

to crack the skull and afford the imprisoned soul a means of exit from the now useless body. The fragments of the cocoanuts which had been used for the liberation of the dead man's soul were, I remember, eagerly sought by the bystanders.

According to the Abbé Dubois, who witnessed similar burials in the southern region of India, bits of coconut cracked on a dead *sannyāsī*'s skull are believed to make barren women bear children.[33] This may be interpreted as a case of death blossoming into the regeneration of life[34] and also of the erotic fertility associated in Hindu thought with controlled sexuality. The cross-legged position simulates meditation, and the *rudrāksh* beads which are customarily hung over a *sannyāsī*'s corpse are believed to contain his spiritual power.[35] Gold and jewels may be thrown into the pit before the exposed head is covered over with salt. If the ascetic who died is a Guru with a large following, a shrine is built above his burial place. This may carry a Shiva *lingam* and often, today, a statue of the Guru cast in bronze or silver. Since the power and presence of an enlightened person are believed to permeate the burial site, the *samādhi* of a well-known saint may become a center of pilgrimage.

In his classic overview of yoga, Mircea Eliade writes, "The exemplary image of the conquerer of death as presented in folklore and literature corresponded precisely with that of the *jivan mukta,* of the man "liberated in life," the supreme goal of all yogic schools."[36] The Sadhu in Swamiji's story who penetrates the mysteries of life and death is a precipitation of this image into folk narrative. He shows how the *sannyāsī* has, through initiation and spiritual practices, gained a cool mastery over Death, who chases householders.[37] In this way, it seems, the figure of the enlightened *sannyāsī* serves to lift uncertainty and terror from death for the culture at large. Through this living example, people learn that there is meaning in death and that it may be controlled; and so fearlessness becomes a possibility for everyone.

Swamiji was still talking about death when I returned to India bearing the dissertation which included a version of this chapter. His health had been steadily failing and doctors advised a coronary bypass, but he felt there was no point for this fuss and expense. "A body is just a body," he said, making me think of Manu, whom I had cited on death. "It's like a house you live in for a while. And this one is getting old. No matter what anyone does, it's falling apart like any old house. Mend the ceiling and a wall caves in, mend the wall and the plumbing goes bad, mend the plumbing and the floor needs repair. This one here is like a peasant's hut, it isn't even made of cement. That's why I need to live beside a craftsman!" We all laughed, knowing that he was referring to his doctors upstairs. "One day though," Swamiji cheerily continued, "it'll just fall down and nobody will be able to do anything about it."

The next morning, he talked not about what could be destroyed but what endured. "The soul [*jīv*] has many experiences," he said. "It should use these to merge with the Absolute [*brahman*] at the top of the head [*sahasrār*]. The soul has come from the Absolute and will return there. When we say *brahmā* what do we mean? First, it can mean delusion, can't it? Or the imagination [*kalpanā*]? And then Brahma is the creator, too. Imagination, you can say, is what creates this universe. The imagination has no form. The creator, too, has no form. Then, if you look into the matter, we aren't born and we don't die. We are born and we die in the mind. . . ." Swamiji went on to say that though forms were in flux, nothing in the universe was ever destroyed. "Forms change, Bhagavan is the same. So why should anyone grieve or cry?"

8. Heaven and Hell

Though Swamiji now lives in Nasik, he visits his old ashram on the Saptashring mountain once a year, at the time of the radiant October moon. The annual visit rolled around toward the end of my second extended trip, and Swamiji had offered to take me along. Freshly bathed and dressed in a silk sari for the occasion, I waited in the carriage area of our family bungalow. In my childhood we had been the last house on the road with a view that swept out toward mountains in the North. But Nasik had grown. As I looked out in the direction we would later drive, I could no longer see any mountains but only the people of an apartment building starting their morning routines. A man chewing at a *neem* stick stared down at me curiously, a woman stepped out to hang a wet towel over the balcony. The sunshine was still cool as it touched the tumble of crimson bouganvillea near our gate. The slant and sharpness of the morning light reminded me that the monsoon was over and winter would soon be here.

A Fiat taxi painted yellow on top, black below, swept into the driveway shortly before seven. This was Vyas Dada's taxi, and he had offered to drive Swamiji the several hours to Saptashring. In the front seat beside Vyas Dada sat Madan and bespectacled Dr. Mukund. Swamiji was cross-legged and grinning in the back seat, ochre cloth drawn over his head. I fit myself and my bag in beside him, keeping my tape recorder and blank cassettes handy just in case I should need them.

Sure enough, Swamiji was in a storytelling mood. As we proceeded past villages, children, and goats scampering off the road, he started in on the legend of Amrish. He had seen an adaptation of this story on television the night before, and now he recounted how Amrish's one-pointed devotion to Bhagavan had remained unswayed through a variety of worldly mishaps. I had been typing and packing the night before, and now I wished I had watched television with my cousins so I could know just how Swamiji revamped the television version of this traditional story. As Swamiji spoke, I mused that Indian folklore was inevitably becoming adapted in its modes of transmission and constituent themes to the circumstances of the twentieth century; this was yet another phase in the ongoing, swirling process of a people's creativity.

Swamiji finished this tale, and then began to muse about a letter he had received from a male disciple in California. The previous afternoon I had read and translated the letter from English to Hindi, barely able to contain my laughter at the disciple's distinctive New Age tone: he had expressed the desire to "vibrate in oneness" with Swamiji, to "dance together in cosmic joy" (a hope that was especially absurd since Swamiji's arthritis had recently taken a turn for the worse). Though I had sputtered with amusement as I tried to translate these idioms, Swamiji had listened with attentive care. Now he reminded me that I had offered to write a reply.

"What's there to write him?" Swamiji looked out over Vyas Dada's shoulder at the road ahead. "On receiving your letter, I was very happy. This is all the Lord's play. You can make the earth heaven and you can also make it hell. . . ." Swamiji coughed. His glasses were off, and turning to me, his eyes had a nearsighted serenity. "On earth there is heaven [*svarg*] and there is hell [*narak*]. Isn't that so?"

"*Jī,*" I agreed.

"Some see this as heaven, some see this as hell. The one who tells you is the heart [*dil*]. There's a story about this . . . when you say heaven and hell are both here. There was a man. . . . Haven't I told you this story before?" he turned to ask me.

"I don't remember heaven and hell, Swamiji," I said.

So Swamiji started into this folktale. The countryside slipped past outside as he spoke, his voice throaty against the hum of the car, the honk of the horn, the wind blowing through the window. The rest of us listened, eyes on the road, caught within the shared space of moving vehicle and progressing tale.

*   *   *

There was a man like me. He sat under a tree. [A prolonged honk to scatter children from the road—honks blare all through the story, but Swamiji is unperturbed.] It came into his head—he was hungry—that if he got one single* coffee,* one pitcher [*loṭā*] of coffee,* then that would be very good. Yes?

["Yes," says Kirin, laughing. Swamiji pronounces "kaa-fee!" with such relish. Kirin continues to punctuate most of the sentences that follow with

a "*hān,*" "yes." With those in the seat ahead watching the road, she feels
the responsibility for audience response.]

Then he got the coffee. "Next, if I got two *vaḍās* and one *iḍlī* [south
Indian snacks] it would be even better." Just then, the *iḍlī-vaḍā* appeared.
He ate them. Then he thought, "This is very good. If I got a *masālā dosā*
[another south Indian snack] that would be very good." The *masālā dosā*
came! He ate it. Then he thought, "This is good, it's very good that I'm
sitting under this tree. And . . . if I got some good food this afternoon, it
would be good. I don't want too much salt. *Dāl* [lentils], *roṭī* [bread], and
a little *bāsmatī* [fine, long-grained] rice. And a little spicy rice. After this
some *kachorīs* [fried dumplings] and other things. . . ." He thought along
these lines. All this appeared there of its own good accord at lunch time.
Twelve—the time he had said. At that very time, the food was all ready on
a plate. He ate it with relish.

He thought, "What's this? Whatever I think about appears here! There's
something special about this tree. When I move from here to a different
tree, nothing comes." He was a clever man.

["Was he a *sādhu,* a holy man?" Kirin asks hopefully, thinking of her
dissertation. "Not a *sādhu* or anything," Swamiji replies. "He was like you;
or think of him like me, a little topsy-turvy. Yes?"]

He thought. . . .

["Think of him as a little like yourself," Swamiji lapses out of the story
again, "as a knowledgeable person [*vidyāvant*], a scientist.* He wasn't a
sādhu, he was a scientist!*" "Yes," Kirin agrees politely, though a little mystified. Could Swamiji mean a social scientist?]

He thought, "People talk about the Wish-Fulfilling Tree [*kalpavriksh*],
the Wish-Fulfilling Tree. The name of this tree is probably Wish-Fulfilling
Tree. For whenever I sat under this, I got everything. But when I tried
sitting under other trees, I didn't get anything." It came into his mind,
"Whatever you ask for under this tree, you get."

He stayed there for one or two days. Yes? On the second day, when he
came and sat down, he thought, "If a Siddh Purush [saint; perfected man]
were to come here, that would be very good." A Siddh Purush appeared.

He thought, "Now what should I ask for from this Siddh Purush who
appeared? I should ask him something!" He had no special business. He
was just testing all this.

The Siddh Purush said, "What brother, what is it that you want?"

"Are you a Siddh Purush?"

"I'm a Siddh Purush" [nodding his head].

"Do you wander in all places?"

"I wander in all places. What do you want?" he asked.

The man said, "This is my desire: to see Heaven [*svarg*]. I want to see Heaven and return; to see what the realm of Heaven [*svargalok*] is like."

The Siddh Purush said, "Look brother, you can see Heaven. If you want to see the realm of Heaven, then that road* which takes you there goes from above Hell [*narak*]. As you go, first you'll come to Hell and then you'll come to Heaven. It's the same road.* Yes? This is the way you'll have to go."

He said, "Certainly! What's there in that? I want to see Heaven, but if I go above Hell then all the better. What's wrong with seeing Hell? I'll get to see both of them. Now if you want to go to America and the way is above England, then you see England and America, too.

["Isn't that so? Someone told me, if you want to go to America, you have to go above England." Swamiji is grinning, head tilted and the lids of his old eyes folded into their sockets. He has the faraway, unfocused look of a blind person. "Yes," laughs Kirin. Then, after slipping effortlessly out of the story frame, Swamiji draws us back inside.]

"I'll see England, too, then I'll got to America!"

"All right," he said.

The two of them sat down. When I say they sat down, I mean that they were going along the road to Siddhalok [Realm of the Perfected Beings]. They were taken there. First they went to the realm of Hell. Yes? It was exactly twelve o'clock: meal time.* *That* meal time.*

When they went there at meal time, then who was staying in Hell? They were all sinners. The bell had rung.

["Have you heard this story?" Swamiji turns to ask congenially. "No, I *never* heard it," Kirin emphatically replies. "And then?"]

There's a *ganṭā*—bell* isn't there? DAIIN, DAIIN, DAIIN, the bell was rung. All the sinners' souls [*pāpi jīv*], you know, souls that have sinned, all these souls came. "HAW, HAW, HAW," they said [mouth wide, head pushed forward from the neck]. How many? Tens and hundreds of thousands of souls came there.

When they came there, large tables had been placed: line* upon line.* On top of these, there were all kinds of food. All kinds of food. What was there? There were all kinds of food: *laḍḍūs*—even in Hell, there's no shortage of things to eat—*laḍḍūs, jalebīs, puraṇ poṛi, halvāh* [all delicious sweets]. All the fine foods—these had all been made and put there.

[We are speeding to pass another car on this narrow road. Swamiji pauses, looking out of the window. His legs are still comfortably tucked under him. He has barely moved since the story starts, and this stillness provides a serene backdrop to what he says. We are now driving toward the mountains with the strange volcanic formations so characteristic of the Deccan plateau.]

Yes?

["Yes," Kirin says once more.]

All this had been put there and all the souls that were there, they had a wooden *ucchāṭan*. Do you understand what *ucchāṭan* is? A wooden stick, bound to the arm [extending a straight arm]. The arm can't bend. The stick is up till here [beyond the hand] and keeps the arm straight. It's lo-o-ng: nine feet. About three feet are covered by this part [tapping his arm] and the rest is out there [extending beyond the fingers and rising above the shoulder].

All the food is there. Everyone is told to eat. All the souls are told to eat. But the arms can't bend. All the souls go to eat. "HAH, HAH, HAH!" they say, and they do this [tossing both stiff arms in the air]. Nothing falls in anyone's mouth. They do this, they do that, they do this [tossing up one arm, then the other, with the head thrown backwards, mouth agape]. Aa-aa [opened mouth strains after imaginary food]. They keep dancing around on top of the food; the food falls under their feet. It's all stamped and crumbled. Nothing falls in a single mouth. Lentils, rice . . . it all falls under the stomach and it's all destroyed. Everything is completely finished off. Then the bell rings again. "Yes, go away!" is called [roughly]. They all go hungry. Even a single grain doesn't reach a single stomach.

["Do you understand?" after all this mimicking, Swamiji returns to his own composed self. "Yes, yes," Kirin nods. "If this is done, then how will anything go in anyone's mouth?" Swamiji asks. "It won't," Kirin agrees.]

"This is Hell, what else can be said? No matter how much is made, nobody can eat a single thing. Everything that could be cooked had been cooked. Not a single person ate. Now let's go to Heaven," the Siddh Purush said. He took him to Heaven.

To go from here to there takes a long time.* The same time that it takes to go from your England to America. England's twelve o'clock to America's twelve o'clock. There, too, it was time to eat. There, too, the bell had rung. Just as these people came, it was exactly time to eat. DAIIN, DAIIN, DAIIN, DAIIN, it rang. There are all the meritorious souls; the ones who have gained merit [*punya*]. All the things that had been cooked in Hell were there in Heaven, too: *laḍḍū, halvāh, imratī, kachorī, puraṇ poḷī.* All these things had been in Hell and they were there, too. Everything had been set out in the same way. The souls there also had their arms bound. Where? In Heaven, they also had their arms bound the same way. The bell had rung for food. Everything had been set at some distance. "Eat, everyone!" was called. They all went. All the people went. They all went to eat. It was twelve o'clock.

Now a *jalebī*, it would be taken like this in one hand [Swamiji lifts his stiff right arm in the direction of Kirin's mouth—a *jalebī* is a golden swirl that crunches under the teeth to release sweet syrup], "Take *jī*, Kirin." It would be put in your mouth. Understand? It would be lifted in one hand and put in. "Take, Madan" [hand outstretched toward Madan sitting in front], and this would be put in like this. A *laddū* would be put like this [toward Dada; a *laddū* is a tightly packed ball of sugar and some other heavier material like flour]. From here another man would be putting food like this [on his right side, where fields slope up to hills, Swamiji conjures up two imaginary men]. That man would lift something and put it in my mouth. Even a single grain wasn't wasted in this process. "Rice, spicy rice; take *jī*, eat," they said. "Take, eat," and they'd feed someone else. Even a single grain didn't fall down.

["Do you understand?" Swamiji turns to ask. "Each one fed the other," Kirin says and nods.]

One feeds another, another feeds him. One feeds another, another feeds her. Here, they all think, "I'll eat it all myself," and not a single thing falls into their mouth. But where they think of feeding the others, the other people feed them. This is the principle [*tattva*] here.

["It's very beautiful," Kirin says. "Yes?" Swamiji asks. "Very," Kirin repeats. Swamiji is smiling to himself and watching the road, so after a moment she asks, "Then did that man return?"]

He went and he came back.

*   *   *

"When I say this is a story of Heaven and Hell," Swamiji emerged from the story frame without a pause, "both are here on earth. If I think 'I alone will experience happiness [*sukh*],' then I don't experience any happiness. If I'm glad when I see others' happiness, then I'll stay happy and make others happy, too. This is what I tell you. This is one principle. One who thinks, 'I alone will be happy,' who considers things that come to him to be his, he can't eat himself, he can't give to others. If I give whatever comes to others, then those others will give things to me. Give those things that come away to others, and take things that others give you: at all times. If you serve others, they serve you. This is the main principle. If I say I want to go to heaven myself, then I have to take others there, too, and keep them there through ties, until no one is left on earth. What, Doctor, is this right?" Swamiji raised his voice to address Dr. Mukund in the front seat.

"Yes, yes," the doctor said.

"At all times, we should be those who serve [sevak]." Swamiji paused, then turned to look at me intently, "This shouldn't just be said from the mouth, but one should become this from the heart [dil]."

"Absolutely," I agreed. I lowered my eyes and considered what he said. I was not sure if this in some way related to my hilarity over yesterday's letter. Maybe Swamiji thought I was appropriating the letter as fuel for my own laughter rather than feeling any genuine concern for the man. Or maybe this story related to some conflict that the disciple had previously confided in Swamiji, and was meant for him rather than me.

We sat silently as the car rattled ahead. Soon we were at the base of the mountain and then weaving along hairpin bends up to the plateau. As we ascended, the fields below assembled into patterns of green and brown like a patchwork quilt extending toward the horizon. Other mountains pushed up through this quilt, keeping company with one another in this expanse of land and sky. Since this would be the first full moon after Navarātrī—"nine nights" sacred to the Goddess—other pilgrims were swarming up the mountain, in vehicles and on foot. When I had last visited there was no paved road and one had to trudge several hours up the mountainside. Now the road took us all the way to the ashram gate.

The crowds grew thicker as we reached the central settlement. We had to honk our way through narrow alleys lined with shops that catered to the needs of pilgrims. Everywhere there were marigold garlands, red mounds of kumkum, piles of coconuts, plastic-wrapped packets of sugar balls, green saris, green blouse-pieces, and row upon row of prints, key chains, amulets, magnetic stickers featuring Saptashring Nivasini Devi with her enormous eyes and many arms. The shopkeepers squatted behind their wares, heads covered with a white Congress cap or the end of a sari. A confusion of bodies milled in the dust around these stalls: peasants, townspeople, hobbling old women, tightly held children, policemen in khaki uniforms, cows, goats, chickens, dogs. The temple bell clanged above us. A man's voice issued instructions to pilgrims over a scratchy sound system. Groups were singing with a clash of cymbals; some were dancing, too. As we drove through the bazaar, people peered in through the window and saluted Swamiji.

The low-beamed hall of the ashram was dark and cool. Swamiji was greeted with garlands which he intercepted before they reached his neck and was led through to a chair set up like a throne with a cushioned stool to rest his feet. Many people had assembled for this welcome. The Adivasi children who now live in the ashram so they may attend the village school were lined up, a jostling group of boys dressed in worn shirts and khaki shorts. As the two Swamis now in charge of the ashram looked on, each boy bowed before Swamiji and accepted a handful of the toffees he had brought along. The boys left, sweets bulging in their cheeks. The group that remained to bow and then sit on the spread cotton dhurries was primarily adult. A uniformed policeman with a round face and moustache stood beside Swamiji making small talk. Smiling, the policeman asked why Swamiji no longer lived at this fine ashram he had built, visiting only once a year for a short time.

"There's a difference," Swamiji said, "between a *sādhu* and a *svādhu* [selfish person]. A *sādhu* doesn't work for himself, to gather happiness to himself. A *sādhu* works to make others happy. He shows them a path [*rāstā*], he makes something for them. Then he should walk on and leave it all behind."

Sitting in the corner by the open door, I pulled out my notebook to write down what Swamiji said. I discerned an overlap in themes between the story that Swamiji had told and the comment he just made. Like those in heaven, the ideal *sādhu* of whom Swamiji spoke thought primarily about the welfare of others. While the Siddh Purush in the story showed the man under the tree the path to Hell and Heaven—in other words, instructed him on right living—the *sādhu* leads people along paths in the world. Having performed the function of transporting the man, the Siddh Purush vanished from the narrative. As the highest of renunciatory ideals, the perfected Siddh Purush walked on: unencumbered, unattached.

Other Versions

Searching back through my field notes, I found references to the story "Heaven and Hell"[1] made two months earlier. Apparently some tensions about preparing the daily communal lunch had erupted among the visiting Westerners. Swamiji came to learn of it, and rather than outright admonishing those concerned, he told this story. I had been away, but later, as I lazily chatted during an afternoon rest with "Gayatri," she told me that hearing this tale made her realize "we had made our own hell." It was "Ahalya Amma," though, who paraphrased the tale: "The difference between Heaven and Hell is that in both places elbows are locked. In Hell, no one can eat. In Heaven each one feeds the other."

While this three-sentence summary carries the gist of the story, such a terse version contrasts with the extended narrative Swamiji told. When the moral is stated like this, one listens and passes on. When a story is spun, one is drawn into a compelling imaginative space, listening with suspense over the outcome and delighting over details. The moral does not stand naked, but swathed in texture and color, it strides through a story into an imaginative landscape.

A determined flipping through motif-indexes from several countries yielded no variants to this story, unlike the other tales in this volume. I ran into a poeticized version quite by chance while searching for soup recipes. In *The Tassajara Recipe Book* was the following poem:[2]

Heaven and Hell

(Adapted from a Japanese folk tale)

Contrary to popular belief
the tables of Hell are laden
with the most exquisite dishes of food.
Whatever you could possibly desire:
soups, salads, stews, sauces, curries
if you want, fruits succulent meats
(grilled to order), pastries, ice cream.
The single unusual factor being that
one must eat with a fork three feet long.
Holding it close to the tines you could manage
to eat, but when you do so, a demon immediately
slaps you (or pokes you with his fork),
and says, "Hold it at the other end!"
So getting the food on the fork up to your mouth
is quite impossible, alas, though an abundance
of delicious food is readily available.

In heaven the situation is exactly the same:
same long tables covered with tasty dishes,

same long forks. The only difference in heaven
is that the people feed the person sitting
across the table from them.

Edward Brown, the author of this cookbook, is also a Zen monk and a
friend of mine. I telephoned him, curious to know where he had found
this tale that he transformed into a poem. He said he had heard the late
Shunryu Suzuki Roshi tell the story in Tassajara, a Zen community in
California. As Suzuki Roshi was a Japanese Zen Master, Ed assumed that
it must be a Japanese folktale.

Several months later, while wading through the literature generated by
Christian theologians on narrative, I came across another variant. The version is in Terence W. Tilley's *Story Theology* and is cited in the context of
Jesus' parables that feature a banquet in the kingdom of heaven. The story
appears in a digression in which Tilley likens this story to the style of the
Gospel writers themselves, who played on key words such as "banquet" to
string stories together.[3]

> A Catholic missionary returning from China was once asked . . . how he ex-
> plained heaven and hell to the Chinese. He responded, "Hell is like a great
> banquet at which everyone is given four-foot-long chopsticks so nobody can
> feed himself; heaven is like a great banquet at which everyone is given four-
> foot-long chopsticks and everybody feeds each other."

Curiosity piqued by these cross-cultural variants, I began to ask friends if
they had heard the story. An American Jew whose parents live in Israel
reported that his mother occasionally told this tale. He referred me to a
rabbi. The rabbi had also heard it, identified it as a Hasidic story, and directed me to a Hasidic scholar. The Hasidic scholar agreed that this was a
well-known tale, but could not recall if he had ever seen it in print. He
suggested Martin Buber's *Tales of the Hasidim,* which I pored through
without luck. But while researching the use of narrative in psychotherapy,
I found a written Hasidic account at last. This occurs in Carl Fellner's article, "The Use of Teaching Stories in Conjoint Family Therapy." He summarizes Sufi, Zen, and Hasidic stories that he has successfully used. On the
second-to-last page, when I was least expecting it, I found the story that
had been eluding me for so long.[4]

> A last example is a Hassidic [*sic*] tale that tells of a rabbi who had a conversa-
> tion with the Lord about Heaven and Hell. "I will show you Hell," said the

Lord and led the Rabbi into a room in the middle of which was a very big round table. The people sitting at it looked famished and desperate. In the middle of the table was a large pot of stew, enough for everyone. The smell of the stew was delicious and made the Rabbi's mouth water. The people around the table were holding spoons with very long handles. Each one found that it was just possible to reach the pot to take a spoonful of the stew, but because the handle of his spoon was longer than a man's arm, he could not get the food back into his mouth. The Rabbi saw that their suffering was terrible. "Now I will show you Heaven," said the Lord, and they went into another room exactly the same as the first. There was the same round table and the same pot of stew. The people, as before, were equipped with the same long-handled spoons, but here they were well-nourished and plump, laughing and talking. At first the Rabbi could not understand. "It is simple, but it required a certain skill," said the Lord, "You see, they have learned to feed each other."

Swamiji, a Hindu Guru; Suzuki Roshi, a Zen Master; a Christian missionary in China; an American family therapist drawing on a rabbinical precedent: all these men use the same story. This was the first example I found of the same folk narrative being used by teachers of different religious traditions. Yet in each case, the story was recast to fit a cultural milieu, represented above all in the choice of food.

Swamiji's souls are eating, like Indians, with their hands (though the presence of tables makes me suspect that this folktale may be imported from elsewhere). Edward Brown's souls eat with forks, and one wonders whether in the version he borrowed from they were brandishing chopsticks. The missionary's souls actually eat with chopsticks. The Jewish souls use spoons to dip into a steaming pot of soup. Swamiji and Edward Brown (both accomplished cooks in their own right) fill the tables with choice dishes. Their choices are culturally marked: while Swamiji's notion of delicacies includes sweets like *laḍḍū, jalebī, puraṇ polī, halvāh,* and savories like rice, lentils, and *kachorīs,* in Brown's paradise there are soups, salads, stews, sauces, curries, fruits, meats, pastries, and ice cream. Tilley's account never lets us know exactly what the souls were eating, but the Hasidic tale describes a delicious-smelling stew. So although the moral of mutual responsibility in these stories spans religious traditions, the conception of what evokes a heavenly taste is clearly culturally relative.

Of all these variants, the Hasidic story matches Swamiji's the closest. In both cases, a spiritual authority leads a human being through Hell and Heaven. The Lord takes a Rabbi (or *rebbe* in orthodox Hasidic usage); the Siddh Purush takes a "seeker after knowledge." The role of the Hasidic *rebbe* and a Hindu Guru is actually very similar in that both serve as mystical mediators and exemplars for believers; they also tend to be consummate storytellers. But neither the Hasidic nor the other versions mention the peculiarly Hindu motif of a wish-fulfilling tree. Either the wish-fulfilling tree was tacked on by Swamiji himself or it existed in the version he had learned.

When I asked Swamiji where he heard this story, his answer was evasive. He'd heard so many stories, he said, he couldn't always remember where each one came from. It is possible that the source was Swamiji's Guru, who toward the end of this life had an enormous multi-national ashram with secretaries who translated stories from various traditions for him to retell in Hindi. It is also possible that this is a Hindu story, and the variants from other religious traditions are due to independent existence rather than diffusion. Yet even if this is a Buddhist, Christian, or Hasidic story, in Swamiji's retelling it is permeated with Hindu themes.

Magic Trees and Food

The folktale "Heaven and Hell" opens with a man sitting under a magic tree. The *kalpavriksh* (or *kalpataru*)—which literally means "wishing tree"—is an entrenched Hindu religious and folkloric motif. As the fulfiller of all desires, it is a symbol of plenty, prosperity, and joy.[5] Apposite to this folktale is Wendy O'Flaherty's observation that "the symbol of paradise is the self-creating source of food, the magic tree."[6] Also, perfected *sādhus* are sometimes likened to wish-fulfilling trees since, through their blessings, the desires of their disciples are fulfilled. Thus several central themes in the story converge in the tree symbol: food, Heaven, and the Siddh Purush.

The man resting under the tree thinks wistfully of coffee. He next moves on to snacks, and then to an entire meal. Swamiji's mouthwatering description of various delicacies reflects his own regional bias and enduring interest in cooking. As a south Indian—in fact from Mysore, home of excellent coffee beans—Swamiji preferred coffee to the strong, sweet tea that was the most common drink in Maharashtra. The snacks, too, are south Indian. Swamiji's hotel-owning disciples from Udipi often arrived with *idli, vaḍā,* or *masālā dosā* neatly wrapped in banana leaves. Swamiji would delightedly distribute these snacks while they were still warm. Because of his high blood pressure and diabetes, Swamiji's own diet was stringently overseen by doctors. The request for just a little salt in the meal is a detail that Swamiji would remember in the course of his everyday life; the time that everyone eats in the story—noon—was also the time that all of us disbanded each day for lunch. The meal that appears for the man is difficult to pin down in terms of regional cuisines; including both wheat and rice, it probably would come from the central region of India.

In both Hell and Heaven, there are staples like lentils and rice, but also sweets galore. Sweets were a recurrent aspect of Swamiji's interactions, for not only did people bring him sweets, but he was always distributing them: the more substantial sweets that are described in this story as well as toffees or spiked white sugar balls. In so doing, he followed the cultural precedent of other *sādhus* who distributed *prasād*. Swamiji was barred from sweets himself because of diabetes, yet he often used sweetness as a metaphor for religious experience. Just as sweetness could not be captured in words, he said, so the encounter with divinity could not be described but only experienced.

Food (*anna*) has an important role in Hindu thought as the provider of nourishment and sustainer of life. The *Vedas* and *Upanishads* are replete with paeans to food.[7] The act of eating together is an expression of social bonding from the earliest texts: "He who eats alone is all sin," declares the *Rig Veda* (X : 117, 6), and the *Bhagavad Gītā* echoes, "Those who prepare food just for themselves are sinful: they eat sin" (III : 13). In this folktale the choice of food as a symbolic expression of reciprocity or selfishness bears resonances that extend far back in the Hindu tradition. Furthermore, as O'Flaherty has commented, in Hindu mythology, the pleasures of heaven are emphasized in terms of food (and not, as she says, sex).[8] Swamiji's souls finding fulfillment as they fed one another off the tables in heaven recapitulated an ancient theme, even as the specific foods they ate anchored the story in a sensual immediacy. I would be surprised if there was anyone present in the car whose mouth was not watering a little as the story was told.

What this story overlooks in regard to food is the manner in which it can express caste divisions. As anthropologists of India who focus on caste know all too well, food bears the potential to carry purity or pollution. Swamiji's *prasād* of bananas or sweets, for example, is supremely pure, charged with the power of the deities at the altar to whom they were offered and with Swamiji's own blessings: to eat *prasād* like this is a means of uplifting one's spiritual condition. On the other hand, food handled by someone who is less pure—a member of a lower caste or a menstruating woman, for example—would carry impurity to the eater. The entire caste system can in fact be arranged in a hierarchy ranging from the most pure to the most impure based on observations of who may accept food from whom.[9] In portraying heaven as a place where all people feed each other, Swamiji is projecting his ascetic "anti-structural" bias against caste.

Yet even if Swamiji did not see food as carrying caste pollution he certainly felt that it carried qualities other than nutritional ones. Since my childhood I had heard my grandmother Ba link food to the mind: pure *ghee* (clarified butter), she assured, wouldn't make you fat but smart, because it went straight to the brain (a theory that my father's blocked arteries now belie). Leftovers were the supreme taboo, for she said food left overnight acquired dark and heavy (*tamas*) qualities that would most positively give you the "intellect of a buffalo" (*bhens ki buddhī*). One of my aunts, in fact, was accused of losing her good sense after eating too much leftover food. *Prasād,* Ba said, would bring blessings directly into your life, and so when Swamiji ushered us into his kitchen one day to eat *dosās* doused in honey, Ba's delight could not be contained. "A *siddh purush* fed me today!" she kept repeating with a girlishly giddy excitement in the rick-shaw taking us home. "Honey from his own hands!" Having been trained by Ba in these traditional views, when Swamiji began to discourse on food as carrying subtle qualities, I did not find what he said strange. One afternoon as he watched over my drinking sweet, rose-scented tea in his kitchen, he observed:

> The qualities of the person who cooks get mixed up in the food. The person who cooks with love fills the food with love. If it's made with anger, though, anger fills the food. If the person who serves the food is angry, after eating it you will get angry, too. One shouldn't eat what's been made or served like this. . . .
>
> If you take milk and set some aside, you can make *ghee* and then butter. You don't see the butter in the milk; if you want to see it you'll have to boil the milk, make curds, churn it, separate it from buttermilk. Food can be transformed like this. In the same way, food becomes blood. If it's served with love, it becomes love in the blood. Then it becomes sexual fluid and the radiance in your body [*ojas*]. After this it becomes the intellect.
>
> Food can help your meditation. Just as butter becomes *ghee,* knowledge [*jnān*] can become wisdom and science [*vijnān*]. Science is a lamp, and knowledge, like *ghee,* lights this lamp. How it's used, though, depends on your relationship to the world. You can make an aeroplane* from science, or you can make a bomb.

In terms of his own life experience, Swamiji's emphasis on the importance of food and feeding others can be traced to the old *sādhu* he met in
his early twenties at the Temple of Madurai Meenakshi. This old man had
urged him to eat and care for the body if he wished to meet the Bhagavan
within. Later, they went traveling together through south India.

> In Rameshwaram we came to a place. All the people had eaten and the leaves
> [used as plates] had been thrown. There was nothing left but the leaves.
> Three or four dogs came up to lick them. Then a beggar [*bhikārī*] appeared,
> scattered the dogs, fought with them, picked up a leaf and began to lick it like
> this [moving an outspread palm up and down in front of his open mouth].
> The Maharaj pointed this out to me and said, "Bhagavan is in the body. Is
> there something else in there, too? There is hunger. The body needs at least
> two mouthfuls of food. The soul [*ātman*] needs this food. The dogs scrabble
> like this for food. Because of his hunger, the beggar comes and licks at
> leaves. Does it seem like tainted leftovers [*jhūṭā*] to him? All distinctions
> vanish in the face of hunger.
> "Now what should a person do? One shouldn't beg for alms, one should
> give food. Any kind of food. The soul sits in the body of all creatures, and
> the body needs food. Give food. Do something for another soul. You will be
> serving and nourishing the soul."

In India, as in most of the third world, much of the population goes
hungry. The chilling sight of human beings competing with animals among
piles of garbage is a familiar one. Swamiji's Maharaj transformed the horror of this sight into a lesson to carry away: survival is bound up with
food, and consuming hunger can push away prior conditioning as to what
is edible and what is not. To feed other people is to serve Bhagavan, for the
indwelling divine spark (*ātman*) resides in all bodies. This is a lesson
Swamiji has carried with him and it finds expression not just in his words
but in his actions. Everyone who meets him takes away at least a banana, if
not a good deal more.

Heaven, Hell, and the Wisdom of a Perfected Being

Heaven and Hell are used allegorically here, but in light of the cycles of
reincarnation from the last story I should point out that heaven and hell
are viewed in Hindu thought not as permanent abodes of dead souls, but
as resting places where souls temporarily stop over before they take an-

other life form. Sins (*pāp*) can land a person in Hell and a lesser birth, while merits (*puṇya*) will lift a person to Heaven and a more spiritually evolved birth. Swamiji's interpretation of Heaven and Hell is that they are states of mind which exist in the day-to-day world. Social relations based on reciprocity create a Heaven; those divided by selfishness make Hell.[10]

Hell, in this story, has the same setting as Heaven. There is the same set-up, the same schedule, the same delicacies served. The souls are encumbered with the same long sticks which, in my reading, represent the binding constraints of every individual existence. In Hell among the "sinners," selfishness predominates and as a result no one is fulfilled. There is delicious food everywhere, yet it is tossed about in frustration. Hell is a chaos of spilled food and hungry souls. The connection between evil and hunger in Hindu thought, as O'Flaherty observes, is ancient.[11] In Heaven, though, altruism has made for orderliness. The souls are bound by the same limitations, yet they have learned how to act with them. Rather than being frustrated in efforts for self-gratification, they feed each other and there is no waste of food or of energy. The souls in Heaven are well fed and content.

The story starts out with the desire for food. Still, on the second day, the man who sits under the tree wishing up vast quantities of food thinks instead of summoning a Siddh Purush. With this step, he moves from gratification on the material plane to spiritual interests. A Siddh Purush is one who has reached the ascetic goal and can now help others across "the ocean of worldliness." Such a person may possess *siddhis*—magical powers—and so the process of perfection within a human form has magical overtones.[12] It is, in fact, akin to an alchemical change.[13] A perfected being is unfettered by the bonds of human existence. He or she has moved beyond the play of opposites: pleasure and pain, merit and sin, Heaven and Hell. As the Siddh Purush in this folktale assures the man, he roams freely in all places, regardless of their difference. Endowed with powers to bestow boons and grant wishes, he can ask the man what he desires. By taking him to Heaven via Hell, the Siddh Purush wordlessly instructs the man on the principles underlying social life. Give and you will receive; don't give and you will go emotionally hungry and unfulfilled.

Outer Life in the Narrative

Although those in the front seat of our car were listening, the story was primarily told to me. In this dialogue, Swamiji compared the man under the tree first to himself—one who drank coffee and was a little "topsy-turvy" (*agaram-bagaram*)—and then to me—a seeker of knowledge and a "scientist." I was puzzled when Swamiji described me as a scientist, but I interpreted the comment as related to my relentless questioning and my affiliation with a distant American university. By sharing the identity of the man between himself and me, Swamiji established a whimsical bond between us. He also underlined that the moral of this story was equally applicable to us both: a *sannyāsī* and someone in the world; a man and a woman; an old person and a young one.

At the end of the story, Swamiji made a mock play of feeding all those present in the car as though we were among the souls in Heaven who addressed each other with the respectful "*jī*." Madan, Dr. Mukund, and Vyas Dada all turned momentarily to grin. We were a small audience, but we were all drawn in. Our shared presence was extended by the story into a shared cooperation. We were reminded that the exhortation to help others involved us directly; seeing ourselves in the story made the possibility of living with such assured selflessness more real.

When Swamiji likened Heaven and Hell to England and America, I was not quite sure what he was commenting on. Was he making a reference to my own air travels between India and the United States, with a stop over in England, or was there any deeper meaning? With his acute interest in current events, Swamiji was certainly aware of the racial discrimination that Indians encounter in England. In his conversations, though, he did not seem to show any particular preference for America as a paradisiacal new world. When speaking of America, he compared it to a *khichṛī*, or mixture of many different ingredients cooked together: "A little rice, a few lentils, some salt, some spices . . . very delicious!" He also joked that the "air and water" (*havā-pāni*) in America had an unfailing power to corrupt Indian Gurus. "Somehow even the best *sādhus* develop an interest in money when they go to America," Swamiji observed. "It just must be something in that air and water." When disciples in America offered him tickets to visit, Swamiji's excuse was always that he dared not encounter that environment. Perhaps there is a correlation between Swamiji's view of America as a land of luxury and plenty and his choice of this realm as Heaven. I suspect, though, that he chose England and America primarily in terms of geographical distance from India. The journey with the Siddh Purush became assimilated to the modern image of air travel, even allowing for changing time zones, so that once more lunch rose up to meet them as they proceeded ahead.

Service

Swamiji's commentary on this story stresses service (*sevā*), an emphasis that extends beyond him to other *sādhus* engaged in interaction with householders. Lacking personal ties that circumscribe responsibility to a family or region, they view themselves as "servants of the entire world" and "servants of all sentient beings."[14] Service of the Guru has long been stressed for the disciples, whether ascetics or householders. The idea of an ascetic serving not just the Guru but the world owes largely to Vivekananda's redefinition of the *sannyāsī* as one who is actively involved in social uplifting. As Swamiji said, a *sādhu* was above all not a *svādhu*, or selfish person. When people came to see him, after the preliminary greetings he often settled back into his chair and comfortably asked, "And now how can I serve you?"

Swamiji is also keen that lay people, not just *sādhus*, view themselves as involved in serving others. The first day I arrived in Nasik in 1983, Swamiji was speaking at length of a young American who had come to him from an ashram, and whom he sent back to his own country. A group of people were sitting around Swamiji, Indians and Westerners alike, and Swamiji drifted onto the subject of ashrams.

"Many people come to me from ashrams," Swamiji said. "I send them all home. Bhagavan is in everyone, I tell them. Work in the world. Serve your nation, serve humanity. Do some work. In some ashrams, people pay as much as 900 rupees a month for food and living quarters. They work at least four hours a day. The money and the work all go to the ashram. Who benefits? The ashram. I tell people, serve your parents, your country, the world."

Here, Swamiji was speaking of the cosmopolitan ashrams of Gurus who have substantial Western followings and charge devotees for accommodation even as these devotees offer their services at the Guru's feet. Ashrams of this sort, Swamiji was to note playfully several months later, were possibly the result of American's past karma with slaves.

"An American boy had come here," Swamiji continued, "whose parents owned an aeroplane* factory.* He had been living in an ashram, and then he came here. 'There's not much point in wasting your life like this,' I told him. 'You can go home and serve your country. What does your family do?' 'We own an aeroplane* factory,' he told me. An aeroplane* factory, now, probably employs about a thousand people. And then, each of those people must have at least four or five members in the family. 'To give these people work is a great service,' I told him. 'Bhagavan is in every person, in every country. To serve people is to serve Bhagavan. Service is not just living in an ashram.'"

The concept of service was also applied by Swamiji to ecological issues: the earth, he said, was like a mother who should be cared for. In Maharashtra, Mother Goddesses are offered green saris. The meaning of this, Swamiji said, was growth; since the earth was a mother, caring for vegetation or even planting a tree would be of greater value than presenting a cloth sari at a shrine. In August 1985, Swami R. had honored Swamiji at his own hermitage, and I had gone with my grandmother to join in the crowds celebrating this happy event. On the way back, we all stopped for breakfast at the home of Swami R.'s disciples. Ba and I went upstairs to chat with Swamiji, who gave us *laḍḍūs* to eat and asked for the latest news of my brother. Swamiji began to reflect on how my mother had immediately left India to nurse Rahoul when it became apparent that he was very ill. "This is the beauty of a mother's love," Swamiji said. Ba stood beside me, tears flowing down her cheeks as Swamiji turned from this sad situation to speak of mothers in more general terms. At this point, he spoke of the earth.

> The earth is also our Mother. Break her, stamp on her; she accepts it all. It makes us happy to see her all green, she's known as the Goddess of Plants [*vasundara*]. In the end, it's she who receives us all. Say you crash in a jumbo* jet* [referring to the Air India jet Kanishka that had blown up shortly before]: where do you go when you fall from the sky? To Mother Earth. Then when people are sick with a terrible illness and die, who takes them in her arms? Mother Earth. No one else will touch them, but she accepts everything and purifies everything. We should look after the earth. We should serve the Mother. To serve anyone is to serve Her.

Swamiji applied this concept of selfless service to my own project. In 1983, after speaking about the necessity to act in the world and yet remain free from attachment to the fruits of action, Swamiji peered at me through his spectacles. "You can't escape action," he said. "Whatever you do, you're acting. If you sleep, that's an action. If you walk, that's an action. If you write, don't do it with the expectation that this will make you a great scholar. If you're writing, then just write well. Don't worry about whether this will be of use to you. It will be of use to someone at some time."

9. The Divine Storyteller

If ever as a child I felt an enchanted world was immanent, it was at Saptashring. Climbing up so high to a space elevated above everyday life gave me the sense of leaving my known world, to enter instead into a landscape charged with sacred meaning. The view from the mountain reduced families, roads, schools, and buses to a minuscule hubbub of activity; what mattered, looking out over the horizon, were the other groups of mountains attired in legend and myth. This mountain was itself criss-crossed with legends of the Goddess's appearance. Rahoul had told me some of these stories, and when visiting with my mother, we heard more. Under this tree, we were told, the Goddess appeared, green sari pulled over Her face so that just one eye showed. Here at the cliff edge were footsteps carved into the mountain and painted orange where people jumped, offering themselves as a sacrifice. There was a story of the child who leapt and was found dazed but unharmed a few days later in the village below: who but She could have caught him? An old *sādhu* camping out in a Shiva temple told us that the plateau was actually hollow, with a system of subterranean passages connecting various temples and shrines. This mountain, with its blue tints of shadow and coolness even in the brightest sunshine, seemed always surrounded by a faint shimmer of mysteries.

These were my memories from childhood, and I had something of the same sense of wondrous possibility when I returned to the mountain with Swamiji. After Swamiji had been greeted, I started up to visit the Goddess with Dr. Mukund. Though the plateau is flat, at its western end the mountain continues to rise into seven curved peaks. Standing outside the ashram, we could look up and see the temple protruding from the cliff-face, a human construction in gray cement amid sheets and folds of rock. The temple is joined to the plateau by steep, winding steps. As we climbed, all around us there were others going up and coming down. Many of these people were peasants from villages in the area, but there were also middle-class townsfolk present. Everyone was going at a different pace: some

A view up to the temple at Saptashring from the plateau.

bounded up, some wheezed and carried staffs, some touched a burner with camphor at each step, some patted down *pān* leaves as offerings, some hauled burlap bags clunking with coconuts and broke one at each landing to trail coconut water over the next series of steps. There were men with two waterpots slung on a staff across their shoulders, groups with drums and cymbals, and a man decked out in women's finery dancing as though possessed. All this activity was to propitiate the Goddess or to fulfill vows made to her.

Nearing the top, the bustle thickened. We were jostled tighter as policemen directed groups of people through, raising and lowering a makeshift gate of bamboo. The shriek of whistles cut through the singing, shouting, ringing of bells. In the past there have been stampedes near this shrine. About thirteen years earlier, the Goddess was apparently displeased by lax worship: a boulder came tumbling off the top of the mountain on such a festival day, and people were crushed both by it and by the panic that ensued. As we finally neared the temple there were women "with Devi in their bodies," loosened hair whirling about them as they rocked and panted, "ahe-ahe."

At last we stood before the image that has been so central to Swamiji's life. At least ten feet tall, Saptashring Nivasini Devi emerges coral-hued from the rock. Her eyes are enormous—riveting, reflective, with black irises rimmed on all sides with white. Eighteen arms surround her like the hood of a snake. For festivals like this one, she is adorned with silver ornaments and wears a sari of rich brocade. She bends slightly to her left, head inclined, with the uppermost left hand cupped beside an ear. She is said to be listening to hymns composed in her praise by the sage Markandeya, who sat facing her from the next mountain over (which carries his name). These hymns comprise the *Durgā Saptashatī*, or *Chaṇḍī Pāṭ*, which Swamiji so often played from his tape recorder during *darshan* hours.

That night brought not only the largest full moon of the year but also the annual trustees' meeting at Swamiji's ashram. At this time each year, a public statement of donations and expenditures was issued, and future plans were collectively discussed. It was to sit in at this meeting that Swamiji had come. When asked why he didn't visit more often than this, Swamiji often quipped, "When a father gives a daughter in marriage, whose is she?" Like a married daughter, the ashram was now in other hands, to be visited only occasionally. Yet Swamiji continued to command a position of respect. He was consulted on major decisions, and when either of the two *sannyāsīs* visited Nasik they always presented extended anecdotal news. Now Swamiji sat with his legs comfortably tucked under him on a chair, observing the ashram proceedings like a genial grandparent. Outside, the moon was radiantly clear and the vast landscape had become patterned with shadow and silver light.

The next morning a group of about twenty-five people, mostly men, had gathered in the hall again. We sat on faded cotton carpets facing Swamiji. He was cross-legged on the chair again, ochre robes bundled misshapenly under a red wool vest. Like all the other walls and beams in this low-roofed hall, the space behind Swamiji was thick with pictures of various gods and holy people, including Swamiji himself. Directly behind his chair, there was a black and white picture of Swamiji, beaming and round-faced. One of the marigold garlands Swamiji had refused to wear the evening before was now honoring the picture instead. The garland made a bright "V" of orange above his freshly shaved head.

Conversations rushed ahead, for Swamiji had not seen many of these people for some time and was full of questions about their lives. Then a white-haired man attired in white and wearing glasses and a Congress cap stood up to leave. He eased through the seated array of people toward Swamiji's chair and began to bow his farewells. Swamiji asked after his family: how were things at home? How was so-and-so's health? Had such-and-such passed his examination? The man mumbled something in an undertone. It must have been about domestic discord, for Swamiji threw back his head to laugh, and then started in on a story that began with the churning of the cosmic ocean, bringing up many precious things including Lakshmi, lovely Goddess of Wealth, who Vishnu desires to marry. But she can only be married, she says, after her shrewish elder sister is. So arrangements are made for this sister to marry a sage. Once married, she persists in doing the exact opposite of whatever she is asked to do. Narad (a cosmic busybody) comes by and advises that the sage tell her to do what he doesn't want, so by default she will do what he does. In this way, domestic harmony is temporarily restored.

The rest of us sat smiling as Swamiji told this story. His depiction of the headstrong wife who cowed her pious husband sent ripples of hilarity through the room. The man who was being addressed sat with his head bowed, a smile on his face, but his fingers nervously twisting. "Some people are like this," Swamiji said with a grin. "They do the opposite thing; they should be told to do the opposite." Looking down at the man he added in a reassuring voice, "Not that it's like this with you. . . ."

"No, no, what you said is right," the man wagged his head.

"If this goes on for years and years then a person is changed to the opposite!" Swamiji said. Voice lowered, he reiterated gently, "Not that it's like this with you. Stay happy at all times, pursue your worldly life [*samsār*] well." He went on to send greetings to various relatives and neighbors of the man.

I sat against the wall at one corner of the room, setting this story within the framework of other stories I had also heard Swamiji tell. Narad, for example, was a favorite character in Swamiji's repertoire. A disciple of Vishnu and a notorious mischief-maker, he often set stories rolling toward misunderstandings that required many further twists in a plot before a resolution could be reached. Recently, this character had appeared in a television series called "*Naṭkhaṭ Nārad*" (Naughty Narad) which was aired over national television on Monday evenings. The series dealt with the comic adventures of Narad when he was sent by Bhagavan Vishnu into the chaos of contemporary urban India with the mission to restore *dharma* since people had gone the way of science. Dressed in a costume appropriate for a mythological hero but in marked contrast to other civilians, Narad good-naturedly made his way through jail, the Bombay underworld, and law courts, with most people mistaking him for a criminal or elderly eccentric. The juxtaposition of mythological worlds and everyday life utterly delighted Swamiji and after watching the program on Mondays he would often retell sequences of the story on Tuesday (with the amused participation of those who had also watched the show). While the stories for television were written by a scriptwriter who improvised on preexisting folk narrative themes, with Swamiji's retellings Narad was reappropriated by the oral tradition.

Narad then, was familiar from a variety of stories. But I also recalled another folktale in which Narad appeared along with a sister of Lakshmi. In the story Swamiji had just told, Lakshmi's sister, the sage's wife, was unnamed. In the story I had heard several times before, she was identified as Daridra Lakshmi, Goddess of Poverty. I asked Swamiji if this perverse sister he had described was the same as Daridra Lakshmi.

"Maybe," Swamiji said, considering my question. "Maybe she has more than one sister." Reminded of this other story, he quickly reviewed it in a few lines. "Would you like to hear this?" he asked, looking around at those of us assembled. He grinned like a grandmother with sweets held behind her back. Of course we wanted to hear it. Nods, smiles, and murmured yesses answered his question. Even the man who had been told the last story and was about to leave now hesitated, then sat down again. "Have you heard this?" Swamiji singled out a particular farmer sitting against the wall at the far end. "No," the farmer shook his head. "You haven't heard it?!" Swamiji's grin grew broader. "This is another story [*kathā*]." Indicating me, Swamiji said, "She asked this, and now I must tell it." Distant sounds of the temple bell, children's laughter, and dishes clattering in the kitchen all wove a background of sound behind his voice.

*   *   *

There was a village. [Swamiji plunges in, then withdraws for a fresh start.] No, not a village. . . .

Bhagavan's hand, Vishnu's hand, is always like this, under his head [cradling the space between cheek and temple]. He lies in the Milk Ocean [*kshīrsāgar*]. Isn't that so? Vishnu is called "He who lies in the Milk Ocean" [*kshīr-sāgar-shayanā*]. Vishnu Bhagavan keeps lying there, doesn't he, on top of the serpent Shesh? One hand is under his head, isn't it? He looks worried. Lakshmi keeps massaging his feet. Lakshmi is always at his feet, massaging away.

[There are photos* like this, aren't there?" Swamiji looks around the walls covered in pictures, as though to spot a print of this familiar scene. Then he scans our faces and repeats his question. "Aren't there a lot of photos* like this?" The room is filled with nodding heads, and one of the men in a Congress cap affirms aloud, "Many, many."]

Narad goes there and extolls Lakshmi. "You are so fortunate, Lakshmi. You are so revered. There is no one else as pure as you. Even for a single moment you don't leave Vishnu. There is no one as devoted to a husband as you. This is very special. And to get such a wife a person must have accumulated great merit!"

[The grins on our faces broaden when Narad is mentioned, for we know that when he appears, complications are sure to arise. Speaking for Narad, Swamiji ripples his fingers through the air as though playing a musical instrument: Narad is known to carry a stringed *vīnā* as he travels through mythological realms.]

"Even though you have such a fine wife. . . ." He asks Vishnu, "Now Bhagavan, there's no one with as beautiful a form as Lakshmi. Among all those faithful to their husbands [*pativrat*], there's no one as chaste as she. Even though you have such a fine wife, why are you always so worried, with your head like this? [Swamiji dejectedly clasps his cheek in his hand.] What's the reason for your being worried?" Narada asks Bhagavan all this.

When he asks this, Bhagavan says, "The one whom you praise is the very cause of my worries."

[Ripples of amusement rise from those of us listening. Swamiji looks around as though enjoying our pleasure.]

"What can I say? My wife is the very cause of my worries."

"Your wife is the cause of your worries! What trouble does your wife give you?"

"It's because of my wife that I'm so worried. She causes me a lot of worry and suffering."

"What do you mean suffering [dukh]? She gives you so much happiness [sukh]! [With a simultaneous smile and shake of the head, Swamiji exudes amused disbelief.] She serves you so much, then how can she worry you?"

He said [gently], "You watch; I'll show you."

Now there was a village.

["Think of it as a place like Saptashring," Swamiji advises, peering out the doorway into the glare of sunshine. "Or a village like your Sukhi," he turns to an older man smiling from the audience. Sukhi is in central Maharashtra. "Any small village (kheṛā gāon)."]

There people didn't take Bhagavan's name; nor did they assemble in the company of pious people [satsang]; nor was there any kind of religious observance [āchār-vichār]. Everyone was involved in a bad line.*

In some villages there is a Maruti [Hanuman] temple, isn't there?

["There is," nods one of the men.]

All over the place. [All over the place," the same man echoes.] There, Bhagavan changed his guise. He transformed his guise and took the form of a man who told stories [kathā karne kā ādmī]. Having changed his form, he took a vīnā in one hand and started to tell stories there. Every day he gave discourses. In the beginning, a few people came. The next day there were some more people. The third day, even a little more. This kept happening, and in eight or ten days the entire town came there. If an ordinary storyteller [kathākār] visits, many people assemble. If Bhagavan himself comes to tell stories think how it will be! The entire town was drawn there.

In the end what used to happen is that everyone would lock up their houses and come sit there. He used to tell stories from three to four o'clock: one hour. Though he told stories for just one hour, people would come there at two o'clock to find a place to sit. This is what happened.

Then in one house. . . . In all the houses people would clean up the dishes after lunch, and then go sit there. They would go sit there. One day what happened is. . . . It's always the work of a daughter-in-law [sūnbāi, Marathi] to put things away in a house. Isn't that so? The mother-in-law and all the others leave first. After eating and drinking, to wash the dishes and clean the house: this is all a daughter-in-law's job. After doing all this work, to close the door and at two o'clock put on the lock. At this very time an old woman came from afar. She was banging her stick and was wearing torn clothes. She came.

She came up and said [in a low, hoarse voice], "Oh daughter, give me some water."

Then, it came into this girl's mind, "Where did this old woman come from? I should go there to listen to the kathā. Our village has improved with this Panditji telling his stories. No one is materialistic. There's no illness in our homes, no sickness: no one falls sick in the entire village. Everyone gathers so nicely in good company. People have abandoned the habit of drinking. No one drinks liquor. Everyone has gone on the path of devotion [bhakti-mārg]. Now this old woman has come for water. The Panditji said in his stories, "Give water to the hungry [with a flick of his head, Swamiji corrects], water to the thirsty, food to the hungry." If I don't give this to her, it will be a sin [dosh]."

Then she says to the grandmother, "I want to go listen to the kathā. It's hard to find space there. Drink the water quickly. I'll give you water."

She said, "I want to drink the water quickly, daughter. I'm very thirsty."

The girl went inside, got some water and gave it to the old woman. The old woman drank the water. She drank it and gave back the vessel. When she gave it back, the vessel was gold.

The girl said, "Grandmother, this isn't the vessel that I gave you. Our vessel is copper. You've made a mistake and given this to me instead."

The old woman said, "This is the very vessel you gave me. I don't have another vessel."

"No, I didn't give you this other one. The vessel I gave you was copper."

She said, "This is the very vessel you gave me."

"No, I gave you a copper one."

She said, "How would I have gold? I don't have clothes to wear. I'm a beggar. Look into my bag; I don't have anything. I gave back what you gave to me."

The girl said, "What are you saying, grandmother, you're telling a lie. There's not a single bit of gold in this house. Even then, we're contented people. It was a copper vessel I gave you. I'm getting late, don't delay me for no reason. Give me our vessel."

Then the old woman said, "What can I do, daughter, whatever I touch turns to gold. It's probably because of this that your copper vessel became gold; from my hands."

"Is that what happens, grandmother?"

"Yes, yes."

"Come forward a little," she said.

"All right."

"Come here."

She came. Then the girl softly said, "Just touch this lock a little." She touched it. It became gold. "Touch this bolt." It became gold. "Come further in," she said. She came. "Touch this vessel." The vessel became gold. She went around turning everything into gold, and never went to hear the *kathā*.

The next day people said, "Why didn't you come yesterday? There was a very fine story told."

"Is a person's stomach filled with a story? A woman [*mātājī*] has come to our house, and what can I say? Everything she touches turns to gold."

"Is that so? She touches things and they turn to gold?"

[A gong is being struck sharp and loud outside, summoning boys living in the ashram dormitories to lunch. We must strain to catch Swamiji's soft voice.]

So then all the women came there: "Grandmother, come to our house, grandmother, come to our house." Within one or two hours, there was a procession following the grandmother around.

After this, by evening you could see that none of the women were going to listen to the stories. The women didn't go, and the men also started following her around. Women and men—everybody—started wandering around after the old woman. "Come to our house, grandmother; come to our house."

Within two days there was no one in the temple. Bhagavan watched, holding cymbals in one hand. He was carrying a *vīnā*. [Swamiji plucks at imaginary strings.] Just then Narad arrived. "How are things going?" he asked.

["Yes?" Swamiji looks genially from face to face, as though to make sure we're all still with the story line. Nods and murmurs of assent rise from the group facing him.]

Bhagavan said to Narad, "Look, when people call out to me, I go to a place. When I go there they're satisfied, they're happy. Wherever I go, my wife follows. Once my wife comes then no one asks after me. I have to stay in a place all alone. Everyone goes after her. They go after her and leave me. Then I must leave that village and move on to another place. Once I've left then my wife comes after me." [Swamiji is laughing.] Then Daridra Lakshmi [Goddess of Poverty] comes. She comes after her.

["You brought up Daridra Lakshmi's name," Swamiji looks around the room. His eyes settle on Kirin, who nods agreement. "It is she who comes."]

When Narayan [Sustainer of the Universe] arrives, Lakshmi [Goddess of Wealth] comes, too. Once Lakshmi comes, don't ever leave Narayan. If you don't let go of Narayan, Lakshmi won't ever leave either. At all times. In some houses, Lakshmi and Narayan are together. In some places, things are that good. Once wealth has come, don't ever forget Narayan. Then Lakshmi won't leave either. She'll stay put. I've told you a true thing. For many people, once they have wealth they forget Bhagavan. Once Bhagavan is forgotten, they're done for. If Bhagavan isn't forgotten then he settles there. But no matter how settled he is, this story can start to happen. Then once you begin to forget him, he leaves of own accord. Once he leaves, then Lakshmi goes, too. This wisdom is well known. Finished."

*   *   *

We sat for a minute in silence as Swamiji emerged from the story. The man with the white cap who had problems at home stood up once more to go. Swamiji rumbled blessings, sending him on his way. Others also chose this break between story and conversation to take their leave. They assembled in a line to touch Swamiji's feet and receive sugar balls as well as triangular packages of sacred *kumkum*. I slipped out into the sunshine. Looking up at the cliff-face, I could see the trail of pilgrims ascending and descending the steps, and could hear the clang of bells from the shrine. In the next few hours I would take the bus back to Nasik; the next day I would depart for Bombay from where I would fly back to San Francisco. This was the last story in my collection. It had also been the first story taped when I arrived in July. Standing in the sunshine sharpened by altitude, I smiled to myself over the unintended symmetry of beginning and ending this year's visit with the same story. Given the theme of my research, this was uncannily appropriate. For Narayan, entertaining and edifying villagers through his use of stories, dramatizes just how storytelling can be a vehicle for religious teaching.

Other Occasions that Evoked this Story

My first memory of this story is from 1980. In the course of a conversation about ashrams that become money-making enterprises, Swamiji had told this story he called "Lakshmi-Narayan." The critique was obvious, though indirect and understated in its narrative form. Telling this story, Swamiji seemed to imply that ashrams which amassed wealth were slipping away from Narayan and toward Lakshmi: by replacing their religious concerns with materialistic ones, they were on the road to both spiritual and monetary bankruptcy. I lacked a tape recorder that day, and though I listened closely, I did not take notes.

In 1983, the issue of money came up when Swamiji told a folktale about how "money earned through hard work buds, swings, and blossoms." This was a folktale about a storyteller who was given a donation of just a few coins but since the coins themselves had been amassed through sincere work, they brought great wealth. The theme of money and storytelling in this folktale reminded me of "Lakshmi-Narayan." The next morning, when Swamiji genially enquired of the assembled group whether there was anything we wanted to hear, I brought out my tape recorder and asked Swamiji if he would retell it. The story had been evoked by my intervention, yet Swamiji adapted it to the situation at hand. "Gayatri," "Bhavani," and "Saraswati" found themselves scrambling after the old woman, calling, "Come to my house!" and "Touch this, touch that!" I was never sure whether Swamiji was teasing them personally or was tossing out an oblique criticism of Western materialism.

Shortly after I arrived for my second bout of fieldwork in early July of 1985, Swamiji addressed "Lakshmi-Narayan" to a clean-shaven young man who visited during the afternoon *darshan* hours. He had come for advice and blessings since his father was ill. His family owned a prosperous provision store nearby. They had visited occasionally in the past, but it appeared to be some time since anyone had dropped in. From what I gathered, the provision store also had a reputation for overblown prices. When Swamiji launched into this story, I assumed that he was rebuking the family for the pursuit of wealth, remembering religion only in times of crisis. As it was almost time for the evening chant when children would arrive, Swamiji announced that he was telling the story "in short." Yet he brought in details from the situation at hand. The Doctor's young daughter was present with a white Pomeranian in her lap. The little dog knew that Swamiji would soon cuddle and feed it, and its beady eyes were intently fixed on him. To illustrate his point that if listeners flocked around ordinary storytellers, of course Bhagavan would draw crowds, Swamiji waved a hand, "Look, even this dog is listening with such love!" He ended with comments about how when people were poor they worshipped Bhagavan a lot, but when they got something, they arrogantly attributed all their accomplishments to their own efforts.

"All of us are going to die one day," Swamiji went on, his voice low and face serious as he looked at the young shopkeeper. "This is all in the Lord's hands. That's why, don't think of yourself as great. Think that Bhagavan is greater than you. There's no one greater than the Lord. I'm telling the truth." Then, slipping with characteristic ease from male to female gender in his references to a divine principle, Swamiji went on to instruct the young man on a ritual with five coconuts to be offered to the Goddess. "She'll do something for you," Swamiji assured. "Things won't stay dark with you." During my stay, I only saw the young man again once, in passing. I never found out how he had interpreted the story or whether he had followed Swamiji's advice. In mid-September, though, I overheard Swamiji discussing the ill father with another old man. This time Swamiji observed outright that since the family had become prosperous everyone had forgotten the Devi and no one dropped in to see Swamiji, not even to ask after his health.

My mother offered examples of the three other occasions when Swamiji had called on this folktale. Once in the mid-1970s, when Swamiji was visiting his guru's large ashram, some visitors complained to him about the opulence of this place. "Swamiji said wealth could be seen as a natural consequence of worship and told this story," my mother recalled, sipping tea in my Berkeley apartment. Another time, Swamiji was visiting Swami R. at his place in the forest. Since the young *sannyāsī* had moved to this place, it had changed from a deserted area where no one visited after sunset to a bustling pilgrimage site with a bus service and resthouse. Swamiji listened to an enumeration of further plans that the government had formulated for the development of the area: a road, a dam, electricity, jobs for the villagers. Then Swamiji told this story. "He was accepting, but he set these changes that had been planned in a mythological framework," my mother said. "He locates everything in the framework of his stories."

The third retelling my mother remembered referred not to *sādhus* but my own family. Years ago when Rahoul had gone off to help with the children at Swamiji's ashram, Swamiji had been amused to see a boy from an educated and fairly prosperous family show an interest in *sādhus*, ashrams, and social service. He remarked that in some families people held to Narayan even when Lakshmi arrived, and that this was a good thing. Then he told the story. Sitting opposite her with my notebook open before me, I looked up to ask my mother how she interpreted the story. She answered readily, "Where there's worship, you get wealth; then wherever there's wealth people's minds turn away from worship. Swamiji is interested in metamorphosis; how things change."

This is a sample of the many occasions on which Swamiji calls on this story, "Lakshmi-Narayan." The three transcriptions that I have from my own collection are all different in their details: the Maruti temple is elsewhere described as a Shiva temple, the vessel (*bhāṇḍī*) touched becomes a waterpot (*loṭā*), the daughter-in-law does not just enquire how stories fill people's stomachs, but what a Swamiji's stories will do for them. Yet in all the cases, the outline remains the same as Swamiji's quick summary before he told the story at Saptashring:

> First Narayan comes, then Lakshmi, then her little sister—or you could see her as the big sister—Daridra Lakshmi. She comes, too. Where there is poverty, where there is suffering: there people call out to Bhagavan. Then, when Bhagavan is called he goes there. After Bhagavan goes to a place, then Bhagavati comes, too—Lakshmi. After Lakshmi comes, people let go of Narayan. When Narayan has been abandoned, he must leave that place. Then Lakshmi goes after him and leaves too. This is the story.

Though this is clearly a folktale with motifs shared with other Indian folk narratives,[1] I have only been able to discover one other related tale. This short fragment was recorded by Susan Wadley in the course of her fieldwork on oral traditions and religion in Karimpur, central India.[2]

The Myth of Vishnu and Lakshmi

Vishnu said that he was bigger. Lakshmi said that she was. They had a fight. Both came into the world where a ritual was taking place. A Pandit was saying *kathā* [ritual stories]. Vishnu became like a Pandit and sat at the *kathā*. There Lakshmi made herself a beggar. She also came to the *kathā*. One man said to the beggar, "Please bring some water." So Lakshmi gave him a golden waterpot. She gave much wealth to all. Later, Lakshmi sat in a big house made for her. So she is bigger. So we always say Sita before Ram, Radha before Krishna.

This story has a different beginning and a different end. Also, with its explanatory ending, it falls more into the genre of myth than folktale. However, there are several common elements indicating that this story may be related to "Lakshmi-Narayan" as Swamiji tells it. Vishnu takes the form of a Pandit or storyteller and is associated with *kathā*; Lakshmi assumes the disguise of an impoverished old woman and is associated with a gold waterpot. Both versions involve a power struggle between Vishnu and Lakshmi. Both concur that in the world, Lakshmi has the power to divert people through wealth. In Swamiji's version there is a cycle of poverty, religion, wealth, and poverty since Lakshmi must follow Narayan. The Karimpur version, on the other hand, closes with Lakshmi's supremacy being established. She ends up settled in a big house to herself, "bigger" than her spouse. Wealth wins out over religion in the world.

While Wadley does not state the source of her story, it is likely (since she mentions no *sādhus* as storytellers) that it was a householder. Stating wealth to be a primary moving force in the world, Wadley's version articulates the householder's perspective. Swamiji's version, on the other hand, is consonant with the goals of renouncers who have stepped aside from worldly concerns and to whom spiritual and moral forces are paramount. Yet, in Swamiji's view, his version is applicable to all people whether householders or renouncers, for all people are susceptible to the lure of materialism represented by gold.

An Allegory of Wealth and Religion

In July 1985, after most of the other visitors had trooped out, I came forward to ask Swamiji where he knew this story from. Balancing at the foot of his deck chair, he paused to think, then said he had heard it at the Nirmal *akhāṛā* on the banks of the Kaveri river. An *akhāṛā* is where militant Naga ascetics live together, and so I asked, "Is this a *sādhu*'s story?" "Not just *sādhus*," Swamiji replied, staring at me as though I'd missed the point. "It's for householders, it's for anyone."

This story, like most others, carries many dimensions of meaning. Depending on the perspective implicit in the context of a telling or the situation of the listeners, different dimensions are highlighted. The themes emphasized in Swamiji's retellings include domestic discord, the haughty self-sufficiency of the wealthy, the dangers of gathering wealth in an ashram, and the value of remaining religious while also being wealthy. Implicit meanings include the disruptive power of women and the power of storytelling to transform people's lives. Swamiji's own exegesis of what teaching the story contains, though, narrows the range of interpretations that people are likely to hear. As he spells out the meaning, in times of poverty people remember religion; religion clears away poverty; however, if wealth becomes a preoccupation, religion's role in people's lives fades and poverty returns. For the best life, religion should be held fast to, even in times of prosperity. In other words this story is an allegory: Lakshmi represents wealth, Narayan religion, and Daridra Lakshmi poverty.

As the Goddess of Wealth, Lakshmi is one of the most popular of Hindu goddesses.[3] A print of her standing in a pink lotus adorns many calendars and appears in many homes. The story "Lakshmi-Narayan" plays on symbols laden with associations to her. As Swamiji pointed out, Lakshmi's devotion to her husband, Vishnu, is well known and is visually depicted in posters that show her massaging his feet as he reclines on his serpent. She appears in other folktales in the disguise of an old woman.[4] In ritual she is associated with a pot (*kalash*) of water.[5] Furthermore, Lakshmi is linked to the "sap of existence,"[6] and women as a category are often symbolically equivalent to water in Hindu mythology.[7] So it is appropriate that Lakshmi requests water from the daughter-in-law in this story, and receives this water in a vessel that she transforms into gold.

Gold is another symbol of Lakshmi; many posters depict her with gold coins showering from one hand. (Silver can also stand in as her symbol: for the Hindu New Year's worship of Lakshmi, for example, my grandmother would bring out a silver coin bearing the image of Queen Victoria as a young woman, which was placed in a pot of water to indicate Lakshmi's attendance.) Just as the women side with Lakshmi in this folktale, she is linked with women in general. In many parts of India when the first-born child is a daughter, the cultural preference for sons is smoothed over with the consolation that "Lakshmi came to the house." Lakshmi's Midas touch can be seen as another instance of the equation "women and gold" (*kāminī-kānchan*) that many ascetics use to describe the primary distractions that lure an earnest spiritual seeker off the path.

This story, in fact, can be read as a statement of women's power to divert and disrupt. Lakshmi draws attention away from her husband. Similarly, the daughter-in-law, lowest in the hierarchy of joint family relations and a symbol of discord,[8] pauses at the threshold of the house she is locking up. This house may perhaps represent the irreligious past which is being left behind. Then, at Lakshmi's request, she unlocks the house and reenters, forgetting all about the storyteller who holds forth in the temple. The daughter-in-law draws her women friends away from the *kathā* as well. Next come the men, for as Swamiji says, "Where women go, there men follow, too." The irony lies in Lakshmi following Narayan because she is a devoted wife; the daughter-in-law dispensing water because the Panditji in the temple instructs that this is a meritorious deed. Even as the story lays the blame on women, it acknowledges that the women were all well intentioned.

Lakshmi is also known to be fickle; she can leave as easily as she comes. For this reason, it is thought to be a good thing if money is allowed to flow out so it may just as easily flow back in. As Swamiji had said the morning before this story was told (reminding me of "The Seth and the Sadhu"), "Money isn't the kind of thing that should be kept. It should be given and received. Don't put it in a trunk and leave it there. It should keep moving. It's called 'movement' [*chalan*] isn't it? If it's kept in one place, then a rich person becomes poor."

Lakshmi's sister, Daridra Lakshmi, is her opposite. If Lakshmi is wealth, Daridra Lakshmi is poverty; if Lakshmi is devoted to her husband, Daridra Lakshmi is a shrew. If Lakshmi departs in the form of a poor old woman, Daridra Lakshmi comes where there is the dross of gold. Musing on the polarization between these two sisters, it struck me that this may be a surfacing of the bifurcated image of the mother which Sudhir Kakar attributes to the Indian male psyche. While the mother is seen as "good," benevolent, and nurturing as Lakshmi, she is also seen as demanding and destroying as Lakshmi's sister.[9]

Swamiji also uses this story as a reflexive commentary on the role of *sādhu*. After relating this tale in July 1985, Swamiji leaned back in his armchair to muse, "Even holy men [*mahātmā*] like me are like beggars in the beginning, wandering here and there. Then when God gives them something they say, 'I did this all myself, it's the result of my hard work!'" Swamiji laughed, rubbing the white stubble on his chin, "I'm telling the truth! 'This was all made by me,' they say. 'God has nothing to do with it. This is the greatness of my hard work.'" Here the story is slanted toward the tension between poverty and wealth that *sādhus* face. A loincloth may lead to the world of a palatial ashram; gathering disciples, *sādhus* gain economic security and power. With this comment, Swamiji reasserted his view that a *sādhu* should be humble, viewing all that happens as part of a larger, divinely orchestrated plan.

In other retellings Swamiji made the storyteller arrive in the guise of a *sādhu* addressed as "Swamiji," "Babaji" or "Maharaj." This figure, a *sādhu* who magnetically draws listeners to hear stories laden with religious teaching that will change their lives, has seemed to me the icon of my research.

Stories in Society

As the daughter-in-law ponders, standing by the door, "I should go there to listen to the *kathā*. Our village has improved with this Panditji telling his stories." She goes on to enumerate the improvements: discarding materialism, no illness, no alcoholics, everyone gathering in good company and following the path of *bhakti*, devotion. Her own altruistic deed of stopping to give the old woman water rather than rushing off to save a place to sit is backed by the storyteller's instructions to give water to the thirsty, food to the hungry.

Though storytelling may change people's lives, this folktale also acknowledges that materialism may ultimately triumph. As the daughter-in-law asks her friends by the well, "Is a person's stomach filled by a *kathā*?" Starting with the women, the entire village is drawn away from storytelling and toward the acquisition of gold. The opposition stated here between storytelling and materialism parallels a comment made by Anna Liberata de Souza, the ayah of Mary Frere, who told the stories reproduced in the first English collection of Indian oral tales, *Old Deccan Days:* "When I was young, old people used to be fond of telling stories; but instead of that, it seems to be that now the old people are fond of nothing but making money."[10] Storytelling, after all, does nothing except shuffle words, and yet through the words' arrangement, new worlds are built filled with an imaginative wealth. As a leisurely activity, it stands counter to capitalist goals.

Folklore is shot through with cultural themes, but it is not ethnography. Its truths are symbolic, not literal. So whether a human *kathākār* in an actual village could have as elevating an effect as Narayan has on ongoing life is open to question. As a city child, I was never much exposed to professional storytellers' performances, and so to place this in a social setting I had to rely on others' reviews. D. N. Majumdar, who did fieldwork in a multi-caste village in Uttar Pradesh, for example, is dubious about the uplifting value of religious stories. After describing *kathā* as "the means whereby religious values are sought to be imparted to the villagers," he goes on to assert: [11]

> Many such stories are recited, but it is doubtful whether the *Kathā* ceremonies have any reformative value in the village. The villagers enjoy the stories all right, but the moral of it fails to arrest their attention: at any rate they do not realize that they should put these morals into practice. . . . So one can, without exaggeration say that *Kathā* ceremonies in the village do not serve their real purpose.

Despite Majumdar's pessimism, I found from other sources that *kathā* and other folk performances (such as dramas, *bhajans,* and so on) are indigenously recognized as a means of implanting values and attitudes.[12] Especially if one looks at a performative tradition through time, the imbedded messages can be seen to change with social concerns. For example, starting from colonial times, *kathā* in Maharashtra were used as a platform for nationalism. As Damle reports in an overview of the Maharashtrian *kathā* tradition, "Even though traditional themes such as that of Krsna and Kamsa or Jarasandha and Bhima were utilized, the purpose was to pinpoint the misdeeds of the British rulers; to spread discontent among the audience, and to goad them to suitable action."[13] Many storytellers were arrested.[14] The famed freedom-fighter Lokmanya Tilak is quoted as once having said that if he had not become a political worker, he would have been a *kathākār*. Today, in Maharashtra, Damle reports, "None should be surprised if mention is made of the Five Year Plan, Development Projects, National Savings Campaign, Literacy Campaign."[15]

Milton Singer, interviewing a Tamil *harikatha* performer, learned that she was planning shortly to incorporate propaganda for the Five Year Plans that emphasized national development. He also found that *harikatha* had been invented around Mahatma Gandhi's life, with Gandhi represented as a manifestation of God who delivered India from the demons of foreign domination.[16] In this way political themes are cast in the structure of older narrative models. In addition, older models may be revamped to highlight alternate points of view. Dravidian chauvinists, for example, have rewritten the *Rāmāyaṇa* with Ravana as the southern hero and Ram as the northern villain.[17]

Philip Singer, who researched charisma among *sādhus,* wrote a passage which earned me glares in a library when, on reading it, I let out a burst of laughter. He describes a *sādhu* he heard lecturing in Punjab in the late 1950s who intertwined telling the *Rāmāyaṇa* with "an indictment of materialism in general and America in particular." Speaking over a public address system to at least 5,000 people, the *sādhu* said:[18]

> When America attacked Korea, the Chinese who were styled by the Americans as apes, made an army out of nothing and threw back the armed might of the Americans. You should also remember that apes defeated Ravana.

Such manipulations are effective when audiences are already familiar with the stories and the associations evoked by characters like the bullying Ravana or resourceful apes. Ved Vatuk reports that in north India, the *bhajnopdeshak,* itinerant preachers who use songs interspersed with story, frequently draw on mythological themes familiar to the audience as they argue for social reforms like the abolition of untouchability, the equality of the sexes, distribution of land to the landless.[19] I learned from a Indian social activist visiting Berkeley that the CHIPKO movement, which fights for ecological rights, has employed the services of a woman *kathākār.* Retelling selected stories from the *Bhagavata Purana,* she also spreads themes of social protest.

In the early 1960s John Gumperz wrote an insightful overview of religious vehicles for social communication in the much-studied north Indian village "Khalapur." He describes how a Muslim actor performing the story of Nala and Damayanti inserted a plea for Hindu-Muslim unity. Similarly, a preacher of the Arya Samaj reform movement who was telling a story from the *Upanishads* described this kingdom as honest, because "All goods in my kingdom are sold at fixed prices." Yet another Arya Samaj singer was employed by the Community Development Block and sang devotional songs about public health, the Japanese method of rice cultivation, and so on. Gumperz concludes, "The roles of the religious preacher and of the secular, social, and economic reformer, which to some Westerners seem quite separate, are closely associated within the Indian social system."[20]

By telling this story in situations that he aims to critique or change, Swamiji is paralleling the role of Narayan within the tale. Though Swamiji's stories contain messages for social reform, he tends to emphasize personal reform as the root of all social improvement. His messages tend to be metaphorically implicit in stories or the situations to which they are addressed, and are not always spelled out. He is content to transmit his views to anyone who comes to listen and has no interest in rounding up a large gathering. But people do listen attentively and, as they will freely acknowledge, they make an attempt to relate these teachings to their own lives.

When Swamiji exhorts people to hold fast to Bhagavan even after they are comfortably provided for, he does not just mean through rituals. He is speaking rather of a moral stance, in which respect for oneself and social responsibility are emphasized. When telling people to lead a good life in *saṃsār*, Swamiji often reminds them that Bhagavan is in their hearts and should be honored. Instructing people to respect and serve others, he says that Bhagavan is in other people, too. Swamiji's exegesis of Bhagavan as a force collectively projected within social relations and monitoring morality reminded me, at first, of Durkheim's classic, *The Elementary Forms of the Religious Life*.[21] There are important differences, of course, that arise from the gap between a spiritual and sociological perspective, yet steeped in recent learning from graduate school, I was thrilled to see an intersection in the humanism of both men. On an afternoon in July 1983, as Swamiji was sitting on a stool in his kitchen, these words made their way through tobacco wadded in one cheek.

SWAMIJI: You can't just say to people that Bhagavan has no form. People can't comprehend the formless. You can talk about Bhagavan in terms of attributes. Then people have something they can grasp, on which they can pin their devotion and allow it to grow. Then they won't act unjustly, they will walk in justice. If you say Bhagavan can't be seen, then people just do whatever comes into their heads.

KIRIN: Yes.

SWAMIJI: Who were all these religions [*dharma*] made for? For people. So they can live in justice, in righteousness, and order, and not do ill to others. This is why *dharma* was created. People made all this, Mataji. It was with the inspiration of the Inner Self [*ātman*]. People thought: "This is good to do, that is good to do." Using their own wisdom, they made rules* of how things should be done. These rules* are Bhagavan.

Take the government. The government is Bhagavan. It's not one person— can you see the government?

KIRIN: No.

SWAMIJI: You can't see it, but you can understand what it is.

Just as the government is an intangible presence monitoring society, in the same way, Swamiji sees Bhagavan as a system of rules that help people live together harmoniously, yet as a human creation based on inspiration from the divine Inner Self. To allow the human mind to grasp this concept, it is symbolically projected in terms of attributes. In order to be sure that I had correctly understood Swamiji, a few days later I broached the subject more directly.

KIRIN: Swamiji, you said that people make religion [*dharma*].

SWAMIJI: What?

KIRIN (leaning forward to enunciate the words with care): That people make religion; that Bhagavan did not make his own form.

SWAMIJI: Yes, I said that.

KIRIN: In the subject I'm studying, anthropology, we read about all kinds of societies. In our books it says that a religion is made up by people and reflects their society. What do you think?

SWAMIJI (who has been listening, hands folded in his lap, shoulders slumped forward, is suddenly animated): That is true! That is just what I said. It's people who make religion. What you read is correct. People make religion; the Lord doesn't make it. Now, the Hindus, the Muslims, the Buddhists, all made their own religions. Actually, there is just one sort of religion: that which is made by people. We think over something, we write it down: "this is a good way to live." All religions are one, they are all equal.

III

Conclusions

10. The World of the Stories

"Give me the atlas," Swamiji called over his shoulder to "Dattatreya." This was in 1980, and Swamiji was sitting, bare-chested, on the floor. Before him sat a man who had just poured out endless tales of difficulties. As the man spoke Swamiji let out "hmms" through a mouth filled with tobacco. He had not said anything. Now when he asked for the atlas it seemed almost as though he had not heard what had been addressed to him. The man tweaked a toe, looking around at the walls filled with pictures. He seemed a little hurt.

A giant atlas was brought out along with a magnifying glass. Swamiji flipped through the pages, still paying no attention to the man. When he came to a dark page swirling with specks of white, he stopped. "This is Bhagavan's creation," he motioned with the rim of the magnifying glass. I scooted over to look. It was a picture of the galaxies. "So many worlds," said Swamiji. "So many suns and different kinds of life."

"Yes," agreed the man.

"Where is our earth in this?"

The man brought out spectacles from his shirt pocket. "I don't know," he said after a few minutes. There was indeed nothing recognizable on the page: no oceans, no land masses, just a vast patterning of lights in the darkness of outer space.

"Hmmm," said Swamiji. He continued his search with the magnifying glass. At one corner of the page there was a tiny arrow. "What does this say?" he asked me.

I read aloud the English, "Our solar system is somewhere here."

"Look, even our sun doesn't show!" Swamiji told the man. "In the entire creation this is so tiny. Then think about how small our earth is, and our countries. Each person sees his own life as the most important thing. Yet there are so many millions of other lives, all with their own worries. Then, too, we're only speaking of our earth. Look at how many other suns there are, how many other worlds. Who knows what life forms they have?

This universe is all made by Bhagavan. Beyond what we know or see, it stretches on and on. It is all connected. When you only see your own difficulties, think about all this."

"Yes, Swamiji," the man had begun to smile.

"That's why I tell people, remember Bhagavan: what is inside you is in the whole universe. Why see yourself as important?"

I remembered this encounter when I had written here about Swamiji's eight stories, and was thinking about their place in the wider Hindu narrative tradition. This, after all, was just a fragment of Swamiji's enormous repertoire; the entire corpus of his stories was in turn a minuscule sampling of folk narratives stretching through time and across space in India. How then could I say anything about them that might relate to the culture at large? Yet, as Swamiji said about the universe, it was all interconnected. Themes that appear in these stories about *sādhus* are spread through wide expanses of folk narratives and reveal some central concerns in the culture. It is worthwhile to stop and arrange the eight stories reproduced so far, to see how they fit together like pieces in a jigsaw puzzle, and to ponder the picture that emerges when they join.

Sādhus and Householders

In this reflexive world of Swamiji's stories about *sādhus,* the first issue to note is that a *sādhu*'s attributes are not fixed but emerge in interaction with other characters. The *sādhu* acts in relation to householders and fellow ascetics. Even his solitude is defined in terms of society. Otherwise, he becomes part of a cluster of people in an ashram or sect: the follower of a Guru, or a Guru gathering disciples himself. He is no flat exemplar of the "mystical East" but a character with many faces.

Like the Prime Minister in "That's Good, Very Good," the *sādhu* assures those in the world that reflection can recast whatever happens in a positive light. He can be a confused man, like the character in "The Sadhu and His Loincloth": attached to his own loincloth, he continues following householders' suggestions until he is as worldly as they. Living outside mainstream society, he may be a naive onlooker to life in the world and easily dazzled by its glittering appearances. Like the Brahmachari in "Falling In," he can mistake newlyweds as deities and decide to get married himself.

As a simpleton the *sādhu* is harmless, but as a scoundrel he abuses the

authority commanded by his role. "The Nose-Cutters" and "The Greatness of Lies" show how a fake *sādhu* can base an entire cult on the tenet of
deceit. Yet while there are confused or unscrupulous *sādhus* who have no
positive effect on the world, there are also genuine *sādhus* who will help
others. Acquiring powers through ascetic practice, the genuine *sādhu,* like
the Babaji in "The Seth and the Sadhu," can even reveal to others the underlying workings of fate. As a perfected being like the Siddh Purush in
"Heaven and Hell," a *sādhu* can demonstrate to others how life is best
lived. Like Bhagavan Vishnu in "Lakshmi-Narayan," he establishes himself
in a sacred place, and through his presence and his stories he uplifts the
people. The *sādhu* emerges variously as simpleton, charlatan, wise man,
and storyteller. The ideal *sādhu* is defined as much by the statement of the
kind of *sādhu* he should not be, as what he is: a saint who represents human perfectibility.

When a *sādhu* acts as a Guru, he is a powerful influence on disciples.
Whether he is genuine or a fraud, his disciples' lives are shaped by his
teachings. Where he treads, others follow: down into pits of deceit or up
to heights illuminated with spiritual understanding. If he is a man of integrity, he may prevent disciples from "falling in" the pit of worldliness manifest as uncontrollable sexuality, blind attachment, and the valuation of self
over others. But as a rogue masquerading in ochre, he can deceive the public and co-opt disciples to construct and sustain elaborate lies. Disciples
may become willing apprentices to deceit and go on to become false Gurus
in their own right. Or else they may lose money, be drawn away from
families to travel with the Guru, and even suffer physical harm.

In these stories the institutions that grow around a Guru are often portrayed in a negative light. When money flows into an ashram, it subverts
attention away from spirituality. A Guru may stand at the center of a large
scale spiritual scam, advertising instant mystical experiences, co-opting
gullible disciples, and setting these disciples to use in maintaining his illusions. The gathering around a Guru can also provide an arena for disciples
to display their own imperfections: that they are gullible, easily intimi-
dated, invested in presenting a positive self-image. Only an outsider with
moral integrity can challenge the institution and destroy its collective
illusion.

Householders, whether disciples or not, extend around the *sādhu* on all
sides. They advise him on material matters ("Get a cat, Maharaj"). They
provide for his needs in the form of food and donations. Though they are
often supportive, they can also subvert the ascetic enterprise through mere

contiguity or more pointed critiques. The servant who is so happily married unwittingly leads the Sadhu to leave behind his loincloth and get married. The betel leaf vendor who mocks the Brahmachari represents a worldly man as anti-Guru, preaching all that is counter to what an ascetic might say. The man whose nose is cut, on the other hand, stands for a worldly man who masquerades as a Guru yet is an anti-Guru who pulls unwitting householders into his web of deceit. Householders, with their human blindness, may also bring laughter to a wise *sādhu*'s lips. Yet while householders enjoy their food and do not worry about death, they may also, like the man who sat under the Wish-Fulfilling tree, think to request a glimpse of a perfected being; like this man, they may find themselves on a journey that bestows insight into the nature of life. They may listen to a *sādhu*'s stories, too. So while *sādhus* are defined in relation to householders, the line between the two states may shift. *Sādhus* must rely on householders, and householders are drawn to *sādhus*. Householders may become *sādhus,* and *sādhus,* if they are not diligent, may land up back in the householder's life.

Caste is not of central significance to these stories, yet the caste stereotypes which pervade Hindu folklore surface in the actions and attributes of certain characters. *Varṇa*—the four major groupings of castes into priestly Brahmans, martial Kshatriyas, merchant Vaishyas, and laborer Shudras—is dramatized more than *jātī* or particular endogamous castes. The King in "That's Good, Very Good," for example, plays out assumptions surrounding Kshatriyas of warrior caste. He is hot-headed, proud, and given to hunting. His Prime Minister, on the other hand, is a Brahman in the best sense of the stereotype: wise, philosophical, and resigned to the workings of a Divine Will.[1]

The Seth who hosts the Brahmachari in town blandly fulfills the role of a wealthy Vaishya who patronizes religion. The Seth who encounters the laughing Sadhu, on the other hand, plays upon particular negative stereotypes; though he capably manages an enormous business, his riches are grasped in a tight fist. As I already stated, this lack of explicit concern with caste appears to represent Swamiji's anti-structural ascetic perspective, emphasizing the essential interrelatedness of all people rather than divisive hierarchy.

The *sādhus* in these stories are all male, and women represent corruption and sexuality. Like the wife of the servant in "The Sadhu and His Loincloth" or the beautiful bride in "Falling In," women can play upon an ascetic's loneliness or naiveté, unwittingly luring him back into the world.

Women are the most gullible, the first to run after a false Guru. They are also untrustworthy and harbor lovers, like the wife of the Seth. Even the faithful Lakshmi is disruptive; the daughter-in-law who gives her water turns the entire village away from worship through what is primarily a pious act. The association of women with gold turns the heads of men, and their sexuality is also distracting. Though in some of Swamiji's other stories women are heroines, sparkling with wit, spunk, and virtue, in all the stories juxtaposing women to ascetics, women are given short shrift. This misogynist ascetic tendency unfortunately extends into the wider culture, where "women and gold" are presented as dangers that can beguile a sincere man off his path. Though women as mothers are revered ("Hail to the Mother of the Universe, Hail!"), women as sexual beings are often reviled and feared.

The polarity and mutual dependence of *sādhu* and householder expressed here is in fact central to Hindu thought. As Wendy O'Flaherty concludes from her study of mythology surrounding Shiva:[2]

> The myths make the Hindu aware of the struggle and its futility. They show him that his society demands of him two roles which he cannot possibly satisfy fully—that he become a householder and beget sons, and that he renounce life and seek union with God.

Swamiji's stories present the resolution to this dilemma in devotion to Bhagavan, acceptance of one's fate, and responsibility for others who ultimately are the same as Bhagavan. The morals apply to both *sādhus* and householders. One need not be a *sādhu* to be a good person, the stories assert. Religion in this view need not involve withdrawal but can be practiced in the world of everyday life.

Characterizations

In Swamiji's retellings, people are often pulled from the audience into the story frame. This is done either through simile or metaphor: the character who enters a story is stated to be "like" a person in the audience, or a person in the audience is thrust directly into the story to become a protagonist. There is an ambiguity to these characterizations that invites listeners to think about themselves and each other. My interpretations of why Swamiji chose to portray a particular person in a particular way are often limited by my inability to fathom the range of conscious and unconscious meanings that might have been touched on in the minds of Swamiji or his listeners. There was a lighthearted nonchalance to the way Swamiji lifted people out of the audience and deposited them in a story, leading several listeners to dismiss their portrayal as a "joke." Yet reflecting on these characterizations, certain patterns do emerge.

As a *sādhu,* Swamiji likens himself to Gurus, to disciples, to old Prime Ministers with nothing to lose, and to "topsy-turvy" men who find themselves under Wish-Fulfilling trees. He is indeed a Guru, a disciple, old, and as he often repeats, "topsy-turvy." By casting himself as a *sādhu*—even when this is a scoundrel—he makes a reflexive statement on the potential performances of his own role. There is a playful, self-demeaning quality to these presentations of his own character. A *sādhu* who appeared in a story as wise and accomplished would always be likened to some other ascetic such as Sadananda or Swami R.[3]

The householders transported into these stories play a variety of roles. Indian men of substance tend to be presented as respectable characters. Responsible Gupta Saheb is likened to a Prime Minister. Wealthy Purshottam Seth finds himself in Nasik with a large house to rent. Other men who are more accessible to Swamiji's teasing might, like Nathu Maharaj, appear in ludicrous roles. While Nathu Maharaj was also cast in a comic light in several other stories I didn't include, in "The Greatness of Lies" he is the first disciple to broadcast the false Guru's accomplishments—a position usually left open to a Westerner.

Westerners tend to be associated with mass movements, allegiance to which represents a lack of discrimination. The women "Gayatri," "Bhavani," and "Saraswati" ran after Lakshmi in a retelling of "Lakshmi-Narayan"; later, "Gayatri" and "Saraswati" were enlisted in the Nose-Cutter sect. "Gayatri," "Gulelal," and "Narahari" all extoll their glimpses of the deity in "The Greatness of Lies." The attitude of a Westerner joining a cult is always presented as petulant and acquisitive: "If so-and-so sees this, then why don't I, too?" Spiritual experience becomes a commodity that must be acquired, a status symbol that leaves an aspirant restless until it is achieved. I have no doubt that Swamiji was parodying the competitive claims on spiritual experience he had observed during his visits to larger ashrams that were patronized by foreign disciples. The Hindu attitude that experiences of great personal worth should be underplayed is here juxtaposed to the contemporary Western sense that if you do not broadcast your own accomplishments, no one else will.

In this collection, I appear in only one story, elliptically compared to the man under the Wish-Fulfilling tree who was a knowledgeable person and "scientist." This seems to comment on my academic affiliation, which Swamiji teased about at other times. In the story of Chandrahasa (not included here), though, I found myself a pious householder who entertained a *sādhu* "like Swami R." in her house. I interpreted this characterization as playing on my grandfather's large house in Nasik, on my family's reputation for patronizing *sādhus,* and also on my own affection for Swami R. In my ambiguous role as both local woman and foreign academic, Swamiji sometimes set me apart on the basis of my education, and sometimes gathered me into the Indian fold.

Locales in the Story World

The geography in which these stories are set extends from this world to mythological realms. In some stories a lost Indian past is brought to life. Kings sit in state, served by their Prime Ministers, occasionally setting off for a hunt or arranging initiations with new sects. A Seth with many gold coins at his disposal builds a mansion adorned with statues. Yet there are also places that could be traveled to in India today. There are villages and towns, jungles, mountains, and rivers. There are houses with verandas, inner sanctums, or meditation halls. There are shops and shop-keepers. There are roads, wells, hermitages, and ashrams. This group of stories ends with places set apart from life in this world. Narayan lies in the cosmic Milk Ocean with Lakshmi pressing his feet; the Siddh Purush takes the man under the Wish-Fulfilling tree on a tour of Heaven and Hell.

The *sādhu* and his followers are mostly depicted on the margins of urban settlements and the bustle of householders' lives. Ascetics live on mountains. They give audience in temples, darkened halls, lonely riverbanks, and under magic trees. *Sādhus* also venture out to interact with householders who will provide alms and advice for the individual *sādhu* or supplies and a source of income for an institution. The noseless Guru takes his disciples dancing through the country, where they camp in parks. While false *sādhus* are eager to attract disciples, the genuine *sādhus* remain aloof.

The settings of these stories are occasionally named, or compared to familiar places. The allusions shift, depending on the listeners present and the places they are likely to know. The disciple who wishes to prove the greatness of lies establishes himself in a town like Nasik, with the distance between two holy sites—Ram Kund and Bhadrakali—measuring the length of the lines of those waiting for *darshan*. These spots in Nasik were familiar to the Nasik audience. The trip to Hell and then Heaven is compared to air travel between England and America, a journey familiar to me, listening to Swamiji in the back seat of the car. The village that Narayan comes to is like Saptashring or Sukhi, both known to the peasants listening as Swamiji told this tale.

Only the location of the Seth in Ujjain who meets with the Sadhu on the banks of the Sipra river seems to be part of the folk narrative as Swamiji learned it. Other comparisons appear to be strategies to make the stories more vivid to listeners. The familiar settings of these stories are a teaching device which underlines that their morals are not floating in some faraway realm but are directly relevant to the here and now. The mundane settings in which listeners' lives unfold become illuminated by the stories. Anything can happen in these places, whether village or town. A rapacious Guru may set up camp, a wise *sādhu* may reveal the karma underlying one's present life, or Bhagavan Narayan may appear in the guise of a storyteller. The understated message is: live vigilantly, for one never knows how sacredness may touch one's life.

Contemporary Life in the Stories

The bridge between narrative space and the here and now of teller and listeners is also strengthened by references to a contemporary reality in the form of digressions,[4] as well as direct inclusion of elements incorporated from surrounding life into the narrative line. The stories are, in fact, sprinkled with artifacts of the modern world. There are cars that carry newlyweds, companies that advertise by radio and television, impressive government buildings, a government that levies high taxes, trucks filled with goods and employees who go on strike. Shards of contemporary, industrialized India with its money economy and consumer tastes have become lodged in the imaginative world of the stories.

At the same time, though, the message of the stories runs counter to capitalism, stressing altruism over self-interest, and mystical understanding over material acquisition. The quest for wealth and its accumulation are invariably portrayed in a negative light. Told in an urban setting to an audience that is predominantly middle class, the stories contest the values associated with industrialization. If the traditional ascetic role has been to challenge the dominant culture of Brahmans and established caste society, these stories told by a contemporary ascetic continue with a subversion of mainstream values of class.[5]

Charlatan Gurus have been well entrenched in Hindu folklore for centuries, but in these stories the trappings of the charlatan have been revamped. He advertises himself, his organization operates like a multinational business, large amounts of money are charged for initiations, and foreigners cluster about him. Versions of the same stories told a hundred years ago certainly do not depict foreign disciples flocking to a Guru. The presence of English words and Westerners underscores the historical moment in which these folk narratives are retold. This is a time in which the meeting, colliding, and blending of different cultures is evident all over the post-colonial world. Swamiji's folk narratives assimilate elements from the juncture of cultures. Yet the underlying themes of the stories are not transformed: they stand on a continuum with the Hindu past.

Religious Themes

Bhagavan is at the hub of these stories: even when they do not directly refer to a divine power, this presence is highlighted in the encircling commentaries. Bhagavan is the orchestrator of fates—whatever happens, Bhagavan has some reason. Attaining Bhagavan is the core of a *sādhu*'s austerities. Earthly happiness may be mistaken as a form of Bhagavan (as the Brahmachari mistakes newlyweds for Ram and Sita); but Bhagavan stands beyond fleeting pleasures of the flesh. Naive people wish to have *darshan* of Bhagavan, and rather than embarking on the path of self-transformation, they hope for instantaneous encounters. Scoundrels prey on the naive by claiming to reveal Bhagavan in various ways. The *sādhu* who is close to Bhagavan understands the patterns of fate and teaches that to serve others is to serve Bhagavan. The good life is defined in terms of submission to Bhagavan's will and a remembrance of Bhagavan through worship. In all these stories Bhagavan emerges as a spiritual power that lies within individuals; furthermore, Bhagavan is a moral force orienting individuals within a collectivity.

In these stories, fate is both preordained by Bhagavan and changed by human action whose moral value is determined in terms of Bhagavan. To act selfishly or irresponsibly entails swerving away from Bhagavan, and this inevitably brings misfortune. Selling sham glimpses of Bhagavan eventually brings retribution. To swindle is to sin, and by clinging to the family line, this sin will bring about a dissolution of wealth that only charity can redeem. To forget Bhagavan Vishnu in favor of the riches offered by his wife brings the departure of both. As fate plays itself out, genuine *sādhus* are endowed with the capacity to intervene and advise, setting individuals straight on their paths.

A cosmic justice operates in these stories. Good is rewarded; evil is always found out. Almost all the stories end with a resolution in terms of what is right. The King understands that whatever happens is truly for the best, the Brahmachari returns to his Guru, the Nose-Cutters are routed, the Guru inciting others to lie unmasks himself. The Seth is told how to alleviate the burden of his sins. The man under the tree is shown that an orientation in terms of others is the secret of Heaven. In the stories where the end leaves people in an awkward position—the Sadhu on the verge of marrying, the villagers poor again—a way of achieving an alternative ending is suggested. And so, the occasional negative ending serves to reinforce the actions which would have allowed the events to turn out right.

The theme of selfishness in opposition to altruism is central to this corpus of stories. The *sādhu* should ideally be emptied of a sense of separateness, of personal attachments and desires. He should live for Bhagavan as a force pervading the universe and present in other people. Yet the *sādhu* does often turn out to be vulnerable to self-interest and the webs it spins. He may hold to his loincloth, wish to discover the pleasures of marriage, think of ways of accumulating money and power over other people. On the other hand, he may embody compassion. Standing outside of events, he appears to transform people's lives. The altruistic *sādhu* illuminates personal fate; he wordlessly instructs on the principles underlying social life; and he tells religious stories.

Sex and money are both portrayed in a negative light. Both threaten the ascetic enterprise, pulling the solitary individual into worldly entanglements. The decision to marry pulls the Sadhu with the loincloth back into the world; curiosity about sex induces the Brahmachari to consider parting company with his Guru and his celibacy. The cutting of noses may represent a cultural suspicion that disciples are abused by the purported celibacy of a false Guru. Money, like sex, is an attribute of the charlatan. He charges exorbitantly for visions of a deity, whether it is himself or an imaginary God that disciples individually or collectively claim to have seen. Money lures people off a spiritual path; it is only harmless when accompanied by righteousness, generosity, and social responsibility.

The issue of egotism and selfishness as opposed to altruism remains important even in the lives of those who are not *sādhus*. The King must learn to discard his habitual haughtiness and accept whatever comes to him. The old Prime Minister must choose whether it is worth sacrificing his nose so the faces of others in the kingdom may remain intact. The Seth, sitting in his shop, must decide whether it is worth parting with the money to free a goat. The daughter-in-law must decide whether to give up a good place for listening to stories or attend to the thirst of an old woman. The souls in Hell and Heaven summarize these isolated dilemmas: seeking their own pleasure they are frustrated and unfulfilled; serving others, they live in peace and plenty. What is given away, this principle states, will also come back bringing merit and happiness.

Spiraling Structures

Other cycles recur in these narratives. Sometimes the cycle is expressed spatially. The King moves from court to jungle and back again; the Brahmachari travels from mountain to town and then returns; the man under the tree goes on a tour of Hell and Heaven only to come back. Often the circularity refers to the reunion of two characters: King and Prime Minister, Guru and disciple, disciple and King, Seth and Sadhu, Bhagavan and Narad. Circularity is also present in terms of principles. A Sadhu leaves the world only to rejoin it. Disciples become Gurus who also gather disciples. Those who deceive others are themselves ensnared. People who assert that they never lie find themselves lying. The sins of fathers are visited on their sons, who become fathers in turn. Feed others and they feed you. Wealth follows worship, but attachment to wealth at the expense of worship means that both depart, only to be replaced by such dire poverty that people return to worship. None of the stories starts at exactly the same place it began, and so the spinning circles are more like spirals, allowing characters to undergo outer experiences and inner transformations even though they appear to be back at the same place.

The spiraling character of these stories may express a deep-rooted principle in Hindu thought. The theories of karma, of death and rebirth, of asceticism and eroticism, of vast cycles of mythological time, all hinge on circularity. The *sādhu* points the way to stepping off this roundabout: spiritual liberation and concern for others rather than one's limited self. The fixed point around which characters and principles whirl in these stories is Bhagavan. The essence of these stories is religion.

11. Storytelling as Religious Teaching

On the Saptashring plateau I presented Swamiji with my tape recorder. This marked the formal end of fieldwork. But this was also the beginning of reflection on all that had occurred. What had I learned about storytelling as religious teaching? The question hummed in my head as I transcribed a few remaining stories; joined my family in gathering around my brother as he spent his last days; organized notes; cut off my braid the day after Rahoul died, dropping with it the demure Nasik girl; attended an anthropology meeting where the discourse brought on another form of culture shock; bought ochre index cards; found an apartment where the word processor could be installed in state; wrote to and received letters from Swamiji; began checking out library books and running down clues from their bibliographies. As index cards spilled out of a shoebox and drafts of chapters grew on the desk, I continued to ask: why stories? Why, all over the world, were stories a form of religious teaching?

When I had sat among the rapt listeners around Swamiji, the answer to this central question had often seemed perfectly clear, almost commonsensical. If I could capture that atmosphere for my readers, I thought, perhaps they too could understand the power of stories from within. Spinning stories around his stories would make my point with the same subtle persuasiveness as Swamiji himself. Yet just as Swamiji often emerged from a story to look back with a few statements about what it all meant, so I knew that for an academic production I would have to end with conclusions that connected the specificity of my experience to more general insights.

After much reading and musing, at the end of a year's writing I began to bring my intuitive understanding of storytelling into conversation with the growing body of literature about narrative. As a "trendy" topic in the 1980s, narrative commands attention in a diversity of disciplines: philosophy, psychology, theology, literary criticism, anthropology, and folklore.[1] In my first few drafts of a concluding chapter I tried to incorporate every last article I had come across, and the result was both cumbrous and confused. Like many scholars, I was essentially being a bricoleur: using bits and ends of other people's thinking to build something that I hoped would be new. Now, many months later, I have lived with these issues so long that, while I am still indebted to others for insights, I am ready to serve as architect for an explanation. I started this project and book with questions. Here, at the other end, is some of the understanding that developed en route.

To begin with, narrative is in the broadest sense a means of organizing experience and endowing it with meaning. To tell what happened is to string together events into a narrative line, and it is possible that experience "is itself is an incipient story."[2] Starting at one point and emerging at another, a story mirrors the dimension of time in human life,[3] though time may be perceived as linear, circular, or spiraling depending on cultural context. The link with time gives narrative an impression of lifelikeness that can recruit imaginative empathy. A plot arranges parts in a unified sequence, and as this unwinds we become bound up with the fates of characters. "And then what happened?" is the driving force from within a story and is what keeps listeners' attention riveted.

A story's lifelikeness also allows events to become believable within it, even if they should never occur in everyday life. For though the world created by a story is often similar to lived cultural reality, it is also full of boundless possibilities.[4] Within a story, received categories can be combined into fantastic new shapes, and time can jump backward, sideways, or far ahead. Men can be born to virgins, gods can fly through the heavens, objects can change shape, and animals can speak. By stretching conceptions of the possible, narrative transcends the here and now. The inherent ambiguity of a story also has a challenging effect, forcing listeners to seek out morals and meanings for themselves.[5] A story can reinforce conceptions of what the world is about; it can also disrupt these conceptions, pointing toward transcendent meanings instead.[6]

Religion also constructs other realities which "correct and complete"[7] the world of everyday life. Just as stories gather up the odds and ends of experience to give them a satisfying form, so religion presents a cosmos within which the arbitrary swings between joy and sorrow make sense. Yet while the world of a story is mostly small and self-contained, the world of a religion is vast and all-embracing. Religion aims for nothing less than complete explanations, for ultimate truths. These truths—which vary within each religion and its cultural idiom—are made comprehensible and persuasive largely through the medium of stories.[8] Narrative provides an "incipiently theoretical level of legitimation"[9] to the propositions of a religion; things are the way they are because that is what stories say.

If religion is defined as a system of symbols,[10] it may equally be defined as a system of stories. Narratives cluster around the central symbols of every religion, whether the Christian cross, the Dogon granary, or the *sādhu's* loincloth. Stories give deities their character, and encircle exemplary religious figures as well. Every prophet and saint who is a symbol of living faith, leaves behind a trail of legends that in turn will guide others. In addition, while religion proposes a system of morality to orient lives in this world, stories dramatize these abstract tenets through character and plot. All of Swamiji's stories, for example, can be summarized in a line or two expressing a principle: "Everything is for the best," "Desire creates a chain of entrapping desire," and so on. Yet by telling a story instead of making a generalized statement, Swamiji endows these principles with a vital immediacy. While enjoying a story and imaginatively participating in its progress, listeners' minds are made pliable to its moral thrust. As the stories become incorporated into listeners' visions of the world, religious belief is bound up with the course of action the morals prescribe.[11]

Of course, not all stories are religious. The association with religion occurs in different ways according to genre and the use to which a story is set.[12] Examples from this collection have shown how the same story can be used for pleasant diversion or potent religious teaching. As far as folk narrative goes, the genre of myth is the most closely allied to religion, for myth, set at the beginning of time, explains how the world constructed by faith came into being.[13] Legends, set in historical time, record religious presences and events adhering to objects, cycles of time, and places. They enshrine the imprints that a saintly character has left on the world, and as long as the religious imagination is alive they are constantly being created.[14] Since both myths and legends are generally viewed as true, what they say strengthens belief. Folktales, on the other hand, are set in a time outside of time and are accepted as fictions rather than sacred narratives. Yet as many of Swamiji's folktales show, the actions of characters in this genre can involve religious roles or themes. Also, folktales can be easily adopted as pithy parables or exempla that communicate religious teaching.

Though stories make up the very fabric of a religion, it should be remembered that they are intertwined with other means of communication and practice.[15] Instead of telling stories, rituals could be performed, straightforward propositions could be stated, or a silent activity like meditation prescribed. Yet rituals are frequently given meaning through myth;

doctrines are linked to accompanying stories; and even rapturous mystical silence where words fall short is often expressed through the metaphorical language of stories. Amid the gamut of possibilities for religious transmission, the emphasis given to stories seems to vary between religions, historical eras, social strata, and the proclivities of particular teachers. The situation I observed around Swamiji, a storytelling Guru in a culture rich with stories, is perhaps on the more extreme end of a continuum along which stories are used.

Often religious stories are not only told but also become enshrined in texts. This act of freezing a particular version in writing bears consequences for both the story and the religion. For while the story remains unchanging, history flows along and thrusts religion against different kinds of social experience. To continue offering meaning to believers, religion must be able to account for these changing experiences, and while some stories can be stretched to accommodate new meanings, others are in danger of becoming irrelevant. When hardened into writing, scriptures require interpretive links to bring them into meaningful conjunction with changing experience. One kind of link is established through exegeses.[16] Christ's parables, for example, have been reread in a variety of ways through time, with each interpretation addressing the concerns of the age.[17] A second kind of link is constructed through new stories. The Old Testament, for example, has sprouted a lush growth of apocryphal stories;[18] eight centuries after the Buddha died, his Dhammapada teachings were explicated in Buddhaghosha's parables;[19] the Koran has generated an ongoing tradition of interpretive tales;[20] a Hindu mythological character like Narad appears in a television series. Finally, a third means of connecting scripture with lived experience involves rewriting ancient stories in an updated vernacular language. Editions of the Bible illustrate this point, as do the English versions of the *Mahābhārata* and *Rāmāyaṇa* which are now read by Westernized, middle-class Indians.

Teachings transmitted orally do not encounter the problem of relevance, for they are made contemporaneous with every retelling. Each time a story is told it can be stretched and moulded to accommodate changing historical circumstances. The value of folk narrative in religious teaching is that oral transmission unselfconsciously accommodates change even as it plays upon cultural themes familiar to listeners from other contexts. The act of performance also brings these themes alive: listeners hear ancient messages coming from a living source, fleshed out with gestures and shaped around the immediacy of a particular situation.[21]

Those who tell religious stories vary between societies: stories may be associated with particular stages of life or may be the province of specialized tellers. In tribal societies it is often old age that defines people as storytellers responsible for communicating religion and its accompanying morality. When someone does wrong among the Jicarilla Apache, they are likely to be impatiently asked, "Did you have no grandparent to tell you stories?"[22] The Athabascan Indians in Alaska recognize that the stories transmitted from the older to the younger generation will serve as a basis for everyday knowledge and religious belief.[23] Among the !Kung Bushmen, an old woman gains respect through her command of the historical and mythic stories which link the present with the past.[24] Many examples exist in the tribal situation, but it must be remembered that even in more complex societies where religion becomes compartmentalized, much of the business of communicating and perpetuating religion takes place in unformalized domestic contexts. Children are told stories of Easter, Passover, or Ram Navami by parents or grandparents. In complex societies religious storytelling may emerge as a specialized profession.[25] Wherever there is the demarcated role of religious teacher, it is likely to be associated with storytelling. This person is already seen as a conduit for ultimate truths, and any stories told are viewed as a part of this flow. The narrator's own sense of divine inspiration can also add to the impact of tales. The folk narratives told are listened to not just because they are the insights of a collectivity—the folk—but also because they have become linked with vital immediacy and power of the teller's presence. Religious authority allows a teller the leverage to improvise on received stories: to refocus their meanings or to create new tales from past models (the parables of Christ, for instance, follow the pattern of Hebrew *mashal*).

Cross-culturally, members of institutionalized religious orders tell narratives about people like themselves, but not quite. Zen masters, Hasidic rabbis, Sufi dervishes, Buddhist monks, and Hindu *sādhus* all tell reflexive tales. While every teller is drawn to stories that depict matters of personal concern, there is more to this reflexive retelling by religious teachers than just a playing out of identification. The stories show extremes of behavior—the most wise, the most debauched—and so they not only uphold ideals but also remind listeners about the potential abuses of powerful roles. It is possible that when religious authority is not monitored by centralized structures, it is taken into the hands of the folk. In the Hindu context, at least, the lack of any overarching institutional framework for monitoring ascetic behavior would seem to make stories about charlatan *sādhus* an important means of setting limits on the extent to which *sādhus* could dupe trusting disciples. Looked at in isolation, each story may present a flat picture of the role, but viewed as an interrelated corpus, the role becomes as multifaceted as in actual life.

When disciples gather around a religious teller, they listen with an intensity and a desire to be edified, not only entertained. The cross-cutting points of view and ambiguity within a story can generate multiple meanings,[26] and so audiences may take away different interpretations of what is being told and why. Listeners who screen these stories with the expectation that they will provide counsel, actively appropriate meanings that speak to their concerns and conflicts. Listening to a religious storyteller, believers find illumination for their disparate paths. As Swamiji said, "Stories, you know, are about people." Story worlds are compelling precisely because they relate back to everyday life.

Epilogue

The news came first through the spoken word. Swamiji, I learned in speaking with my family over the phone, had "left." I was absorbed in revising this manuscript at the time. It was disorienting to think that the relaxed, amused presence I conjured up daily no longer had a physical counterpart; that I could not go back to Nasik and find Swamiji leaning back against cushions near the altar and calling out his usual greeting: "Come in, Mataji, come in." Letters from India gradually arrived and I pieced together a picture of what had happened. On June 11, 1988, after joining the children for *āratī*, Swamiji went into his room, then came out perspiring and with severe chest pains. When the doctors rushed in, he said serenely, "There's nothing anyone can do for me now." His pulse faded away. To use his own idiom, his "ticket going up" was validated; the crumbling house had finally crashed. The letters said he had entered "the Great Union" (*mahāsamādhi*), had "merged with the Absolute." His body was taken to Saptashring and interred in what for years had been his meditation room and would now serve as his *samādhi* shrine. And so, Swami Prakashananda—"the joy of light"—Saraswati joined his Mother: on the mountain, in the earth.

One of the last letters I received from Swamiji bore an ancient prayer he wanted me to include in this book. "This prayer is for all living things," he wrote, "not just human beings." The prayer was sung in Sanskrit each morning by everyone who gathered around Swamiji's altar. When I connect this prayer to Swamiji I think of him with palms joined, eyes closed, brows furrowed with intensity as he repeats the words. Here is my translation of the prayer. It is Swamiji's benediction to all of us who remain in the world.

PRAYER

May the wicked become good, may the good attain peace,
May the peaceful be freed from bonds, may the freed set others free.

Blessings on the subjects and those who govern,
   may the great lords rule according to the path of justice,
May auspiciousness always be with cows and scholars,
   may all people be happy.

May it rain at the right time, may the earth's granaries be full.
May this country be free from agitation, may knowledge
   of the Absolute flow without fear.

May everyone be happy, may everyone be healthy.
May everyone see auspicious things, may no one partake of sorrow.

May everyone surmount difficulties,
   may everyone see auspicious things.
May everyone's desires be fulfilled,
   may everyone everywhere be glad.

May blessings be with the mother, the father,
   blessings on the cows and workers in this world.
May everything in this universe flourish, an aid to knowledge.
   Long may we see the sun!

Om. Peace. Peace. Peace.

Appendix I: Glossary of Commonly Used Hindi Terms

The words that follow are not always italicized in my text, especially if they are in common English usage or employed as a form of address. Nonetheless, this assemblage is designed to provide a key to pronunciation and meaning.

āshram: the religious institution of a particular Guru where disciples visit or stay. The word literally means "without toil."

bābājī: "respected father"; a term of address for holy men.

bhagavān: God; a term of male gender that can be used for God in an abstract sense or in reference to particular deities.

bhagavatī: Goddess; feminine form of Bhagavan.

bhakti: devotion to a personal deity.

brahmachārī: a novice ascetic who, though not fully ordained, is expected to be celibate.

darshan: "to view" is the act of obtaining audience from a more powerful being, whether a respected elder, holy person, or image of a deity.

dharma: religion; moral duty.

guru: teacher; generally refers to a religious teacher.

jī: an honorific form often tagged onto the end of a name to show respect.

karma: consequences of past actions, the force of which propels individuals along to successive rebirths.

kathā: story; refers especially to a religious story, which may be tied to a ritual.

kathākār: professional storyteller.

kumkum: red vermillion associated with Bhagavati, distributed at temples and other centers of worship. It is often placed in a dot at the center of the forehead, and means different things according to the context and region. It may indicate that a woman is married, that a man or unmarried girl has just been involved in a ritual of some sort, or that the person wearing *kumkum* worships the Goddess.

mahārāj: "great king"; a term of address used for holy men, Brahmans, cooks, and men of substance in a community.

mahātmā: "great soul"; a term of address used for saintly men.

mantra: a sacred formula, often saluting a particular deity. A Guru imparts this to a disciple during initiation and it is thereafter recited as a part of spiritual practice.

mātājī: respected mother.

moksh: liberation; release from the cycle of births and deaths by shedding *karma* and achieving union with the supreme divinity.

paṇḍit: learned scholar; a Brahman; an astrologer.

prasād: consecrated food offered to a deity or powerful being, and then distributed.

sādhu: a holy man; an ascetic.

sādhvī: a female ascetic.

samādhi: "union"; a state of indrawn consciousness in which the individual self is absorbed within a larger Self, and all distinctions fall away.

saṃsār: the phenomenal world of illusion; refers to "worldliness" and the state of being married and contributing to the perpetuation of social life.

sannyās: renunciation of the world; asceticism; the fourth stage of the traditional Hindu life cycle.

sannyāsī: a renouncer who has undergone the *sannyās* initiation.

siddh: a perfected being; one who has achieved the ascetic goal.

swāmī: "lord"; a prefix used in the names of ascetics initiated into the Saraswati branch of the Dashanami order of ascetics.

Appendix II: Map of India

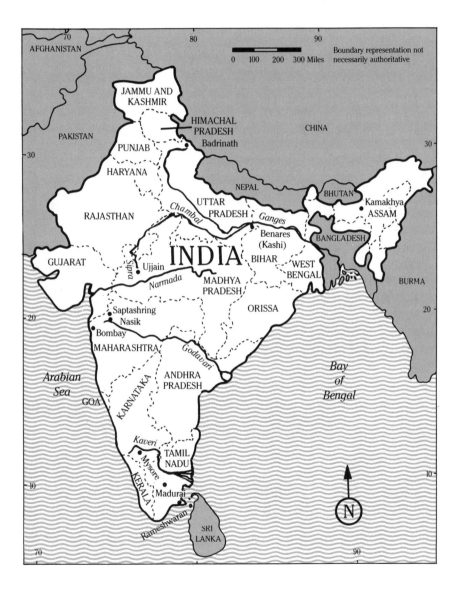

Notes

Introduction

1. I am not alone in recognizing the importance of narrative in the transmission of Hinduism. To introduce key Hindu concepts to non-Hindus, textual versions of narratives used to instruct children and adults have been assembled with commentaries by several scholars. These include Amore and Shinn (1981); Coomaraswamy and Nivedita (1913); Dimmitt and van Buitenen (1978); Kirk (1972); R. K. Narayan (1964). Folk narratives—loosely termed "myths"—have also provided background material for studies of Hindu culture and personality, as in Kakar (1981); Spratt (1966). For narrative as an illustration of the Hindu world view, see Ramanujan (1982, 1983); O'Flaherty (1973, 1976, 1980, 1984, 1985); Zimmer (1946).
2. Unlike other authors, I use "story" and "narrative" interchangeably; story does not just refer to an underlying abstract sequence of events which manifests through telling in discourse. See Chatman (1978); Gennette (1980).
3. Aung (1966).
4. Fabian (1977).
5. Mintz (1968).
6. Tubach (1962, 1979); Welter (1927); for the Jewish exempla tradition, see Gaster (1924).
7. Rosenberg (1970).
8. The term "tool-box approach" is borrowed from O'Flaherty (1980), pp. 5–7, who in turn cites Daniel (1983).
9. For more on "native" anthropologists see Fahim, ed. (1982); Kondo (1986); Nakhleh (1979); Ohnuki-Tierney (1984); Srinivas (1967).
10. See for example Griaule (1965); Price (1983); Stoller (1987).
11. For key works on experimentation in ethnographic writing, see Clifford (1983); Clifford and Marcus, eds. (1986); Dwyer (1983); Marcus and Cushman (1982); Marcus and Fisher (1986).

Chapter One: There's Always a Reason

1. Much of this background on Nasik is from the *Maharashtra State Gazetteer: Nasik District* (1975), pp. 917–73.
2. See Bakhtin (1981) on heteroglossia.
3. On *darshan* see Babb (1981) and Eck (1981).

4. For the concept of "frame," see Bateson (1955); Goffman (1974).

5. *Prasād* can be described as a God's "leavings"—what is left after a tasting, thus allowing a participant to incorporate some of the beneficial qualities which have rubbed off from the deity to the food.

6. Key sources on folklore as performance are: Abrahams (1968); Arewa and Dundes (1964); Bascom, ed. (1977); Bauman, ed. (1977); Ben Amos (1982); Ben Amos and Goldstein (1975); Jansen (1955); Malinowski (1954); Paredes and Bauman (1972); Toelken (1979).

7. The following motifs were located through the indexes appended to Stith Thompson's monumental *Motif-Index of Folk Literature* (1955–58), which is cross-cultural in orientation, and were then followed into the Indic motifs enumerated by Stith Thompson and Jonas Balys, *The Oral Tales of India* (1958). When alerted by these indexes that a particular folk narrative was also a recognized Indic tale type, I made an excursion into *Types of Indic Oral Tales* (1960). The value of this exercise is that one can locate variants of a particular folk narrative and also gain a sense of the distribution of certain motifs. While I have followed up related folk narratives from Indian collections, I have not attempted a cross-cultural exploration.

N25.2   Minister always says "It is for the best when anything happens."
P12.13 King quick to anger.
N771   King lost on hunt has adventures.
V11.9   Sacrifice to deity.
V14   Sacrifice must be without a blemish.
P111   Banished minister found indispensable and recalled.
J21.52.8 Nothing happens that does not work for one's good.

K. Sahal (1965), pp. 38–49, remarks that a recurring theme in Indian folk narrative is expressed in the saying "whatever is meant to be will be" (*honi hoy so hoy*).

8. While a "version" indicates any retelling, the use of "variant" assumes that this is a version of the same narrative, but with some different features. "Variant" is thus a comparative term.

9. Natesa Sastri (1908), pp. 274–76.

10. See Propp (1968); Dundes (1962, 1982).

11. For the image of tribals as inverting Hindu social order see Lannoy (1971), pp. 177–89; Selwyn (1982).

12. On "Bhagavan" see Berreman (1972), pp. 83–86; Wadley (1975), pp. 116–21.

13. On *dharma* as a category distinct from "religion" see Planalp (1956), pp. 149–51; Prabhu (1963), pp. 67–68, 74–83. For a historical orientation see Kane (1933–58); Creel (1977).

14. For introductory histories of Hinduism see the succinct articles by Madan (1977); Thapar (1985). For longer treatments see Hopkins (1971); Kinsley (1982); Sen (1961); Weber (1958).

15. Srinivas (1952, 1962).

16. Marriott (1955).

17. Babb (1986).

18. Singer (1972).

Chapter Two: Lives and Stories

1. Benjamin (1968); pp. 91–92. On creativity in storytelling see also Azadovskii (1974); Degh (1969). Swamiji's improvisations can only be understood within the context of folklore in India. For an overview of folklore scholarship here, see Blackburn and Ramanujan, eds. (1986).
2. Ong (1982).
3. The dates I cite are taken from O'Flaherty (1975), pp. 16–18. As she points out, these dates are somewhat arbitrary, because oral versions may have preceded written ones by several hundred years; furthermore, the written texts not only lack dates for the original writing, but also were often added to through the centuries ahead.
4. Mookerji (1947), p. 112.
5. Pocock (1985).
6. Coburn (1984), p. 445.
7. On this point about the *Bhagavad Gītā*, see Agehananda Bharati (1970c), 274–75.
8. For more on Katha literature see Walker (1968), Vol. I, pp. 535–37.
9. Ryder (1956), p. 16.
10. W. N. Brown (1919).
11. For a meticulous study of the performance dynamics and transmission of one *kathā* tradition, see Lutgendorf (1987). From at least the sixth century B.C. there appear to have been wandering storytellers in India—because they traveled with pictures to illustrate their stories, they were known as *chitrakathi*, "picture showmen." See Coomaraswamy (1929); Raghavan (1936). On more contemporary professional storytellers see Damle (1955, 1960); Raghavan (1958); M. Singer (1972), pp. 150–70.
12. For absorbing collections of *vrat kathā* see Gupte (1919); Neogi (1916). For rigorous ethnographic accounts see Wadley (1975, 1978, 1983).
13. Bhagat (1976), p. 330. For more on contemporary *sādhu*'s use of *kathā*, see Gross (1979), pp. 233, 435.
14. Gross (1979), p. 159.
15. Oman (1905), p. 157.
16. For a study of how significant biographical themes are reflected in an individual's folklore repertoire, see Oring (1984). For more on repertoire, see Pentikainen (1978), and on life history, Langness and Frank (1981).
17. For what I was up to in Kangra, see K. Narayan (1986).
18. On this point see Geertz (1968).

Chapter Three: Sādhus

1. See the lists in P. Singer (1961), p. 33; Miller and Wertz (1976), p. 34.
2. Mahadevan (1980), p. 58. He points out that actually this verse is ascribed to Totaka, one of the four main disciples of Shankaracharya.
3. For further details on the diversity of *sādhus* and discussions of sectarian dif-

ferences, see Ghurye (1953); Wilson (1828). For an account from within by an initiated ascetic turned anthropologist, see Agehananda Bharati (1980).

4. Gross estimates this figure, calculating the entire ascetic population to over three million in the late 1970s (1979), pp. 165–69. Also see Babb (1984), (1986), pp. 93–155; Ojha (1981, 1985), for more information on female ascetics.

5. For historical overviews of asceticism, see Bhagat (1976); Chakraborti (1973); Chattopadhyaya (1970); Gross (1979), ch. 1–2; Sharma (1939); Thapar (1978); Tiwari (1977).

6. Thapar (1975).

7. Heesterman (1964).

8. On the four stages of life see Kakar (1978); Thapar (1982).

9. On ethnographic observations of religiosity becoming more pronounced in old age, see Carstairs (1955), pp. 51, 96–97; Mines (1981); Roy (1975), pp. 134–47.

10. Cenkner (1982); Sadananda Giri (1976).

11. On the differences between Shaiva and Vaishnava sects, see Bhandarkar (1933); Gonda (1970).

12. Stein (1968).

13. For more on the tradition of devotion which flourished especially in the fifteenth and sixteenth centuries, yet continues today, see Gold (1987).

14. Farquhar (1925); Lorenzen (1978); Sarkar (1950).

15. Cohn (1964); Kolff (1971); Lorenzen (1978).

16. Ghosh (1930).

17. Gross (1979), pp. 102–3.

18. This phrase is from Pennell (1909), p. 211, but the rhetoric is pervasive in other colonial accounts of *sādhus*, as in Campbell (1905); O'Malley (1935), as well as American accounts such as Zumbro (1913).

19. King (1978); Madan (1977), pp. 264–65; Nandy (1983), pp. 80–85.

20. Marshall (1970), p. 118.

21. For a sourcebook of readings see Ellwood, ed. (1987).

22. Oman (1905), p. 275.

23. G. Das (1908), p. 178.

24. Madan (1977), pp. 264–68.

25. French (1974), p. 63.

26. Khare (1984).

27. For a precursor of the large-scale Western quest see Brunton (1935). For commentators on the era I mention see Brent (1972); G. Mehta (1979). On the American developments see Cox (1977); Harper (1972).

28. Appadurai (1986); Inden (1986).

29. Heesterman (1964); V. Das (1982), pp. 43–45.

30. Dumont (1970a) and more particularly (1970b).

31. Dumont (1970b), p. 46.

32. Turner (1969), especially p. 107. "Nowhere has this institutionalization of liminality been more clearly marked and defined than in the monastic and mendicant states in the great world religions."

33. For applications of liminality to *sādhus,* see V. Das (1982), p. 126; Parry (1982), p. 82.

34. Gross (1979), p. 272 and passim.
35. Olivelle (1975).
36. Kolenda (1983), p. 331, makes this point within an impressive argument for the existence of hierarchy in traditions of renunciation, pp. 330–36.
37. Sinha and Saraswati (1978), ix.
38. Van der Veer (1987), pp. 689, 692.
39. Tripathi (1978), pp. 116–19.
40. Burghart (1983a).
41. Burghart (1983b).
42. Agehananda Bharati (1970b), p. 89.
43. See the discussion on the "democratization of suffering" in the discourse of Gurus in Kakar (1982), p. 132.
44. Gonda (1965), pp. 229–83; Mlecko (1982); Padhye (1946).
45. For the miracles performed by Gurus, see especially descriptions of Sathya Sai Baba in Babb (1986); Swallow (1982); White (1972).
46. Staal (1975).
47. Eliade (1958).
48. For a cogent critique of the use of "sect" in Hinduism, see Eschmann (1974); McLeod (1978).
49. Miller (1976–77).
50. Bhattacharya (1896), p. 278.
51. Bharati (1970c).
52. Madan (1977), p. 275.
53. Pocock (1973), pp. 158–63.
54. For a similar interpretation of the Guru in the universe, see Gold (1987), pp. 104–9.

Chapter Four: The Listeners

1. The concern of these literary critics is titled "reception theory" in its German strain and "reader response criticism" in the cluster of Anglo-American writings. For an excellent overview see Holub (1984) and the articles in Suleiman and Crosman, eds. (1980).
2. Dundes (1976), p. 80. This point is an elaboration of Dundes (1966).
3. Jacobs (1959, 1960).
4. For examples of the various ways narratives can be transcribed to express action, intonation, and rhythm, see Fine (1982); Glassie (1982); Seitel (1980); Tedlock (1983). I diverge from these performance-oriented transcriptions that read more like poetry: Swamiji, to me, does not recite his stories, but rather narrates them in a garrulous, flowing fashion to which a prose form is most suited.
5. This folktale is No. 761 in Bødker (1957), and tale type No. 75 in Thompson and Roberts (1950).
6. For more on *shakti* see Abbott (1932); Wadley (1975).
7. Goffman (1961), pp. 7–10.

8. The term "polyphony" is borrowed from Clifford (1983).
9. Fish (1980).
10. Mink (1978).
11. For the contrast of narrative and analytic modes of understanding, see Bruner (1986).
12. H. White (1980).
13. For discussions of ethics in Christian narratives, see Hauerwas (1983); Hauerwas and Burrell (1977); Nelson (1987); and in terms of a philosophical conception of unified self, MacIntyre (1984), pp. 204–25.
14. Abrahams (1968), p. 146.
15. Basso (1983).
16. Kirschenblatt-Gimblett (1975).
17. Bettelheim (1977), p. 25.
18. See Kermode (1979), pp. 24–47, for a further discussion on this incident as presented in the two gospels.
19. Fellner (1976), p. 249.
20. For more on Milton Erickson's use of therapeutic storytelling, see Barker (1985); Haley (1972); Rosen (1982). For an alternative form of story that takes off from the imaginative tales elicited from patients themselves, see Gardner (1971). For a sampling of different approaches to narrative in psychology, see Hoffman (1986), ch. 3; Sarbin (1986).
21. For discussions of the Guru as an indigenous therapist, see Carstairs (1965); Kakar (1982); Neki (1973).
22. Lévi-Strauss (1963).
23. Benjamin (1968), p. 104.

Chapter Five: Loincloths and Celibacy

1. Griaule (1965); Ginzburg (1982).
2. Von Sydow (1948), pp. 12–15.
3. In the Indic indexes this is the tale type No. 1045 A, and the motif is Z49.12: Hermit must get cat to kill rats in hut, cow to give milk, etc.
4. Raju (1901), pp. 102–3.
5. Ananthamurthy (1978), p. 92.
6. "M" (1942), p. 435. A longer, embellished retelling can be found in Sri Ramakrishna (1967), pp. 18–21.
7. Dumont attributes this point to Frits Stahl in (1970b), p. 43.
8. Gross (1979), p. 294.
9. *Stotra Ratnavali,* pp. 298–99.
10. Gross (1979), p. 642.
11. This review of different kinds of loincloths has been assembled from the following sources: Gross (1979), pp. 452–53, 470–72; Burghart (1983a), p. 648; Parry (1985), p. 67; Van der Veer (1987), p. 687. All of these studies focus on male ascetics, and I have been unable to find out anything at all about the under-clothes of female ascetics.

12. Gross (1979), p. 453.
13. Gross (1979), p. 472.
14. Gross (1979), p. 642.
15. This is one of the few tales for which I could not find any variants. The constituent motifs, though, are:

 T617 Boy reared in ignorance of the world.
 T330 Anchorites under temptation.
 J2133 Numbskull falls.
 R131 Rescue from well.

16. Kane (1941), Vol. II, pp. 548, 769.
17. See the discussion of the "erotic sphere" in Weber (1958a), pp. 343–50.
18. For an influential statement on purity and impurity in the caste hierarchy, see Dumont (1970a).
19. Carstairs (1961), pp. 84–86.
20. Cantlie (1977), p. 265; O'Flaherty (1973), pp. 355–57, and (1980), pp. 43–48.
21. Eliade (1958), pp. 248–68. Agehananda Bharati (1970a), p. 265, differs, stating that it is mainly in the Tibetan tantric tradition that semen is not supposed to be spilled, whereas in the Hindu tradition it may be emitted with a ceremonial "*svāhā!*"
22. O'Flaherty (1973).
23. See Bloomfield (1924); O'Flaherty (1971), pp. 276–79, and (1983), pp. 64–68; Ramanujan (1982), Veltheim-Osso (1959).
24. Tripathi (1978), p. 141.
25. Weber (1958a), p. 332.

Chapter Six: False Gurus and Gullible Disciples

1. For more on the *Durgā Saptashatī*, also known as the *Devī Māhātmya*, see Coburn (1985).
2. Narayan (forthcoming).
3. Dayananda Saraswati (1963), pp. 503–11, for the Hindi and (1970), pp. 367–71, for the English translation of this tale.
4. Williams (1984), p. 15.
5. This is No. 1707 in Thompson and Roberts (1960), "*The Noseless Man:* A man who has lost his nose persuades others that they too can see God if they will cut their noses off. They do so, whereupon he scoffs at them."

 Motifs:
 K 1286 Mock initiation for dupe.
 K 1826.2 Disguise as ascetic.
 (K 1829 Disguise as holy man; K 1961.1.5 Sham holy man.)
 K 2285.1 Ascetic as villain.
 J 758.1 Noseless man persuades others to cut off their noses.
 K 1286 Wisdom of an old man.

6. Robinson (1885), pp. 31–32.
7. *North Indian Notes and Queries* IV (1894), no. 301.

8. Upreti (1894), pp. 50–51.
9. Dayananda (1963), p. 511, and (1970), p. 370.
10. Kakar (1981), p. 99.
11. Tawney (1968), p. 45.
12. Spratt (1966).
13. Goldman (1978).
14. Mitra (1917).
15. Dubois (1978), pp. 466–74.
16. Swynnerton (1882), pp. 56–62. In Swamiji's story, the central motifs are:

K 1961.1.5 Sham holy man.
K 445.1   God to reveal self to those of legitimate birth. All afraid to admit to not seeing God.

For those familiar with the European tradition, this is reminiscent of "The Emperor's New Clothes," with the motif K 445 in European indexes, and tale type 1620. Significantly, in the European tale, it is a child rather than an old person who unveils the deception, which emphasizes the value accorded to age in India.

17. Cited in Pocock (1973), pp. 100–1.
18. For anthropologists admitting to having posed as *sādhus,* see Gross (1979), pp. 115–34; Sinha and Saraswati (1978), p. 25; Tripathi (1978), pp. 8–10.
19. Kautilya (1951), pp. 18–20.
20. Gross (1979), p. 156.
21. S. Stevenson (1920), pp. 421–22.
22. Padhye (1946), p. 106.
23. Miller and Wertz (1976), p. 89.

Chapter Seven: Death and Laughter

1. For more on formalized requests for alms, see Crooke (1910).
2. For detailed case histories of children who stated they remembered past lives, see I. Stevenson (1975).
3. For more on the karma concept, see Keyes and Daniel, eds. (1983); Neufeldt, ed. (1986); O'Flaherty, ed. (1980).
4. Weber (1958b), p. 121.
5. See for example Sharma (1973), as well as articles in Keyes and Daniel, eds. (1983).
6. See Rocker (1980).
7. Wadley (1983).
8. Miller (1986).
9. Marriott has asserted that the *sannyāsī* engages in minimal transactions (1976), p. 132, but as Potter (1980), pp. 264–65, points out, the *sannyāsī* does continue to act and transact in the world; what distinguishes the liberated *sannyāsī* is an inner distance stemming from the lack of attachments.
10. For an excellent introduction to the differences between the folk narrative genres, see Bascom (1965); on the problem of establishing these genre distinc-

tions cross-culturally, see Ben Amos (1969). This story, which falls between folktale and legend, carries the following motifs:

N456	Enigmatical smile (laugh) reveals secret knowledge.
V223.6	Saint as prognosticator.
Q551.5.1	Reincarnation into degraded form as punishment.
E611.4	Man reincarnated as goat.
Q411.0.1.2	Man kills wife's lover.
E693	Reincarnation for revenge.
M341.1	Death at a certain time.
Z 71.5	Formulistic number: seven.

11. For a mention of Ujjain's holy sites, see Bhardwaj (1973), p. 130.
12. Dubois (1978), pp. 524−25.
13. This is my own translation from the Sanskrit.
14. Stokes (1879), pp. 114−18.
15. *North Indian Notes and Queries* V (1895): no. 339.
16. W. N. Brown (1920).
17. Daniel (1983).
18. Babb (1983).
19. This apt phrase is borrowed from Obeyesekere (1968), p. 21.
20. For the Indian emphasis on the perspective of parents in the Oedipal relationship, see the provocative article by Ramanujan (1983).
21. Mandelbaum (1970), Vol. I, pp. 67−71; Wadley (1976).
22. Goldman (1978).
23. Carstairs (1957), pp. 45, 71.
24. Bloomfield (1917).
25. Douglas (1968). For more on humor see Apte (1985).
26. This is an interesting inversion of Robert Hertz's (1960) thesis that, cross-culturally, biological death is followed after a period of time by a social death, freeing the liminal spirit and reintegrating mourners back into society.
27. Cantlie (1977).
28. Carstairs (1957), p. 233.
29. For more on these and other Maharashtrian saints, see Ranade (1985).
30. "We were struck by the frequency of their early experiences with death in the family" write Miller and Wertz of their interviews with *sādhus* in Orissa (1976), pp. 77−78. Masson (1976), who unsympathetically views asceticism as a neurosis, actually ascribes the adoption of a *sannyāsī's* lifestyle to childhood trauma with death, sexual molestation, or cold parents. A direct equation between childhood experiences with death and becoming a *sādhu* is surely too simplistic. People who have not experienced death become *sādhus,* people who have experienced death may not become *sādhus,* and furthermore, a wide variety of motivations (down to roguish ones) may underlie the adoption of an ascetic pursuit. But it should be noted that for Swamiji, the correlation with early experiences of death is accurate since he lost his mother when he was ten years old.
31. Parry (1982), pp. 74−110, and V. Das (1982), p. 123.
32. Oman (1905), pp. 156−57.
33. Dubois (1978), pp. 538−41.

34. On this theme see Bloch and Parry (1982).
35. S. Mehta (1919).
36. Eliade (1958), p. 317.
37. Long (1977).

Chapter Eight: Heaven and Hell

1. Motifs:

D950	Magic Tree.
D1472.1.3	Magic Tree Supplies Food.
F0	Journey to other world.
F2	Translation to Otherworld without dying.
F183	Foods in Otherworld.
Q560.1	Punishments in land of dead.

2. E. Brown (1985), p. 120.
3. Tilley (1985), p. 88.
4. Fellner (1976), pp. 430–31.
5. Upadhyaya (1965).
6. O'Flaherty (1976), p. 29–30.
7. Pannikar (1977), p. 38.
8. O'Flaherty (1985), p. 38.
9. For a classic study of caste ranking, see Marriott (1968).
10. For a theory of reciprocity in society, see Mauss (1967).
11. O'Flaherty (1976), p. 30.
12. Eliade (1958), p. 303.
13. D. White (1984).
14. Gross (1979), p. 231.

Chapter Nine: The Divine Storyteller

1. "Laxmi-Narayan" carries the following motifs:

T210	Faithfulness in marriage.
K1811	Gods in disguise visit mortals.
N114	Fortune as an old woman.
D565.1	Midas' golden touch.

2. Wadley (1975), pp. 133–34.
3. Kinsley (1986), pp. 19–34.
4. For example, see Neogi (1916), pp. 135–36.
5. Gupte (1919), p. 53.
6. Kinsley (1986), p. 31.
7. The equation of women with water is No. 17 in the list of motifs that O'Flaherty lists for the mythology of Shiva (1973), p. 25.
8. Mandelbaum (1970), Vol. I, pp. 70–72.
9. Kakar (1981), pp. 79–103.

10. Frere (1898), p. xxvii.
11. Majumdar (1958), pp. 292–93.
12. For an excellent overview of performative traditions from the various corners of India, see Parmar (1975).
13. Damle (1960), p. 68.
14. Damle (1955), p. 18.
15. Damle (1955), pp. 15–19.
16. M. Singer (1972), p. 170.
17. M. Singer (1972), p. 80.
18. P. Singer (1961), p. 90.
19. Vatuk (1979), pp. 137–60.
20. Gumperz (1964), p. 96.
21. Durkheim (1965).

Chapter Ten: The World of the Stories

1. There is also a prevalent stereotype of a greedy, overweight Brahman more intent on money than on religious duties—a figure similar in some ways to the fake ascetic, but who does not appear in this selection.
2. O'Flaherty (1973), p. 38.
3. This was the story of Chandrahasa in which a *sādhu* makes only a brief appearance.
4. For more on storytelling digressions, see Başgöz (1986); Georges (1983).
5. For more on folklore as a source of opposition to the dominant order, see Lombardi-Satriani (1974); Limon (1983, 1984).

Chapter Eleven: Storytelling as Religious Teaching

1. The literature is immense, but for good overviews of the trend, see the article by Randall (1984), the interdisciplinary convergence in Hoffman (1986), the edited collection by Mitchell (1980), and the thorough, if dry, survey by Polkinghorne (1988). In the realm of ethnography, see Bruner (1986); Schweder (1986); Webster (1983).
2. Crites (1971), p. 297, echoed by many others including Bruner (1986, 1987); MacIntyre (1982).
3. Ricouer (1984).
4. Wilder (1983).
5. Beardslee (1978); Jackson (1975).
6. Crossan (1975).
7. Geertz (1973), p. 122.
8. R. M. Brown (1974); Crites (1967); Goldberg (1982); Kort (1975); Slater (1978); Tilley (1985).
9. Berger (1969), p. 31.
10. Geertz (1973); see the forceful critique by Asad (1983).

11. Braithewaite (1955), pp. 32–35; Hauerwas (1983).
12. In an overview of developments within Christian theology, Fackre (1983) distinguishes three foci of research: canonical stories, life stories, and community stories.
13. See the collection edited by Dundes (1984) for varied analytic approaches to myth.
14. See for example Delehaye (1982); Ginzberg (1950–69); Loomis (1948).
15. The limits of equating story with religion have been discussed by Estess (1974); Lischer (1984); Wesley (1980).
16. Van Baaren (1972).
17. For all the varied scholarship on Christ's parables, see Kissinger (1979).
18. Ginzberg (1950–69).
19. Buddhaghosha (1870).
20. Baljøn (1973).
21. On the sacred power of the word, see Ong (1982), pp. 74–75.
22. Opler (1938), p. xii.
23. Rooth (1976), p. 88.
24. Shostak (1983), p. 325.
25. Apart from the *kathākār* discussed in Chapter 9, see Prusek (1938).
26. Bakhtin (1981); Bruner and Gorfain (1983).

Bibliography

Abbott, J. 1932. *The Keys of Power: A Study of Indian Ritual and Belief.* London: Methuen.

Abrahams, Roger D. 1968. "Introductory Remarks to a Rhetorical Theory of Folklore." *Journal of American Folklore* 81:143–58.

Agehananda Bharati, Swami. 1970a. *The Tantric Tradition.* New York: Doubleday.

———. 1970b. "Pilgrimage Sites and Indian Civilization." In *Chapters in Indian Civilization,* edited by J. W. Elder, 85–126. Dubuque: Kendall Hunt Publishing Co.

———. 1970c. "The Hindu Renaissance and Its Apologetic Patterns." *Journal of Asian Studies* 29:267–87.

———. 1980. *The Ochre Robe: An Autobiography.* 2nd rev. ed. Santa Barbara: Ross Erickson.

Amore, Roy C., and Larry D. Shinn. 1981. *Lustful Maidens and Ascetic Kings: Buddhist and Hindu Stories of Life.* New York: Oxford University Press.

AnanthaMurthy, U. R. 1978. *Samskara: Rites for a Dead Man.* Translated by A. K. Ramanujan. Delhi: Oxford University Press.

Appadurai, Arjun. 1986. "Is Homo Hierarchicus?" *American Ethnologist* 13:745–61.

Apte, Mahadev. 1985. *Humor and Laughter: An Anthropological Approach.* Ithaca and London: Cornell University Press.

Arewa, E. Ojo, and Alan Dundes. 1964. "Proverbs and the Ethnography of Speaking Folklore." *American Anthropologist* (special issue) 66:70–85.

Asad, Talal. 1983. "Anthropological Conceptions of Religion: Reflections on Geertz." *Man* (n.s.) 18:237–59.

Aung, Maung Hin. 1966. *Burmese Monks' Tales.* New York and London: Columbia University Press.

Azadovskii, Mark. 1974. *A Siberian Tale Teller.* Translated by James Dow. Austin: University of Texas Press.

Babb, Lawrence A. 1975. *The Divine Hierarchy: Popular Hinduism in Central India.* New York: Columbia University Press.

———. 1981. "Glancing: Visual Interaction in Hinduism." *Journal of Anthropological Research* 37:387–401.

———. 1983. "Destiny and Responsibility: Karma in Popular Hinduism." In *Karma: An Anthropological Enquiry,* edited by C. Keyes and E. V. Daniel, 163–81. Berkeley: University of California Press.

———. 1984. "Indigenous Feminism in a Modern Hindu Sect." *Signs* 9:399–416.

———. 1986. *Redemptive Encounters: Three Modern Styles in the Hindu Tradition.* Berkeley: University of California Press.

Bakhtin, M. M. 1981. *The Dialogic Imagination*. Edited by Michael Holquist. Translated by Caryl Emerson and Michael Holquist. Austin: University of Texas Press.

Baljøn, J. M. S. 1973. *A Mystical Interpretation of Prophetic Tales by an Indian Muslim*. London: E. J. Brill.

Barker, Philip. 1985. *Using Metaphors in Psychotherapy*. New York: Brunner/Magel.

Bascom, William. 1965. "The Forms of Folklore: Prose Narratives." *Journal of American Folklore* 78 : 3–20.

———, ed. 1977. *The Frontiers of Folklore*. Boulder, Colorado: Westview Press.

Başgöz, Ilhan. 1986. "Digression in Oral Narrative: A Case Study of Individual Remarks by Turkish Romance Tellers." *Journal of American Folklore* 99 : 5–23.

Basso, Keith H. 1983. "'Stalking with Stories': Names, Places and Moral Narrative among the Western Apache." In *Text, Play and Story*, edited by E. Bruner, 19–55. Washington, D.C.: American Ethnological Society.

Bateson, Gregory. 1955. "A Theory of Play and Fantasy." *Psychiatric Research Reports* 2 : 39–51.

Bauman, Richard. 1977. *Verbal Art as Performance*. Rowley, Massachusetts: Newbury House.

Beardslee, William. 1978. "Parable, Proverb and Koan." *Semeia* 12 : 151–77.

Ben Amos, Dan. 1969. "Analytical Categories and Ethnic Genres." *Genre* 2 : 275–301 (reprinted in Ben Amos, 1982).

———. 1982. *Folklore in Context: Essays*. New Delhi, Madras: South Asian Publishers.

Ben Amos, Dan, and Kenneth S. Goldstein, eds. 1975. *Folklore: Performance and Communication*. The Hague and Paris: Mouton.

Benjamin, Walter. 1968. "The Storyteller: Reflections on the Works of Nikolai Leskov." In *Illuminations*, edited by Hannah Arendt, 83–109. New York: Harcourt, Brace and Jovanovich.

Berger, Peter L. 1969. *The Sacred Canopy: Elements of a Sociological Theory of Religion*. Garden City, New York: Doubleday.

Berreman, Gerald D. 1972. *Hindus of the Himalayas: Ethnography and Change*. Berkeley: University of California Press.

Bettelheim, Bruno. 1977. *The Uses of Enchantment: The Meaning and Importance of Fairy Tales*. New York: Alfred A. Knopf.

Bhagat, M. G. 1976. *Ancient Indian Asceticism*. Delhi: Munshiram Manoharlal.

Bhandarkar, R. G. 1933. *Vaishnavism, Saivism and Minor Religious Systems*. Poona: Bhandarkar Oriental Research Institute.

Bhardwaj, Surinder Mohan. 1973. *Hindu Places of Pilgrimage in India: A Study in Cultural Geography*. Berkeley and Los Angeles: University of California Press.

Bhattacharya, J. N. 1896. *Hindu Castes and Sects*. Calcutta: Thacker, Spink and Co.

Blackburn, Stuart A., and A. K. Ramanujan, eds. 1986. *Another Harmony: New Essays on the Folklore of India*. Berkeley: University of California Press.

Bloch, Maurice, and Jonathan Parry, eds. 1982. *Death and the Regeneration of Life*. Cambridge: Cambridge University Press.

Bloomfield, Maurice. 1917. "On Recurring Psychic Motifs in Hindu Fiction and the Laugh and Cry Motif." *Journal of the American Oriental Society* 36 : 54–89.

————. 1924. "On False Ascetics and Nuns in Hindu Fiction." *Journal of the American Oriental Society* 44 : 202–42.

Bødker, Laurits. 1957. *Indian Animal Tales: A Preliminary Survey*. Folklore Fellows Communications 170. Helsinki: Suomalainen Tiedeaketemia.

Braithwaite, R. B. 1955. *An Empiricist's View of the Nature of Religious Belief*. Cambridge: Cambridge University Press.

Brent, Peter. 1972. *Godmen of India*. Chicago: Quadrangle Books.

Brown, Edward Espe. 1985. *The Tassajara Recipe Book*. Boston and London: Shambhala.

Brown, Robert Mc Afee. 1974. "Story and Theology." In *Philosophy, Religion and Theology*, edited by James W. McClendon, 55–72. Missoula: Scholar's Press.

Brown, W. Norman. 1919. "The Pañcatantra in Modern Indian Folklore." *Journal of the American Oriental Society* 39 : 1–54.

————. 1920. "Escaping One's Fate: A Hindu Paradox and Its Use as a Psychic Motif in Hindu Fiction." In *Studies in Honor of Maurice Bloomfield*, 89–104. New Haven: Yale University Press.

Bruner, Edward M. 1986. "Ethnography as Narrative." In *The Anthropology of Experience*, edited by V. W. Turner and E. M. Bruner, 139–55. Urbana: University of Illinois Press.

Bruner, Edward M., and Phyllis Gorfain. 1984. "Dialogical Narration and Paradoxes of Masada." In *Text, Play, and Story*, edited by E. M. Bruner, 56–79. Washington, D.C.: American Ethnological Society.

Bruner, Jerome. 1986. "Two Modes of Thought." In *Actual Minds, Possible Worlds*, 11–43. Cambridge, Massachusetts: Harvard University Press.

————. 1987. "Life As Narrative." *Social Research* 54 : 11–32.

Brunton, Paul. 1935. *A Search in Secret India*. New York: E. P. Dutton.

Buber, Martin. 1948. *Tales of the Hasidim*. New York: Schocken.

Buddhaghosha. 1870. *Buddhaghosha's Parables*. Translated by Capt. T. Rogers. London: Trubner and Co.

Burghart, Richard. 1983a. "Renunciation in the Religious Traditions of South Asia." *Man* (n.s.) 18 : 635–53.

————. 1983b. "Wandering Ascetics of the Ramanandi Sect." *History of Religions* 22 : 361–80.

Cantlie, Audrey. 1977. "Aspects of Hindu Asceticism." In *Symbols and Sentiments*, edited by I. Lewis, 247–68. London: Academic Press.

Carstairs, G. Morris. 1961. *The Twice-Born: A Study of a Community of High Caste Hindus*. Bloomington: Indiana University Press.

————. 1965. "Cultural Elements in Response to Treatment." In *CIBA Symposium on Transcultural Psychiatry*, edited by A. V. S. de Reuch and P. Porter, 169–75. London: J. and A. Churchill.

Cenkner, William. 1982. *A Tradition of Teachers: Shankara and the Jagadgurus Today*. New Delhi: Motilal Banarsidas.

Chakraborthy, Haripada. 1973. *Asceticism in Ancient India in Brahmanical, Buddhist, Jaina and Ajivika Societies*. Calcutta: Punthi Pustak.

Chatman, Seymour. 1978. *Story and Discourse*. Ithaca, New York: Cornell University Press.

Chattopadhyaya, Sudhakar. 1970. *Evolution of Hindu Sects up to the Time of Sam-karacarya*. New Delhi: Munshiram Manoharlal.

Clifford, James. 1983. "On Ethnographic Authority." *Representations* 1:118–146.

Clifford, James, and George E. Marcus, eds., 1986. *Writing Culture: The Poetics and Politics of Ethnography*. Berkeley: University of California Press.

Coburn, Thomas B. 1984. "'Scripture' in India: Towards a Typology of the Word in Hindu Life." *Journal of the American Academy of Religion* 52:435–59.

———. 1985. *Devi Mahatmya: The Crystallization of the Goddess Tradition*. Delhi: Motilal Banarsidas.

Cohn, Bernard S. 1964. "The Role of the Gosains in the Economy of Eighteenth and Nineteenth Century Upper India." *Indian Economic and Social History Review* 1:175–82.

Coomaraswamy, Ananda K. 1929. "Picture Showmen." *Indian Historical Quarterly* 5:182–87.

Coomaraswamy, Ananda K., and Sister Nivedita, 1913. *Myths of the Hindus and Buddhists*. London: Harrap.

Cox, Harvey. 1977. *Turning East: The Promise and Peril of the New Orientalism*. New York: Simon and Schuster.

Crane, Thomas Frederick. 1867. *The Exempla or Illustrative Stories from the Sermones Vulgares of Jacques de Vitry*. Publications of the Folklore Society 26. Nedeln Lichtenstein: Kraus Reprint.

Creel, Austin B. 1977. *Dharma in Hindu Ethics*. Columbia, South Carolina: South Asia Books.

Crites, Stephen D. 1967. "Myth, Story, History." In *Seminar on Parable, Myth and Language*, 66–73. Cambridge, Massachusetts: The Church Society for College Work.

———. 1971. "The Narrative Quality of Experience." *Journal of the American Academy of Religion* 39:291–311.

Crooke, William. 1910. "Mendicant's Cries in North India." *Indian Antiquary* 39:346–50.

Crossan, John Dominic. 1975. *The Dark Interval: Towards a Theology of Story*. Niles, Illinois: Argus Communications.

Damle, Y. B. 1955. "A Note on Harikatha." *Bulletin of the Deccan College Research Institute* 17:15–19.

———. 1960. "Harikatha: A Study in Communication." *Bulletin of the Deccan College Research Institute* 20:63–107.

Daniel, Sheryl. 1983. "The Tool Box Approach of the Tamil to the Issues of Moral Responsibility and Human Destiny." In *Karma: An Anthropological Enquiry*, edited by C. Keyes and E. V. Daniel, 27–62. Berkeley: University of California Press.

Das, Govinda. 1908. *Hinduism and India: A Retrospect and a Prospect*. London and Benares: Theosophical Publishing Society.

Das, Veena. 1982. *Structure and Cognition: Aspects of Hindu Caste and Ritual*. 2nd ed. Delhi: Oxford University Press.

Dayananda Saraswati, Swami. 1963 (1884). *Satyarth Prakash* (Hindi). Delhi: Govindram Hasanand.

———. 1970 (1908). *The Light of Truth: An English Translation of the Satyarth Prakash*. Translated by Durga Prasad. New Delhi: Gnan Prakashan.

Dégh, Linda. 1969. *Folktales and Society: Story Telling in a Hungarian Peasant Community*. Translated by Emily M. Schossberger. Bloomington: Indiana University Press.

Delehaye, Hippolyte. 1962. *The Legends of the Saints*. New York: Fordham University Press.

Dimmitt, Cornelia, and J. A. B. van Buitenen. 1978. *Classical Hindu Mythology: A Reader in the Sanskrit Puranas*. Philadelphia: Temple University Press.

Douglas, Mary. 1968. "The Social Control of Cognition: Some Factors in Joke Perception." *Man* (n.s.) 3 : 361–76.

Dubois, Abbé J. A. 1978 (1906). *Hindu Manners, Customs and Ceremonies*. Translated and edited by Henry K. Beauchamp. 3rd ed. Delhi: Oxford University Press.

Dumont, Louis. 1970a. *Homo Hierarchicus: An Essay on the Caste System and Its Implications*. Chicago: University of Chicago Press.

———. 1970b. "World Renunciation in Indian Religions." In *Religion / Politics and History in India*, 33–61. The Hague and Paris: Mouton.

Dundes, Alan. 1962. "From Etic to Emic Units in the Structural Study of Folktales." *Journal of American Folklore* 75 : 95–105.

———. 1966. "Metafolklore and Oral Literary Criticism." *The Monist* 60 : 505–16.

———. 1976. "Structuralism and Folklore." *Studia Fennica* 20 : 75–93.

———. 1982. "The Symbolic Equivalence of Allomotifs in the Rabbit Herd (AT 570)." *Arv: Scandinavian Yearbook of Folklore* 36 : 91–98.

———, ed. 1984. *Sacred Narrative: Readings in the Theory of Myth*. Berkeley: University of California Press.

Durkheim, Emile. 1965. *The Elementary Forms of the Religious Life*. Translated by Joseph W. Swain. New York: The Free Press.

Dwyer, Kevin. 1982. *Moroccan Dialogues: Anthropology in Question*. Baltimore and London: The Johns Hopkins University Press.

Eck, Diana. 1981. *Darśan: Seeing the Divine Image in India*. Chambersburg, Pennsylvania: Anima Books.

Eliade, Mircea. 1958. *Yoga: Immortality and Freedom*. Bollingen Series 56. Princeton: Princeton University Press.

Ellwood, Robert S., ed. 1987. *Eastern Spirituality in America*. New York: Paulist Press.

Eschmann, Anncharlott. 1984. "Religion, Reaction and Change: The Role of Sects in Hinduism." In *Religion and Development in Asian Societies*, 142–57. Colombo: Marga Publications.

Estess, Ted. 1974. "The Innarrable Contraption: Reflections on the Metaphor of Story." *Journal of the American Academy of Religion* 42 : 415–35.

Fabian, Johannes. 1977. "Lore and Doctrine: Some Observations on Storytelling in the *Jamaa* Movement in Shaba (Zaire)." *Cahiers d'Etudes africains* 66–67 (17) : 307–29.

Fackre, Gabriel. 1983. "Narrative Theology: An Overview." *Interpretation: A Journal of Bible and Theology* 37 : 340–52.

Fahim, Hussein, ed. 1982. *Indigenous Anthropology in Non-Western Countries.* Durham, North Carolina: Carolina Academic Press.

Farquhar, J. N. 1925a. "The Organization of the Sannyasis of the Vedanta." *Journal of the Royal Asiatic Society of Great Britain and Ireland* July: 479–86.

———. 1925b. "The Fighting Ascetics of India." *The Bulletin of the John Rylands Library.*

Fellner, Carl. 1976. "The Use of Teaching Stories in Conjoint Family Therapy." *Family Process* 15: 427–31.

Fine, Elizabeth C. 1984. *The Folklore Text from Performance to Print.* Bloomington: Indiana University Press.

Fish, Stanley. 1980. *Is There a Text in This Class? The Authority of Interpretive Communities.* Cambridge, Massachusetts: Harvard University Press.

French, Harold W. 1974. *The Swan's Wide Waters: Ramakrishna and Western Culture.* Port Washington, New York: Kennikat Press.

Frere, Mary. 1898 (1868). *Old Deccan Days or Hindoo Fairy Legends Current in Southern India.* 3rd ed. London: John Murray.

Gardner, Richard A. 1971. *Therapeutic Communication with Children: The Mutual Storytelling Technique.* New York: Jason Aronson.

Gaster, Moses. 1924. *The Exempla of the Rabbis: Being a Collection of Exempla, Apologues and Tales.* London: The Asia Publishing House.

Geertz, Clifford. 1968. "Thinking as a Moral Act: Ethical Dimensions of Anthropological Fieldwork in the New States." *Antioch Review* 28: 139–58.

———. 1973. "Religion as a Cultural System." In *The Interpretation of Cultures,* 87–125. New York: Basic Books.

Gennette, Gerard. 1980. *Narrative Discourse.* Ithaca, New York: Cornell University Press.

Georges, Robert A. 1983. "Do Narrators Really Digress? A Reconsideration of Audience Asides in Narrating." *Western Folklore* 40: 215–42.

Ghosh, Jaimini. 1930. *Sannyasi and Fakir Raiders in Bengal.* Calcutta: Bengal Sectarian Book Depot.

Ghurye, Govind Sadashiv. 1953. *Indian Sadhus.* Bombay: Popular Prakashan.

Ginzberg, Louis. 1950–69. *Legends of the Jews.* 7 vols. Philadelphia: Jewish Publication Society.

Ginzburg, Carlo. 1982. *The Cheese and the Worms: The Cosmos of a Sixteenth-Century Miller.* Harmondsworth: Penguin.

Glassie, Henry. 1982. *Passing the Time in Balleymenone: Culture and History in an Ulster Community.* Philadelphia: University of Pennsylvania Press.

Goffman, Erving. 1961. *Encounters: Two Studies in the Sociology of Interaction.* Indianapolis: Bobbs Merrill.

———. 1974. *Frame Analysis: An Essay on the Organization of Experience.* New York: Harper and Row.

Gold, Daniel. 1987. *The Lord as Guru: Hindi Sants in the Northern Indian Tradition.* New York: Oxford University Press.

Goldberg, Michael. 1982. *Theology and Narrative: A Critical Introduction.* Nashville: Abingdon.

Goldman, Robert P. 1978. "Fathers, Sons and Gurus: Oedipal Conflict in the Sanskrit Epics." *Journal of Indian Philosophy* 6: 325–92.

Gonda, Jan. 1965. *Change and Continuity in Indian Religion*. The Hague: Mouton.
————. 1970. *Vishnuism and Sivaism: A Comparison*. London: The Athlone Press.
Griaule, Marcel. 1965. *Conversations with Ogotemmêli: An Introduction to Dogon Religious Ideas*. London: Oxford University Press.
Gross, Robert. 1979. Hindu Asceticism: A Study of the Sadhus of North India. Ph.D. dissertation, Department of Anthropology, University of California, Berkeley.
Gumperz, John J. 1964. "Religion and Social Communication in Village North India." In *Religion in South Asia*, edited by E. B. Harper, 89–97. Seattle: University of Washington Press.
Gupte, Rai Bahadur. 1919. *Hindu Holidays and Ceremonies with Dissertations on Origin, Folklore and Symbols*. Calcutta and Simla: Thacker, Spink and Co.
Harper, Marvin Henry. 1972. *Gurus, Swamis and Avataras: Spiritual Masters and their American Disciples*. Philadelphia: The Westminster Press.
Hauerwas, Stanley. 1983. "Casuistry as a Narrative Art." *Interpretation* 37 : 377–88.
Hauerwas, Stanley, and David Burrell. 1977. "From System to Story: An Alternative Pattern for Rationality in Ethics." In *Truthfulness and Tragedy*, 15–39. Notre Dame, Indiana: University of Notre Dame Press.
Heesterman, J. C. 1964. "Brahman, Ritual and Renouncer." *Wiener Zeitschrift für die Kunde Süd- und Ostasiens* 8 : 1–31.
Hertz, Robert. 1960 (1907). "A Contribution to the Study of the Collective Representation of Death." In *Death and the Right Hand*. Translated by Rodney and Claudia Needham, 27–86. Aberdeen: Cohen and West.
Hoffman, John C. 1986. *Law, Freedom and Story: The Role of the Narrative in Therapy, Society and Faith*. Waterloo: Wilfrid Laurier University Press.
Holub, Robert C. 1984. *Reception Theory: A Critical Introduction*. London and New York: Methuen.
Hopkins, Thomas. 1971. *The Hindu Religious Tradition*. Encino, California: Dickensen Publishing Co.
Hultkranz, Åke. 1960. "Religious Aspects of the Wind River Shoshoni Literature." In *Culture in History: Essays in Honor of Paul Radin*, edited by Stanley Diamond, 552–69. New York: Columbia University Press.
Inden, Ronald. 1986. "Orientalist Constructions of India." *Modern Asian Studies* 20 : 1–46.
Jackson, Michael. 1982. *Allegories of the Wilderness: Ethics and Ambiguity in Kuranko Narrative*. Bloomington: Indiana University Press.
Jacobs, Melville. 1959. *The Content and Style of an Oral Literature: Clackamas Chinook Myths and Tales*. Chicago and London: University of Chicago Press.
————. 1960. *The People Are Coming Soon: Analyses of Clackamas Chinook Myths and Tales*. Seattle: University of Washington Press.
Jansen, William Hugh. 1957. "Classifying Performance in the Study of Verbal Folklore." In *Studies in Folklore*, edited by W. Edson Richmond, 110–18. Bloomington: Indiana University Press.
Jordens, J. T. F. 1978. *Dayananda Sarasvati: His Life and Ideas*. Delhi: Oxford University Press.
Kakar, Sudhir. 1978. "Setting the Stage: The Traditional Hindu View and the Psy-

chology of Erik H. Erikson." In *Identity and Adulthood*, edited by Sudhir Kakar, 3–12. Delhi: Oxford University Press.

———. 1981. *The Inner World: A Psychoanalytic Study of Childhood and Society in India*. 2nd ed. Delhi: Oxford University Press.

———. 1982. *Shamans, Mystics and Doctors. A Psychoanalytic Enquiry into India and Its Healing Traditions*. New York: Alfred A. Knopf.

Kane, P. V. 1930–62. *History of Dharmashastra*. 5 vols. Poona: Bhandarkar Oriental Research Institute.

Kautilya. 1951. *Kauṭilya's Arthaśāstra*. Translated by R. Shamashastry. Mysore: Sri Raghuveer Printing Press.

Kermode, Frank. 1979. *The Genesis of Secrecy: On the Interpretation of Narrative*. Cambridge, Massachusetts: Harvard University Press.

Keyes, Charles, and E. Valentine Daniel, eds. 1983. *Karma: An Anthropological Enquiry*. Berkeley: University of California Press.

Khare, R. S. 1984. *The Untouchable as Himself: Ideology, Identity and Pragmatism among the Lucknow Chamars*. Cambridge: Cambridge University Press.

King, Ursula. 1978. "Indian Spirituality, Western Materialism: An Image and Its Function in the Reinterpretation of Modern Hinduism." *Social Action* 28 : 62–86.

Kinsley, David. 1982. *Hinduism: A Cultural Perspective*. Englewood Cliffs, New Jersey: Prentice Hall.

———. 1986. *Hindu Goddesses: Visions of the Divine Feminine in the Hindu Religious Tradition*. Berkeley: University of California Press.

Kirk, James A. 1972. *Stories of the Hindus: An Introduction Through Texts and Interpretations*. New York: Macmillan.

Kirshenblatt-Gimblett, Barbara. 1975. "A Parable in Context: A Social Interactional Analysis of Storytelling Performance." In *Folklore: Performance and Communication*, edited by Dan Ben Amos and Kenneth S. Goldstein, 105–30. The Hague: Mouton.

Kissinger, Warren S. 1979. *The Parables of Jesus: A History of Interpretation and Bibliography*. New York: Garland.

Kolenda, Pauline. 1983. "The Hierarchical Renouncer and the Dutiful Person." In *Caste, Cult and Hierarchy: Essays on the Culture of India*, 290–340. New Delhi: Manohar.

Kolff, D. H. A. 1971. "Sannyasi Trader-Soldiers." *Indian Economic and Social History Review* 8 : 213–20.

Langness, L. L., and Gelya Frank. 1981. *Lives: An Anthropological Approach*. Novato, California: Chandler and Sharp.

Lannoy, Richard. 1971. *The Speaking Tree*. London: Oxford University Press.

Lévi-Strauss, Claude. 1963. "The Effectiveness of Symbols." In *Structural Anthropology*, 168–205. New York: Basic Books.

Limon, José E. 1983. "Western Marxism and Folklore: A Critical Introduction." *Journal of American Folkore* 96 : 34–52.

———. 1984. "Western Marxism and Folklore: A Critical Reintroduction." *Journal of American Folklore* 97 : 337–44.

Lischer, Richard. 1984. "The Limits of Story." *Interpretation: A Journal of Bible and Theology* 38 : 26–38.

Lombardi-Satriani, Luigi. 1974. "Folklore as a Culture of Contestation." *Journal of Folklore Institute* 11 : 99–121.

Long, J. Bruce. 1977. "Death as a Necessity and a Gift in Hindu Mythology." In *Religious Encounters With Death,* edited by F. Reynolds and D. Capps, pp. 73–96. University Park and London: Pennsylvania State University Press.

Loomis, C. Grant. 1948. *White Magic: An Introduction to the Folklore of Christian Legend.* Cambridge, Massachusetts: Harvard University Press.

Lorenzen, David N. 1978. "Warrior Ascetics in Indian History." *Journal of the American Oriental Society* 98 : 61–95.

Lutgendorf, Philip. 1987. The Life of a Text: Tulsīdās' Rāmcharitmānas in Performance. Ph.D. dissertation, Department of South Asian Languages and Civilization, University of Chicago.

"M." 1942. *The Gospel of Sri Ramakrishna.* Translated by Swami Nikhilananda. New York: Ramakrishna-Vivekananda Center.

MacIntyre, Alasdair. 1984. *After Virtue: A Study in Moral Theory.* 2nd ed. Notre Dame: University of Notre Dame Press.

Madan, T. N. 1977. "The Quest for Hinduism." *International Social Science Journal* 19 : 261–78.

Mahadevan, T. M. P. 1980. *The Hymns of Śankara.* Delhi: Motilal Banarsidas.

Maharashtra State Gazetteer. 1975. *Nasik District.* Bombay: Government Central Press.

Majumdar, D. N. 1958. *Caste and Communication in an Indian Village.* New York: Asia Publishing Co.

Malinowski, Bronislaw. 1954. "Myth in Primitive Psychology." In *Magic, Science and Religion and Other Essays,* 93–148. Garden City, New York: Doubleday Anchor.

Mandelbaum, David. 1970. *Society in India.* 2 vols. Berkeley: University of California Press.

Manu. 1886. *The Laws of Manu.* Translated by G. Bühler. Sacred Books of the East, Vol. 25. Oxford: Clarendon Press.

Marcus, George E., and Dick Cushman. 1982. "Ethnographies as Texts." *Annual Review of Anthropology* 11 : 25–69.

Marcus, George E., and Michael M. J. Fischer. 1986. *Anthropology as Cultural Critique: An Experimental Moment in the Human Sciences.* Chicago: University of Chicago Press.

Marriott, McKim. 1955. "Little Communities in an Indigenous Civilization." In *Village India,* edited by McKim Marriott, 171–222. Chicago: University of Chicago Press.

———. 1968. "Caste Ranking and Food Transactions: A Matrix Analysis." In *Structure and Change in Indian Society,* edited by Milton Singer and Bernard S. Cohn, 133–72. Chicago: Aldine Publishing Co.

———. 1976. "Hindu Transactions: Diversity Without Dualism." In *Transaction and Meaning,* edited by Bruce Kapferer, 109–42. Philadelphia: ISHI.

Marshall, Peter J. 1970. *The British Discovery of Hinduism in the Eighteenth Century.* Cambridge: Cambridge University Press.

Masson, J. Moussaieff. 1976. "The Psychology of the Ascetic." *Journal of Asian Studies* 35 : 611–26.

Mauss, Marcel. 1967. *The Gift: Forms and Functions of Exchange in Archaic Societies*. Translated by Ian Cunnison. New York: W. W. Norton and Co.

McCormack, William. 1958. "The Forms of Communication in Vīraśaiva Religion." *Journal of American Folklore* 71 : 325–35.

McLeod, W. H. 1978. "On the Word *Panth:* A Problem of Terminology and Definition." *Contributions to Indian Sociology* (n.s.) 12 : 287–95.

Mehta, Gita. 1979. *Karma Cola: Marketing the Mystic East*. New York: Simon and Schuster.

Mehta, S. S. 1919. "The Sitting Posture of the Corpse in the Bier Before Burial Among Hindus." *Journal of the Anthropological Society of Bombay* 11 : 636–38.

Miller, David. 1976–77. "The Guru as the Centre of Sacredness." *Studies in Religion* 6/5 : 527–33.

———. 1986. "Karma, Rebirth and the Contemporary Guru." In *Karma and Rebirth*, edited by R. W. Neufeldt, 61–81. Albany: State University of New York Press.

Miller, David M., and Dorothy C. Wertz. 1976. *Hindu Monastic Life: The Monks and Monasteries of Bhubaneshwar*. Montreal: McGill Queens University Press.

Mines, Mattison. 1981. "Indian Transitions: A Comparative Analysis of Adult Stages of Development." *Ethos* 9 : 95–121.

Mink, Louis. 1978. "Narrative Form as a Cognitive Instrument." In *The Writing of History*, edited by R. Canary and H. Kozicki, 129–49. Madison: University of Wisconsin Press.

Mintz, Jerome R. 1968. *Legends of the Hasidim: An Introduction to Hasidic Culture and Oral Tradition in the New World*. Chicago: University of Chicago Press.

Mitchell, W. J. T., ed. 1980. *On Narrative*. Chicago: University of Chicago Press.

Mitra, Sarat Chandra. 1917. "A Note on the Rise of a New Hindu Sect in Bihar." *Journal of the Anthropological Society of Bombay* 11 : 48–52.

Mlecko, Joel D. 1982. "The Guru in Hindu Tradition." *Numen* 29 : 33–61.

Mookerji, Radhakumud. 1947. *Ancient Indian Education: Brahmanical and Buddhist*. London: Macmillan and Company.

Nakhleh, Khalil. 1979. "On Being a Native Anthropologist." In *The Politics of Anthropology: From Colonialism and Sexism Toward a View from Below*, edited by G. Huizer and B. Mannheim, 343–52. The Hague: Mouton.

Nandy, Ashis. 1983. *The Intimate Enemy: Loss and Recovery of Self Under Colonialism*. Delhi: Oxford University Press.

Narayan, Kirin. 1986. "Birds on a Branch: Girlfriends and Wedding Songs in Kangra." *Ethos* 14 : 47–75.

———. (forthcoming.) "On Nose Cutters, Gurus and Storytellers." In *Creativity: Self and Society*, edited by R. Rosaldo, S. Lavie, and K. Narayan. Ithaca, New York: Cornell University Press.

Narayan, R. K. 1958. *The Guide*. Mysore: Indian Thought Publications.

———. 1964. *Gods, Demons and Others*. New York: The Viking Press.

Natesa Sastri, Pandit S. M. 1908. *Indian Folk Tales*. Madras: Guardian Press.

Neki, J. S. 1973. "Guru-Chela Relationship: The Possibility of a Psychotherapeutic Paradigm." *American Journal of Orthopsychiatry* 43 : 755–66.

Nelson, Paul. 1987. *Narrative and Morality*. University Park: Pennsylvania State University Press.

Neogi, Dwijendra Nath. 1916. *Sacred Tales of India*. London: Macmillan and Co.

Neufeldt, Ronald W., ed. 1986. *Karma and Rebirth: Post-Classical Developments*. Albany: State University of New York Press.

Obeyesekere, Gananath. 1968. "Theodicy, Sin and Salvation in a Sociology of Buddhism." In *Dialectic in Practical Religion*, edited by E. R. Leach, 7–40. Cambridge: Cambridge University Press.

O'Flaherty, Wendy Doniger. 1971. "The Origin of Heresy in Hindu Mythology." *History of Religions* 10 (4) : 271–333.

———. 1973. *Asceticism and Eroticism in the Mythology of Siva*. London: Oxford University Press.

———. 1975. *Hindu Myths*. New York: Penguin.

———. 1976. *The Origins of Evil in Hindu Mythology*. Berkeley: University of California Press.

———. 1980. *Women, Androgynes and Other Mythical Beasts*. Chicago: University of Chicago Press.

———. 1984. *Dreams, Illusions and Other Realities*. Chicago: University of Chicago Press.

———. 1985. *Tales of Sex and Violence: Folklore, Sacrifice and Danger in the Jaiminiya Brahmana*. Chicago: University of Chicago Press.

———, ed. 1980. *Karma and Rebirth in Classical Indian Traditions*. Berkeley: University of California Press.

Ohnuki-Tierney, Emiko. 1984. "Native Anthropologists." *American Ethnologist* 11 : 584–86.

Ojha, Catherine. 1981. "Feminine Asceticism in Hinduism: Its Traditions and Present Condition." *Man in India* 61 : 254–85.

———. 1985. "The Tradition of Female Gurus." *Manushi* 6(1) : 2–8.

Olivelle, Patrick. 1975. "A Definition of World Renunciation." *Wiener Zeitschrift für die Kunde Süd- und Ostasiens* 19 : 75–83.

O'Malley, L. S. S. 1935. *Popular Hinduism: The Religion of the Masses*. London: Cambridge University Press.

Oman, J. C. 1905. *The Mystics, Ascetics and Saints of India*. London: T. Fisher Unwin.

Ong, Walter J. 1982. *Orality and Literacy: The Technologizing of the Word*. London and New York: Methuen.

Opler, Morris E. 1938. *Myths and Tales of the Jicarilla Apache Indians*. American Folklore Society 31. New York: G. E. Steichert and Co.

Oring, Elliott. 1984. *The Jokes of Sigmund Freud: A Study in Humor and Jewish Identity*. Philadelphia: University of Pennsylvania Press.

Padhye, K. A. 1946. "Guru-Cult in India." *Journal of the Anthropological Society of Bombay* (n.s.) 1 : 101–9.

Pannikar, Raimundo. 1977. *The Vedic Experience: Mantramañjarī*. Berkeley: University of California Press.

Paredes, Américo, and Richard Bauman, eds. 1972. *Towards New Perspectives in Folklore*. Austin and London: University of Texas Press.

Parmar, Shyam. 1975. *Traditional Folk Media in India*. New Delhi: Gekha Books.

Parry, Jonathan. 1982. "Sacrificial Death and the Necrophagous Ascetic." In *Death and the Regeneration of Life,* edited by M. Bloch and J. Parry, 74–110. Cambridge: Cambridge University Press.

———. 1985. "The Aghori Ascetics in Benares." In *Indian Religion,* edited by R. Burghart and A. Cantlie, 51–71. London: Curzon Press.

Pennell, T. L. 1909. *Among the Wild Tribes of the Afghan Frontiers*. London: Seeley and Co.

Pentikäinen, Juha. 1978. *Oral Repertoire and World View: An Anthropological Study of Marina Takalo's Life History*. Folklore Fellows Communications 219. Helsinki: Suomalainen Tiedeakatemia.

Planalp, Jack M. 1956. Religious Life and Values in a North Indian Village. Ph.D. dissertation, Department of Anthropology, Cornell University.

Pocock, David F. 1973. *Mind, Body and Wealth: A Study of Belief and Practice in an Indian Village*. Totowa, New Jersey: Rowman and Littlefield.

———. 1985. "Art and Theology in the Bhagavata Purana." *Contributions to Indian Sociology* (n.s.) 19 : 9–39.

Polkinghorne, Donald E. 1988. *Narrative Knowing and the Human Sciences*. Albany: State University of New York Press.

Potter, Karl H. 1980. "Karma Theory in Some Indian Philosophical Systems." In *Karma and Rebirth in Classical Indian Traditions,* edited by W. O'Flaherty, 241–67. Berkeley: University of California Press.

Prabhu, Pandharinath H. 1963. *Hindu Social Organization: A Study of Socio Psychological and Ideological Foundations*. 4th ed. Bombay: Popular Prakashan.

Price, Richard. 1983. *First Time: The Historical Vision of an Afro-American People*. Baltimore and London: The Johns Hopkins University Press.

Propp, Vladímir. 1968. *Morphology of the Folktale*. 2nd rev. ed. Translated by Lawrence Scott. Austin and London: University of Texas Press.

Prusek, Jaroslav. 1938. "The Narrators of Buddhist Scriptures and Religious Tales in the Sung Period." *Archiv Orientalni* 10 : 375–89.

Raghavan, V. 1936. "Picture Showmen: Mankha." *Indian Historical Quarterly* 12 : 524.

———. 1958. "Methods of Popular Religious Instruction in South India." *Journal of American Folklore* 71 : 336–44.

Ramakrishna, Sri. 1967. *Tales and Parables of Sri Ramakrishna*. Sri Ramakrishna Math. Mylapore: Madras.

Ramanujan, A. K. 1982. "Hanchi: A Kannada Cinderella." In *Cinderella: A Folklore Casebook,* edited by A. Dundes, 259–75. New York: Garland.

———. 1983. "The Indian Oedipus." In *Oedipus: A Folklore Casebook,* edited by L. Edmunds and A. Dundes, 234–61. New York: Garland.

Ramaswami Raju, P. V. 1901. *Indian Fables*. 2nd ed. London: Swan, Sonnenschein and Co.

Ranade, R. D. 1985 (1933). *Mysticism in India: The Poet Saints of Maharashtra*. Purchase: State University of New York Press.

Randall, Frederika. 1984. "Why Scholars Become Storytellers." *New York Times Book Review* January 29 : 1, 31.

Renou, Louis, ed. 1963. *Hinduism*. New York: Washington Square Press.

Ricouer, Paul. 1984. *Time and Narrative*. Chicago: University of Chicago Press.

Robbins, J. Wesley. 1980. "Narrative, Morality and Religion." *Journal of Religious Ethics* 8 : 161–76.

Robinson, E. J. 1885. *Tales and Poems of South India*. London: T. Woolmer.

Rocker, Ludo. 1980. "Karma and Rebirth in the Dharmashastras." In *Karma and Rebirth in Classical Indian Traditions*, edited by W. O'Flaherty, 61–89. Berkeley: University of California Press.

Rooth, Anna B. 1976. *The Importance of Storytelling: A Study Based on Field Work in Northern Alaska*. Uppsala: University Stockholm Acta Universitatis Upsaliensis.

Rosen, Sidney. 1982. *My Voice Will Go with You: The Teaching Tales of Milton Erickson*. New York: W. W. Norton.

Rosenberg, Bruce A. 1970. *The Art of the American Folk Preacher*. New York: Oxford University Press.

Roy, Manisha. 1975. *Bengali Women*. Chicago: University of Chicago Press.

Ryder, Arthur W. 1956. *The Panchatantra*. Chicago and London: University of Chicago Press.

Sadananda Giri, Swami. 1976. *Society and Sannyāsi: A History of the Daśnāmi Sannyāsis*. Varanasi: Chowkamba Vidya Bhavan.

Sahal, Kanhaiyalal. 1965. *Lok Kathaon ke kuchh rudh tantu* [Hindi]. Allahabad: Kitab Mahal.

Sarbin, Theodore, ed. 1986. *Narrative Psychology*. New York: Praeger.

Sarkar, Jadunath. 1950. *A History of the Daśnāmi Nāgā Samnyāsis*. Daraganji: Sri Panchayati Akhara Mahanirvani.

Schafer, Roy. 1983. *The Analytic Attitude*. New York: Basic Books.

Schweder, Richard A. 1986. "Storytelling Among the Anthropologists." *New York Times Book Review* September 21 : 1, 38–39.

Seitel, Peter. 1980. *See So That We May See: Performances and Interpretations of Traditional Tales from Tanzania*. Bloomington and London: Indiana University Press.

Selwyn, Tom. 1982. "Adharma." In *Way of Life: King, Householder, Renouncer*, edited by T. N. Madan, 382–401. New Delhi: Vikas.

Sen, A. M. 1961. *Hinduism*. Hammondsworth: Penguin.

Sharma, Haradatta. 1939. *Contributions to the History of Brahmanical Asceticism (Samnyāsa)*. Poona Oriental Series 64. Poona: Oriental Book Agency.

Sharma, Ursula. 1973. "Theodicy and the Doctrine of Karma." *Man* (n.s.) 8 : 347–64.

Shostak, Marjorie. 1983. *Nisa: The Life and Words of a !Kung Woman*. New York: Vintage Books.

Singer, Milton. 1972. *When a Great Tradition Modernizes: An Anthropological Approach to Indian Civilization*. London: Pall Mall Press.

Singer, Philip. 1961. Hindu Holy Men: A Study in Charisma. Ph.D. dissertation, Department of Anthropology, Syracuse University.

Sinha, Surajit, and Baidyanath Saraswati. 1978. *Ascetics of Kashi: An Anthropological Investigation*. Varanasi: N. K. Bose Memorial Foundation.

Slater, Peter. 1979. *The Dynamics of Religion: Meaning and Change in Religious Traditions*. New York: Harper and Row.

Spencer, Robert F. 1966. "Ethical Expression in a Burmese Jataka." In *The Anthro-*

pologist Looks at Myth, edited by Melville Jacobs and John Greenway, 278–302. Austin and London: University of Texas Press.

Spratt, Philip. 1966. *Hindu Culture and Personality.* Bombay: Manaktalas.

Srinivas, M. N. 1952. *Religion and Society Among the Coorgs of South India.* New York: Asia Publishing House.

———. 1962. *Caste in Modern India and Other Essays.* New York: Asia Publishing House.

———. 1967. "The Study of One's Own Society." In *Social Change in Modern India,* 147–63. Berkeley: University of California Press.

Staal, Frits. 1975. *Exploring Mysticism: A Methodological Essay.* Berkeley and London: University of California Press.

Stein, Burton. 1968. "Social Mobility and Medieval South Indian Hindu Sects." In *Social Mobility in the Caste System of India,* edited by James Silverberg, 79–94. The Hague: Mouton.

Stevenson, Mrs. Sinclair. 1920. *The Rites of the Twice Born.* London: Oxford University Press.

Stokes, Maive. 1879. *Indian Fairy Tales.* London: Ellis and White.

Stoller, Paul. 1987. *In Sorcery's Shadow.* Chicago: University of Chicago Press.

Stotra Ratnavali. n.d. [Hindi]. Gorakhpur: Gita Press.

Suleiman, Susan, and Inge Crosman, eds. 1980. *The Reader in the Text: Essays on Audience and Interpretation.* Princeton: Princeton University Press.

Swallow, D. A. 1982. "Ashes and Powers: Myth, Rite and Miracle in an Indian God-man's Cult." *Modern Asian Studies* 16 : 128–58.

Swynnerton, Charles A. 1892. *Indian Night's Entertainment or Folktales from the Upper Indus.* London: Paternoster Row.

Tawney, C. H., trans. 1968 (1880). *The Kathāsaritsāgara or Ocean of the Streams of Story.* New Delhi: Munshiram Manoharlal.

Tedlock, Dennis. 1983. *The Spoken Word and the Work of Interpretation.* Philadelphia: University of Pennsylvania Press.

Thapar, Romila. 1975. "Ethics, Religion and Social Protest in the First Millenium B.C. in North India." *Daedalus* (Spring), 119–32.

———. 1978. "Renunciation: The Making of a Counter-culture?" In *Ancient Indian Social History: Some Interpretations,* 63–104. New Delhi: Orient Longmans.

———. 1982. "The Householder and the Renouncer in the Brahmanical and Buddhist Traditions." In *Way of Life, King, Householder, Renouncer,* edited by T. N. Madan, 273–98. New Delhi: Vikas.

———. 1985. "Syndicated Moksha." *Seminar* 13 : 14–22.

Thompson, Stith. 1955–58. *Motif Index of Folk Literature.* 6 vols. Bloomington: Indiana University Press.

Thompson, Stith, and Jonas Balys. 1958. *The Oral Tales of India.* Folklore Series 10. Bloomington: Indiana University Press.

Thompson, Stith, and Warren E. Roberts. 1960. *Types of Indic Oral Tales: India, Pakistan and Ceylon.* Folklore Fellows Communications 180. Helsinki: Suomalainen Tiedeakatemia.

Tilley, Terence W. 1985. *Story Theology.* Wilmington, Delaware: M. Glazier.

Tiwari, Kapil N. 1977. *Dimensions of Renunciation in Advaita Vedanta.* Delhi: Motilal Banarsidas.

Toelken, Barre. 1979. *The Dynamics of Folklore*. New York: Houghton Mifflin.

Tripathi, B. D. 1978. *The Sadhus of India: The Sociological View*. Bombay: Popular Prakashan.

Tubach, Frederic C. 1962. "Exempla in the Decline." *Traditio* 18:407–17.

———. 1969. *Index Exemplorum: A Handbook of Medieval Religious Tales*. Folklore Fellows Communications 204. Helsinki: Suomalainen Tiedeakatemia.

Turner, Victor. 1969. *The Ritual Process: Structure and Anti-Structure*. Chicago: Aldine Publishing Company.

Upadhyaya, K. D. 1965. "Indian Botanical Folklore." In *Tree Symbol Worship in India,* edited by S. Sen Gupta, 1–18. Calcutta: India Publications.

Upreti, Pandit Ganga Datt. 1894. *Proverbs and Folklore of Kumaun and Garhwal*. Lodiana: Lodiana Mission Press.

Van Baaren, Th. P. 1972. "The Flexibility of Myth." *Studies in the History of Religions* 22:199–206 (reprinted in Dundes, ed., 1984).

Van der Veer, Peter. 1987. "Taming the Ascetic: Devotionalism in a Hindu Monastic Order." *Man* (n.s.) 22:680–95.

Van Gennep, Arnold. 1960. *The Rites of Passage*. Translated by Monika B. Vizedom and Gabrielle L. Caffee. Chicago: University of Chicago Press.

Vatuk, Ved Prakash. 1979. *Studies in Indian Folk Traditions*. New Delhi: Manohar.

Veltheim-Osso, Hans Hasso Von. 1959. *Echte und falsche Heiligie, Der Atem Indien, Tagebücher aus Asian*. 3rd rev. ed. Hamburg: Claasen.

Von Sydow, C. W. 1948. "On the Spread of Tradition." In *Selected Papers in Folklore*, 11–43. Copenhagen: Rosenhilde and Bagger.

Wadley, Susan Snow. 1975. *Shakti: Power in the Conceptual Structure of Karimpur Religion*. Chicago: Department of Anthropology, University of Chicago.

———. 1976. "Brothers, Husbands and Sometimes Sons: Kinsmen in North Indian Ritual." *Eastern Anthropologist* 29:149–67.

———. 1978. "Texts in Contexts: Oral Traditions and the Study of Religion in Karimpur." In *American Studies in the Anthropology of India,* edited by Sylvia Vatuk, 309–41. New Delhi: Manohar.

———. 1983. "*Vrats:* Transformers of Destiny." In *Karma: An Anthropological Enquiry,* edited by C. F. Keyes and E. V. Daniel, 147–62. Berkeley: University of California Press.

Walker, Benjamin. 1968. *The Hindu World: An Encyclopedic Survey of Hinduism*. 2 vols. London: George Allen and Unwin.

Weber, Max. 1958a. *From Max Weber: Essays in Sociology*. Translated and edited by H. H. Gerth and C. Wright Mills. New York: Oxford University Press.

———. 1958b. *The Religion of India: The Sociology of Hinduism and Buddhism*. Translated and edited by H. H. Gerth and D. Martindale. New York: The Free Press.

Webster, Stephen. 1983. "Ethnography as Storytelling." *Dialectical Anthropology* 8:185–206.

Welter, J. Thomas. 1927. *L'exemplum dans la litterature religieuse et didactique du moyen âge*. Paris and Toulouse: E. H. Guitard.

White, Charles S. J. 1972. "The Sai Baba Movement: Approaches to the Study of Indian Saints." *Journal of Asian Studies* 31:863–78.

White, David Gordon. 1984. "Why Gurus Are Heavy." *Numen* 31:40–73.

White, Hayden. 1981. "The Value of Narrativity in the Representation of Reality." In *On Narrative,* edited by W. J. T. Mitchell, 1–24. Chicago: University of Chicago Press.

Wicker, Brian. 1975. *The Story Shaped World: Fiction and Metaphysics: Some Variations on a Theme.* Notre Dame, Indiana: University of Notre Dame Press.

Wiggins, James B., ed. 1975. *Religion as Story.* New York: Harper and Row.

Wilder, Amos. 1983. "Story and Story-World." *Interpretation* 37 : 353–64.

Williams, Raymond. 1984. *A New Face of Hinduism: The Swaminarayan Religion.* New York: Cambridge University Press.

Wilson, H. H. 1828. *Religious Sects of the Hindus.* London: Trubner and Co.

Zimmer, Heinrich. 1946. *Myths and Symbols in Indian Art and Civilization.* Princeton: Princeton University Press.

Zumbro, Rev. W. M. 1913. "Religious Penances and Punishments Self-Inflicted by the Holy Men of India." *The National Geographic Magazine* 24 (12) : 1258–1313.

Index